The Vegetarian
meat and potatoes
C O O K B O O K

Also by Robin Robertson

Pasta for All Seasons

Rice & Spice

The Sacred Kitchen (with Jon Robertson)

The Vegetarian Chili Cookbook

Some Like It Hot

The Soy Gourmet

366 Simply Delicious Dairy-Free Recipes

365 Healthful Ways to Cook Tofu and Other Meat Alternatives

The Vegetarian
meat and potatoes
COOKBOOK

ROBIN ROBERTSON

THE HARVARD COMMON PRESS
BOSTON, MASSACHUSETTS

FOR JON

━*mm*━

THE HARVARD COMMON PRESS
535 ALBANY STREET
BOSTON, MASSACHUSETTS 02118
WWW.HARVARDCOMMONPRESS.COM

Printed in the United States of America

Printed on acid-free paper

Library of Congress Cataloging-in-Publication Data

Robertson, Robin (Robin G.)
    The vegetarian meat and potatoes cookbook : 275 hearty and healthy meat-free recipes for
burgers, steaks, stews, chilis, casseroles, pot pies, curries, pizza, pasta, and other stick-to-
your-ribs favorites / Robin Robertson.
      p. cm.
    Includes index.
    ISBN 1-55832-204-3 (cloth : alk. paper) -- ISBN 1-55832-205-1 (pbk. : alk. paper)
    I. Vegetarian cookery. II. Title.

    TX837.R62624 2001
    641.5'636--dc21   2001047048

Special bulk-order discounts are available on this and other Harvard Common Press books.
Companies and organizations may purchase books for premiums or resale, or may arrange a
custom edition, by contacting the Marketing Director at the address above.

10 9 8 7 6 5 4 3 2 1

COVER DESIGN BY NIGHT & DAY DESIGN
BOOK DESIGN BY DEBORAH KERNER / DANCING BEARS DESIGN
ILLUSTRATIONS BY PAUL HOFFMAN

Contents

Acknowledgments

Many thanks to my family, friends, and colleagues for their help during the writing of this book. I am especially grateful to my husband, Jon, for inspiring this project, as well as for his tasting, testing, and technical assistance; and to my dear friends who served as recipe testers, tasters, and my general support system: Gloria Seigel, Kerri Kyle, Kay and Larry Sturgis, Samantha Ragan, Lochlain Lewis, John and Kathy Mein, Todd Ewen, Pat Davis, B.J. Atkinson, and Lisa Lange; my sister, Carole Lazur; and my agent, Stacey Glick of Jane Dystel Literary Management. Special thanks go to Karen Davis of United Poultry Concerns. I also wish to express my gratitude to Bruce Shaw, for his enthusiasm for this project; Pam Hoenig, for her insightful editing; Judith Sutton, for her thorough copyediting; and the entire staff at the Harvard Common Press.

Introduction

When I married him in 1971, my husband, Jon, was a "meat and potatoes" kind of guy. He remains so today, even though he has been a vegetarian since 1986. The answer to this seeming paradox can be found in the pages of this book. *The Vegetarian Meat and Potatoes Cookbook* is written to appeal to everyone, but especially to reluctant vegetarians—people who have said, "I could never go vegetarian. I'm a meat-and-potatoes person."

To many Americans, "meat and potatoes" is synonymous with stick-to-your-ribs comfort food, from indulgent appetizers and hearty entrées to rich desserts. The problem is that the health risks associated with these foods can be anything but comforting. As more people cut down on or eliminate meat from their diets, vegetarians and nonvegetarians alike need sources for nutritious and satisfying meatless meals that are every bit as flavorful as their meaty counterparts.

Despite high-protein fad diets that encourage liberal meat intake, a well-balanced, plant-based diet that emphasizes grains, beans, vegetables, and fruits continues to be a wise choice over the long run. The trend toward healthy eating is moving away from meat and dairy products, because their high fat and cholesterol content have been linked to heart disease and other maladies. There are also concerns over ingesting the pesticides, antibiotics, and other additives commonly found in animal products. In addition, medical studies now recommend that we eat more soy protein. Endorsed by the USDA, they suggest that 25 grams per day can reduce the risk of heart disease.

That's where *The Vegetarian Meat and Potatoes Cookbook* can help. It's a "meat and potatoes" cookbook without the meat that will change the way people think about vegetarian food, a cuisine not usually associated with comfort foods. This book offers a collection of recipes inspired by popular American dishes, as well as those of other cuisines, while celebrating the diversity of vegetarian ingredients.

Some vegetarians object to "meat-like" recipes, while meat eaters may wonder why vegetarians would want such recipes. But it has never made sense to me that just because I choose not to eat meat, I should be deprived of the flavors and textures of traditional dishes. After all, meat eaters haven't cornered the market on the great-tasting sauces, textures, and accompaniments associated with meat. Early on in my vegetarian lifestyle, I began adapting my favorite meat-centered recipes into vegetarian versions. My husband and I have never looked back, and my friends and family never feel deprived. We still enjoy all the tastes and textures of our former favorite meat dishes, but now they are made meatless.

As you will discover in these pages, the word "meat" can mean more than beefsteak and pork chops. The vegetable kingdom, too, offers a variety of "steaks": mushroom steaks, eggplant steaks, and, of course, beefsteak tomatoes. Herein you will find creative "meat and potatoes" recipes using these vegetable "steaks," along with protein-rich meat alternatives such as tempeh (compressed soybeans), seitan ("wheat-meat"), and tofu (bean curd), called "meat without the bone" in China. To me, tofu is the *real* other white meat.

In this book, you will find the mouthwatering nuances of traditional and contemporary comfort foods that vegetarian recipes often lack. These recipes provide all the full, rich flavors associated with nonvegetarian recipes, but are made healthy with plant-based ingredients. *The Vegetarian Meat and Potatoes Cookbook* is for anyone who is looking for ways to cut back on meat

Vegetarians Can Be Well-Meated

Although we usually associate the word "meat" with animal flesh, the original meaning was merely "meal." In fact, the correct meaning of "meat" is food in general: anything eaten for nourishment, by man or beast. Meat is the edible part of anything, as in the meat of a crab, a nut, or a tomato.

This was the meaning of "meat" for Chaucer, as well as for King James I, the first to have the Bible translated into English. The words of God in Genesis 1:29, "Behold, I have given you every herb bearing seed . . . to you it shall be for meat," show that Adam was initially given a vegetarian diet.

Not long ago, it was correct to "sit at meat" when it was time for dinner. When you get up from the table, having enjoyed a nutritious vegetarian meal, you may consider yourself "well-meated."

and dairy products. It is also for vegetarians, vegans, and others who want to prepare traditional dishes in healthful new ways. It can be especially helpful in bridging the gap when both vegetarians and meat eaters live in the same household.

In these pages you will discover the comfort foods you grew up with—retooled vegetarian-style. There are flaky potpies, burgers, hearty stews, casseroles, "meat" loaf and gravy—even roasts and "steaks"—as well as a selection of international favorites like *Thai Tofu Curry with Potatoes and Pineapple* and *Double Eggplant Moussaka*.

The vegetarian roasts feature stuffing and gravy, while the "thick, juicy steaks" are presented with delectable sauces and potatoes on the side. There are hearty soups and substantial sandwiches for casual meals and, for special occasions, a generous sprinkling of fancier fare, including *Almond-Crusted Tempeh Cutlets with Strawberry Mango Salsa* and *Crispy Stuffed "Fillets" of Soy with Spicy Ginger Sauce*. There are also elegant appetizers such as *Roasted Red Pepper and Potato Napoleons* and rich desserts like *Soy Good Lemon Cheesecake* and *Pecan-Studded Chocolate Brownies*.

It was important to me that the recipes in this book be fun and easy to make, simple enough for beginners, yet sophisticated enough for seasoned cooks. You will find the recipes to be user-friendly, calling for ingredients that are readily available in supermarkets, natural food stores, and ethnic grocers. Alternatives are given for any unusual or hard-to-find ingredients. Special attention is paid to offering timesaving ingredients and methods to help you get dinner on the table in record time. In addition, the recipes do not rely on eggs and dairy for their flavor the way many vegetarian cookbooks do. In this book, both dairy and dairy-free options are offered in the ingredients list, making the recipes accessible to everyone. I encourage those who are new to soy foods to try them in place of eggs and dairy as explained in the recipes. If you do use eggs and dairy, however, consider using only organic products from free-range animals.

If you're looking for a new approach to putting healthy foods on the table, then dig into *The Vegetarian Meat and Potatoes Cookbook*. The cutting-edge vegetarian comfort cuisine in this book will provide you with delicious ways to create family-style dishes, gourmet specialties, and ethnic favorites—all in one volume. Let this book help you serve up what many people want: satisfying "meat and potatoes" meals without the meat.

About the Oils Used in This Book

The use of particular cooking and salad oils in this book is a matter of both function and personal preference. Olive oil, with its great taste and proven health benefits, is used wherever possible. Peanut oil is used in recipes that call for high-heat frying, because it is stable at high temperatures. I use flavorful corn oil in baking and wherever a "buttery" flavor is desired. In Mediterranean salads, I use extra virgin olive oil, and to add an Asian flavor to salads, I use dark, or toasted, sesame oil. If you need a mild-flavored salad oil, flaxseed oil is a wise choice because it contains omega trans-fatty acids that are essential for good health. (Do not use flaxseed oil for cooking, though, because it is unstable at high temperatures.) The best-quality oils are labeled "cold-pressed," "expeller-pressed," or "unrefined," which means they are naturally extracted without the use of chemicals or extreme heat. These high-quality oils are available at natural food stores and some supermarkets and can be quite expensive. But many of the cheaper vegetable oils found on supermarket shelves use harsh chemical solvents and high temperatures during the extraction process, and for that reason I do not recommend them.

CHAPTER ONE

Just for Starters

Appetizers play a challenging role. As the name implies, an appetizer should stimulate the appetite for what is to come and set the tone for the meal by expanding its variety and scope, while complementing the main course. Appetizers are often reserved for special occasions or restaurant dining and, as such, are frequently thought of as indulgences or splurges. Sometimes appetizers are served apart from the meal, especially when entertaining at home. They may range from salsa and corn chips or a simple crudités platter to a silver tray of fancy hors d'oeuvres.

Most of the appetizers in this chapter are substantial enough to enjoy as a lunch entrée or light supper. Served in small portions, they are equally at home as a first course on a dinner menu or as an offering on a buffet table.

In these pages you will find a number of appetizers that are whimsical variations on some of the classics. There is *Fauxscargot*, a garlicky shiitake mushroom appetizer in the style of escargot, *Vegetable Carpaccio*, made with thinly sliced beefsteak tomatoes, and *Angels Back in the Saddle*, quick-fried dulse-wrapped oyster mushrooms, playfully mimicking the bacon-wrapped oysters called Angels on Horseback.

There are also a number of hearty appetizers where potatoes take center stage, including *Tapenade-Stuffed Red Potatoes*, *Potato-Scallion Pakoras*, and *Mini Potato Galettes*. In addition, you will find an eclectic mix of tempting international starters ranging from *Artichoke Crostini* to *Spice Island Plantain Bites* that are surprisingly simple to prepare.

Wild Mushroom Bruschetta

Artichoke Crostini

Spiced Vegetable Samosas

Hoisin Eggplant Balls

Spice Island Plantain Bites

Potato-Scallion Pakoras

Mini Potato Galettes

Tapenade-Stuffed Red Potatoes

Wheat-Meat Satays with Spicy Peanut Sauce

Polenta Triangles with Chipotle Salsa

Roasted Red Pepper and Potato Napoleons

Fauxscargot

Balsamic-Glazed Stuffed Mushrooms

Angels Back in the Saddle

Mushroom Rumaki

Vegetable Carpaccio with Remoulade Sauce

Spiced Nut Collection

Spicy Steamed Vegetable Dumplings

Baba Ganoush Roll-Ups

Oven-Baked Potato Chips

Chipotle-Avocado Dip

Texas Caviar

Red Pepper—Walnut Pâté

Three-Stripe Vegetable Pâté

Country-Style Lentil Pâté

Wild Mushroom Bruschetta

A variety of wild mushrooms is now available in most supermarkets. Use cremini, porcini, or shiitake mushrooms, or any combination. Regular white button mushrooms can be substituted for all or some of the wild mushrooms, but the flavor will be less intense.

Eight 1/2-inch-thick slices Italian bread

2 tablespoons olive oil, plus extra for brushing

1 pound wild mushrooms

2 shallots, minced

1 garlic clove, minced

2 tablespoons dry white wine

1/2 teaspoon dried thyme

1/4 teaspoon dried marjoram

1/2 teaspoon salt

1/8 teaspoon freshly ground black pepper

1 Lightly brush both sides of the bread with oil and set aside. Clean and trim the mushrooms, discarding the stems from shiitakes, if using. Mince the mushrooms and set aside. Preheat the broiler.

2 Heat I tablespoon of the olive oil in a large skillet over medium heat. Add the shallots and garlic and cook, stirring frequently, until softened, 2 to 3 minutes. Stir in the reserved mushrooms, the wine, thyme, marjoram, salt, and pepper and cook, stirring several times, until the mixture is hot and the liquid the mushrooms release evaporates, about 5 minutes.

3 While the mushroom mixture is cooking, toast the bread under the broiler until browned on both sides, about 30 seconds per side.

4 Spoon the hot mushroom mixture over the toasted bread and serve immediately.

Serves 8

Mad About Mushrooms

Not long ago, the only mushrooms widely available were the ordinary cultivated white ones. These days, however, rows upon rows of mushroom varieties can be found in the market, from the tiny enoki to the giant portobello. Woodsy shiitakes, golden chanterelles, and delicate oyster mushrooms may be flanked by intensely flavored cremini, cone-shaped morels, or pricey porcini. Each mushroom variety has its characteristic flavor as well as texture. Whether stuffed, sautéed, or grilled, these fabulous fungi are savored by food lovers the world over.

Because of their meaty texture, mushrooms are especially prized by vegetarian cooks. While the smaller varieties lend texture and flavor to stewed, sautéed, and baked dishes, it is the portobello—with its wide flat cap—that is most often thought of as a vegetarian "meat." Widely available in supermarkets, the portobello is actually a large cremini mushroom. Its dark brown gills, while entirely edible, can lend a slightly bitter taste and are sometimes removed before cooking. Portobello caps can be cooked in much the same way as a steak and are especially delicious grilled or pan-seared.

Artichoke Crostini

These flavorful bites can be assembled ahead of time and popped into the oven just before serving. Fresh or canned artichoke hearts can be substituted for the frozen, but avoid the marinated kind, as the flavor would overpower the other ingredients. Soy mayonnaise is available in well-stocked supermarkets and natural food stores, or you can make your own using the recipe on page 309.

One 9-ounce package frozen artichoke
    hearts

2 garlic cloves, minced

$1/3$ cup regular or soy mayonnaise

2 tablespoons freshly grated Parmesan
    cheese or soy Parmesan

1 teaspoon fresh lemon juice

1 teaspoon minced fresh oregano leaves
    or $1/2$ teaspoon dried

Tabasco sauce

Salt

Eight $1/2$-inch-thick slices French bread

$1/4$ cup olive oil

Fresh oregano sprigs (optional) and
    capers for garnish

1 Preheat the oven to 400 degrees F. Cook the artichoke hearts according to the package directions and drain well; let cool slightly.

2 Finely chop the artichoke hearts and place them in a medium-size bowl. Add the garlic, mayonnaise, Parmesan, lemon juice, oregano, and a splash of Tabasco. Season with salt to taste and mix until well blended.

3 Lightly brush both sides of the bread with the olive oil and place on a baking sheet. Bake until lightly browned, 1 to 2 minutes. Remove from the oven, spread the artichoke mixture on the bread, and return to the baking sheet.

4 Bake until the topping is heated through and the tops are lightly browned, 3 to 5 minutes. Garnish each crostini with a small sprig of fresh oregano, if using, and a caper and serve hot.

Serves 4

Spiced Vegetable Samosas

~~~

Fragrant spices punctuate the potatoes and other vegetables surrounded by a flaky crust in this satisfying appetizer from India. I leave the peels on the potato for extra flavor and nutrition. Instead of being fried in oil, as is traditional, these samosas are baked in the oven. Serve with your favorite chutney. Garam masala spice mixtures are available at Indian markets and specialty grocers.

---

1 cup all-purpose flour

1/4 cup water

1 tablespoon plus 2 teaspoons peanut
   oil, plus extra for brushing

1 small onion, minced

1 small carrot, minced

1 large Yukon Gold potato, diced,
   parboiled for 10 minutes, and drained

1/2 cup frozen green peas

1 garlic clove, minced

1 teaspoon garam masala, or to taste

2 tablespoons minced fresh cilantro
   leaves

1/2 teaspoon salt, or more to taste

1/8 teaspoon cayenne, or more to taste

1 In a medium-size bowl, combine the flour and water with 2 teaspoons of the oil and stir until a dough forms. Cover and let stand for 30 minutes.

2 Meanwhile, heat the remaining 1 tablespoon oil in a large skillet over medium heat. Add the onion and carrot and cook, stirring, until softened, about 5 minutes. Stir in the potato, peas, garlic, garam masala, cilantro, salt, and cayenne. Cook until all the vegetables are soft, about 10 minutes. Set aside to cool.

3 Preheat the oven to 400 degrees F. Roll out the dough on a floured board into a thin 16-inch square and cut into 4-inch squares. Place a small amount of the filling in the center of each square and fold the dough in half over the filling to make a triangular shape. Seal the edges with a little water.

4 Place the samosas on a lightly oiled baking sheet and brush them lightly with oil. Place in the oven and bake, turning once, until browned on both sides, 12 to 15 minutes. Serve hot, warm, or at room temperature.

Serves 4 to 6

Hoisin Eggplant Balls

These tasty nuggets coated with hoisin sauce are a great way to enjoy eggplant and an interesting alternative to that chafing dish filled with little meatballs on the buffet table. Garlic, sesame paste, and peanuts add depth, substance, and great flavor to the eggplant mixture.

1 large eggplant

3 garlic cloves, halved lengthwise

1/2 cup ground peanuts

1/4 cup tahini (sesame paste)

2 tablespoons minced fresh parsley
  leaves

Salt and freshly ground black pepper

About 3/4 cup dry bread crumbs

Peanut oil for baking or frying

3 tablespoons hoisin sauce

1 Preheat the oven to 400 degrees F. Cut 6 slits in the eggplant and place a piece of garlic in each slit. Place the eggplant on a lightly oiled baking sheet and bake until soft, about 45 minutes. Remove the eggplant from the oven and allow to cool. Reduce the oven temperature to 375 degrees F if you will be baking the eggplant balls.

2 Halve the eggplant lengthwise and scrape out the pulp. Squeeze the pulp between your palms to remove any excess liquid, and place in a bowl. Add the peanuts, tahini, parsley, and salt and pepper and blend well. Add just enough bread crumbs to hold the mixture together when shaped into balls. Roll the mixture into I- to I 1/2-inch balls and coat with the remaining bread crumbs.

3 Bake on a lightly oiled baking sheet until browned and firm, about 20 minutes; or fry, in batches, in a large skillet in 1/4 inch of hot oil over medium-high heat until brown on all sides, 2 to 4 minutes.

4 Place the eggplant balls in a bowl with the hoisin sauce, stirring gently to coat. Skewer with toothpicks and serve at once.

Serves 6 to 8

Grinding and Chopping Nuts

Whether you chop nuts by hand or machine may depend on several factors. If you need coarsely chopped nuts, a sharp knife may be the best choice, as it allows for more control over the size of the chopped nuts. For finely ground nuts, or if you are in a hurry, a food processor may suit your needs. Just be careful not to overprocess the nuts, or you may end up with nut butter. Other ways to grind nuts are in a blender, coffee mill, or a nut grinder, made specifically for the job.

Roasting Nuts

To roast nuts, preheat the oven to 350 degrees F. Spread the nuts evenly in a single layer on a baking sheet. Place in the oven and roast for 7 to 10 minutes, depending on the nut, until lightly golden and fragrant. Watch carefully, so that the nuts do not overbake.

Spice Island Plantain Bites

Plantains, sometimes called cooking bananas, are available in most supermarkets. The skins of ripe plantains are almost black, but they are creamy white inside. Their mildly sweet flavor is accented by the lime juice, peanut butter, and spices in this recipe, which hint at a taste of the islands.

---

2 garlic cloves, pressed

1 tablespoon creamy natural peanut
   butter

1 teaspoon fresh lime juice

$1/_4$ teaspoon salt

$1/_4$ teaspoon dried oregano

$1/_4$ teaspoon dried mint

$1/_8$ teaspoon ground allspice

$1/_8$ teaspoon cayenne

$1/_8$ teaspoon freshly ground black pepper

3 medium-size ripe plantains, peeled and
   mashed

2 tablespoons olive oil

1 Preheat the oven to 200 degrees F. In a medium-size bowl, combine the garlic, peanut butter, lime juice, salt, oregano, mint, allspice, cayenne, and pepper and blend into a paste. Add the mashed plantains and mix until well combined. Shape the mixture into 1-inch balls, using about 1 tablespoon of the mixture for each.

2 Heat the oil in a large skillet over medium heat. Place the balls in the hot oil, in batches, and press down on them lightly with a metal spatula. Fry, turning once, until golden brown on both sides, about 2 minutes per side. Transfer to paper towels to drain, then place in the oven until all the plantain bites are cooked. Serve hot.

Serves 6 to 8

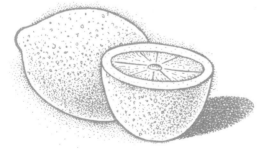

Potato-Scallion Pakoras

These yummy Indian fritters, coated in a scallion-flecked chickpea flour batter, can be made with a variety of vegetables, but this version with potatoes is hard to beat for comfort food at its finest. It's especially good served with a tamarind or mango chutney. Chickpea flour is available at natural food stores and Indian and Middle Eastern grocers.

2 large or 3 medium-size Yukon Gold or other all-purpose potatoes (about 1 pound)

$1/2$ teaspoon brown mustard seeds

$1/2$ cup all-purpose flour

$1/2$ cup chickpea flour

1 teaspoon salt

$1/8$ teaspoon cayenne

$1/4$ cup finely minced scallions

$1/2$ cup regular or soy yogurt

About $3/4$ cup water

Peanut oil for frying

1 In a medium-size saucepan, boil the potatoes in salted water to cover until just tender, 20 to 25 minutes. Drain and allow to cool, then cut the potatoes into $1/4$-inch-thick slices and set aside.

2 Toast the mustard seeds in a dry skillet over medium heat until they pop. Remove from the heat and place in a medium-size bowl, along with both flours, the salt, and cayenne. Stir in the scallions, yogurt, and as much water as needed to achieve a smooth batter.

3 Heat about I inch of oil in a large skillet over medium-high heat. In batches, add the potato slices to the batter to coat, then let any excess drip off and place them in the hot oil. Do not crowd the pan. Cook, turning once, until golden brown on both sides, about 2 minutes. Transfer to paper towels to drain, and serve hot.

Serves 4

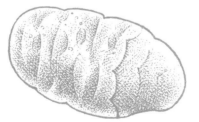

Mini Potato Galettes

These lovely galettes are surprisingly light, despite the fact that they're made with potatoes. Although thyme is used here, you can substitute a different fresh herb according to personal preference or to complement another dish being served with the meal.

1 pound small new potatoes

2 tablespoons olive oil

1/4 cup grated yellow onion

Salt and freshly ground black pepper

1 tablespoon minced fresh thyme leaves,
   plus 4 sprigs for garnish

1 Preheat the oven to 375 degrees F. Using a mandoline or other vegetable slicer or a sharp knife, cut the potatoes into very thin round slices.

2 Arrange enough slices on a lightly oiled baking sheet, overlapping them slightly, to form 4 circles about 5 inches in diameter. Brush with olive oil and sprinkle with the grated onion, thyme, and salt and pepper, then continue layering, brushing and sprinkling each layer, until all the potatoes are used up.

3 Drizzle with a little more olive oil and bake until the potatoes are tender and browned, 30 to 40 minutes. Place each galette on a serving plate and garnish with a sprig of thyme.

Serves 4

Tapenade-Stuffed Red Potatoes

The salty earthiness of tapenade is the perfect complement for sweet red potatoes. For the most appealing presentation, try to find small red-skinned potatoes of uniform size, $1^1/_2$ to 2 inches in diameter.

12 small red potatoes

2 tablespoons olive oil

$1/_4$ cup Black Olive Tapenade (page 312)

$1/_2$ teaspoon salt

$1/_8$ teaspoon cayenne

1 tablespoon minced fresh chives

1 Preheat the oven to 350 degrees F. Prick the potatoes with a fork to keep them from bursting and bake until soft, about 30 minutes. Let cool slightly.

2 Cut the potatoes in half and, using a melon baller, gently scoop out some of the potato flesh from each one and place it in a bowl; set the potato halves aside. Mash the potato flesh with the olive oil, tapenade, salt, and cayenne until well combined.

3 Cut a small slice off the bottom of the potato halves if necessary for stability. Place the stuffing in the potato halves and arrange the potatoes on a serving tray. Garnish with the chives and serve at once.

Serves 6

Wheat-Meat Satays with Spicy Peanut Sauce

Sliced seitan readily absorbs the flavorful marinade, but tempeh, tofu, or a "meaty" vegetable, such as eggplant or mushrooms, can be substituted if you prefer. The bamboo skewers, available in well-stocked supermarkets, should be soaked in water for 30 minutes before using to prevent them from burning. Rather than baking the satays, you can grill or broil them until lightly browned.

1 shallot, chopped

2 garlic cloves, chopped

2 teaspoons peeled and minced fresh ginger

2 tablespoons tamari or other soy sauce

2 tablespoons fresh lime juice

1 tablespoon toasted sesame oil

2 tablespoons firmly packed light brown sugar

$1/2$ teaspoon Asian chile paste

12 ounces seitan, cut into $1/4$-inch-wide strips

1 small head romaine lettuce, cut into chiffonade

Spicy Peanut Sauce (page 305)

1 In a food processor, combine the shallot, garlic, ginger, tamari, lime juice, sesame oil, brown sugar, and chile paste and process until smooth. Transfer to a large bowl. Add the seitan strips and toss to coat. Cover and marinate for 30 to 45 minutes at room temperature.

2 Preheat the oven to 450 degrees F. Remove the seitan from the marinade, reserving the marinade. Thread the seitan onto bamboo skewers and place on a lightly oiled baking sheet. Bake, turning once and brushing with the marinade, until lightly browned, about 10 minutes.

3 Place the satays on individual plates lined with the lettuce strips. Serve at once, with individual bowls of the peanut sauce.

Serves 4

An Asian Pantry

These days, the pantry of virtually any well-stocked kitchen will include an arsenal of Asian ingredients—exotic sauces, pastes, and powders that can turn an everyday meal into something special. Although by no means exhaustive, here is a basic list of the Asian pantry ingredients used in this book. Look for these and other Asian ingredients in well-stocked supermarkets, natural food stores, and Asian markets.

- **Chile paste:** A prepared blend of ground chile peppers that can include garlic, vinegar, ginger, or other seasonings, which varies in flavor and heat intensity; sometimes called chile sauce. There are Thai, Chinese, Korean, and Vietnamese varieties, as well as an Indonesian version called sambal oelek.

- **Coconut milk:** A thick, creamy liquid made from coconuts, used to flavor Thai and Indian curries.

- **Five-spice powder:** An aromatic Chinese seasoning blend most often made from cinnamon, cloves, fennel seeds, star anise, and Szechwan peppercorns.

- **Hoisin sauce:** A thick brown Chinese condiment, also used as a marinade, made from soybeans, chiles, garlic, sugar, vinegar, and aromatic spices.

- **Mirin:** A sweet Japanese rice wine used in cooking.

- **Oyster sauce:** A thick brown cooking sauce made with oyster extract, used in Asian stir-fries. The vegetarian version of this sauce may be labeled "Vegetarian Oyster Sauce" or "Vegetarian Stir-fry Sauce."

- **Peanut oil:** A flavorless oil used for stir-fry cooking because it has a high smoking point.

- **Rice vinegar:** A light clear vinegar made from fermented rice, used to season sushi rice and to make salad dressings.

- **Sambal oelek:** An Indonesian condiment that contains ground chile peppers, sugar, salt, and vinegar. (See chile paste, above.)

- **Sesame oil:** Toasted or "dark" sesame oil is an aromatic and flavorful oil pressed from toasted sesame seeds. It is used as a seasoning rather than a cooking oil.

- **Sesame paste:** The popular thick Middle Eastern paste made from ground sesame seeds is called tahini; Asian sesame paste or sauce is similar but not as thick and does not contain added sesame oil. It is used in sauces, dips, and dressings.

- **Tamari soy sauce:** Also called shoyu, tamari is a traditionally made naturally aged Japanese soy sauce that contains no additives or artificial ingredients, unlike many of the chemically processed, inexpensive brands found on supermarket shelves. Tamari has a mellow salty flavor and can be used as an all-purpose seasoning.

- **Wasabi:** Often called "Japanese horseradish," this root is used to make the fiery green sushi condiment. It is most often available as a powder to mix into a paste with water.

Polenta Triangles with Chipotle Salsa

Polenta is the perfect foil for the bold flavors of this spicy salsa. Chipotle chiles are dried jalapeños. They are commonly found canned in adobo sauce, a thick, dark red sauce made from ground chiles, vinegar, and herbs, and add a smoky richness to recipes. This salsa is best when made several hours in advance to allow the flavors to mingle.

Salsa:

1 pound ripe tomatoes, seeded and
    chopped

1/4 cup chopped yellow onion

2 scallions, chopped

2 canned chipotle chiles in adobo sauce,
    chopped

1 teaspoon cider vinegar

1 teaspoon fresh lime juice

1/4 teaspoon salt

Polenta:

3 3/4 cups vegetable stock (see page 36)

3/4 teaspoon salt

1 cup medium-coarse yellow cornmeal

2 tablespoons freshly grated Parmesan
    cheese or soy Parmesan

Olive oil for brushing

1 Make the salsa: In a medium-size bowl, combine the tomatoes, onion, scallions, chipotles, vinegar, lime juice, and salt. Cover and refrigerate until ready to serve.

2 Make the polenta: Place the stock and salt in a large saucepan over high heat and bring to a boil. Add the cornmeal to the boiling water in a slow, steady stream, stirring constantly with a wooden spoon. Reduce the heat to low and continue to cook, stirring frequently, until the polenta is very thick, 30 to 35 minutes.

3 Stir in the cheese. Spoon the polenta onto a lightly oiled baking sheet, spread it with a wet spatula to a 1/2-inch thickness, and refrigerate for at least 45 minutes, until cooled and firm.

4 Preheat the broiler. Cut the polenta into 6 equal squares, then cut the squares on the diagonal to create 12 triangles. Place on a lightly oiled baking sheet. Brush with olive oil and broil, turning once, until golden brown on both sides, 1 to 2 minutes per side Serve immediately, with the salsa.

Serves 6

Roasted Red Pepper and Potato Napoleons

L ayers of roasted bell peppers and potatoes stack up to create a show-stopping appetizer that is surprisingly simple to make. A flavorful basil pesto sauce provides the perfect complement.

4 small red bell peppers

2 large Yukon Gold or other all-purpose
    potatoes

Olive oil

Salt and freshly ground black pepper

1/4 cup Basil Pesto (page 313), thinned
    with a little olive oil

Fresh basil leaves for garnish

1   Roast the peppers over an open flame or under the broiler, turning often, until the skin is blackened on all sides. Place in a paper bag, seal the bag, and let steam for 5 minutes. Remove the peppers from the bag and cut lengthwise in half. Scrape the charred skin from the peppers and remove the stems and seeds. Set aside.

2   Preheat the oven to 425 degrees F. Cut 4 large 1/4-inch-thick round slices from the center portion of each potato (you can cook off the remaining potatoes and reserve for another use). Place the potatoes on a lightly oiled baking sheet, brush the tops with olive oil, and season with salt and pepper. Roast, turning once, until soft, about 20 minutes.

3   To assemble, place 1 slice of potato on a plate and top with a bell pepper half, another slice of potato, and another bell pepper half. Repeat the procedure on three more plates to make 4 stacks in all. Surround each with a drizzle of the pesto sauce and garnish with basil leaves.

Serves 4

Fauxscargot

Reminiscent of escargot, these delectable shiitake mushrooms are sautéed in a garlicky herb sauce and served in tiny nests of angel hair pasta. If you have actual escargot dishes, they add an elegant, if whimsical, touch to this flavorful appetizer. Toss the hot cooked pasta with a little oil after cooking to prevent it from sticking together. If you can't find small shiitakes, use larger ones and cut them in halves or quarters to make 24 pieces.

1/4 cup olive oil, plus extra for the pasta

2 garlic cloves, minced

1 tablespoon minced shallot

24 small shiitake mushroom caps

1/2 teaspoon dried oregano

1/2 teaspoon dried basil

1/3 cup dry white wine or dry sherry

1 tablespoon fresh lemon juice

1 tablespoon minced fresh parsley leaves

Salt and freshly ground black pepper

4 ounces angel hair pasta

1 Heat the oil in a large skillet over medium heat. Add the garlic and shallots and cook until fragrant, about 30 seconds. Add the mushrooms, oregano, basil, wine, lemon juice, parsley, salt and pepper to taste and simmer until the mushrooms are tender and the liquid is reduced slightly, about 4 to 5 minutes.

2 Meanwhile, cook the pasta in a large pot of boiling salted water until *al dente*, 2 to 4 minutes. Drain well and toss with a little olive oil.

3 To serve, coil 4 to 6 hot pasta strands each in the six hollows of four escargot dishes, or make 6 coils each on small plates. Place a mushroom in the center of each pasta nest and drizzle the pan sauce over them. Serve hot.

Serves 4

Balsamic-Glazed Stuffed Mushrooms

The syrupy sweet-and-sour richness of reduced balsamic vinegar adds a sophisticated taste to these stuffed mushrooms.

1 pound small white button mushrooms

3 tablespoons olive oil

1 garlic clove, minced

1/4 cup dry bread crumbs

1 tablespoon freshly grated Parmesan
    cheese or soy Parmesan

1 tablespoon minced fresh basil leaves

Salt and freshly ground black pepper

1/2 cup balsamic vinegar

1 Trim the mushroom stems and remove them from the mushrooms; set the caps aside. Chop the stems. Heat 1 tablespoon of the olive oil in a small skillet over medium heat. Add the garlic and cook until fragrant, about 30 seconds. Add the mushroom stems and cook until softened, about 1 minute. Transfer to a bowl and add the bread crumbs, Parmesan, basil, and salt and pepper to taste. Set aside.

2 Pour the balsamic vinegar into a large skillet and simmer over medium-high heat until it reduces by about two-thirds and is syrupy. Add the mushroom caps and cook until slightly softened, about 2 to 3 minutes. Remove the mushrooms from the skillet with a slotted spoon and let them cool slightly.

3 Preheat the broiler. Stuff the mushroom caps with the bread crumb mixture and place on an ungreased baking sheet. Drizzle with the remaining 2 tablespoons olive oil and place under the broiler until lightly browned on top. Serve hot.

Serves 4 to 6

Angels Back in the Saddle

Inspired by the oyster and bacon appetizer called "angels on horseback," these flavorful nuggets are made with oyster mushrooms and dulse, a peppery reddish sea vegetable that becomes crispy when fried. Dulse is available in natural food stores.

8 ounces oyster mushrooms

2 ounces dulse sea vegetable

2 tablespoons olive oil

1 Trim the mushrooms into uniform bite-size pieces. Wrap each in a piece of dulse, securing it with a toothpick.

2 Heat the olive oil in a large skillet over medium-high heat. Add the dulse-wrapped mushrooms and fry quickly, turning to crisp on all sides, about 2 minutes per side. Drain on paper towels. Serve hot.

Serves 4 to 6

Mushroom Rumaki

The flavors and textures of these tasty tidbits, made with mushrooms, vegetarian bacon, and water chestnuts, are inspired by traditional rumaki, which is made with chicken livers and bacon. Sliced canned water chestnuts are available in supermarkets and Asian markets.

24 canned water chestnut slices, rinsed

$1/2$ cup port wine

1 tablespoon olive oil

12 small mushroom caps, halved

1 tablespoon tamari or other soy sauce

8 slices vegetarian bacon, cut into 2-inch
   lengths

1 Place the water chestnuts in a shallow bowl and add the port. Marinate for 30 minutes at room temperature.

2 Heat the oil in a small skillet over medium heat. Add the mushrooms and soy sauce and cook until the mushrooms are slightly softened, about 1 minute. Remove from the heat.

3 Position a rack about 6 inches from the heat source and preheat the broiler. Wrap a slice of water chestnut and a mushroom half in a piece of bacon and secure with a toothpick. Repeat with the remaining ingredients and arrange on a baking sheet. Place under the broiler and broil until the bacon is crisp. Serve hot.

Serves 6 to 8

Vegetable Carpaccio with Remoulade Sauce

T raditional carpaccio is thinly sliced raw beef, but I prefer mine made with juicy red beefsteak tomatoes. Arranged on a plate with cucumber slices for crunch, this makes an elegant appetizer when homegrown tomatoes are at the peak of their season.

---

2 large ripe beefsteak tomatoes

1 English cucumber

1 teaspoon capers, drained

1 tablespoon snipped fresh chives

Extra virgin olive oil

Salt and freshly ground black pepper

Ragin' Remoulade Sauce (page 311)

1 Cut the tomatoes and cucumber into paper-thin slices (use a mandoline or other vegetable slicer if you have one). Fan them out in overlapping rings on a large serving platter or individual plates, depending on your preference for presentation.

2 Sprinkle with the capers, chives, a drizzle of olive oil, and salt and pepper to taste. Serve with the remoulade sauce.

Serves 4

Spiced Nut Collection

Nuts are high in protein and vitamins and loaded with taste, especially these, which are flavored with a variety of spices and seasonings. For a striking presentation, serve them along with an assortment of dried fruit in a partitioned shadowbox used as a tray. Begin with unsalted raw nuts.

Tamari Almonds

1 teaspoon peanut oil

1 teaspoon tamari or other soy sauce

$1/8$ teaspoon cayenne

1 cup unblanched raw almonds

Salt

Curried Pecans

1 teaspoon peanut oil

1 teaspoon curry powder

1 cup raw pecans

Salt

Maple Walnuts

1 teaspoon peanut oil

1 teaspoon maple syrup

1 cup raw walnuts

Chili-Spiced Peanuts

1 teaspoon peanut oil

1 teaspoon chili powder

1 cup raw peanuts

Salt

1 Preheat the oven to 300 degrees F.

2 *For the almonds:* In a small bowl, whisk together the oil, tamari, and cayenne. Add the almonds and toss to coat. Spread the almonds on a baking sheet, sprinkle with salt, and bake until browned and dry, about 20 minutes. Let cool completely.

For the pecans: In a small bowl, whisk together the oil and curry powder. Add the pecans and toss to coat. Spread the pecans on a baking sheet, sprinkle with salt, and bake until browned and dry, about 20 minutes. Let cool completely.

For the walnuts: In a small bowl, whisk together the oil and maple syrup. Add the walnuts and toss to coat evenly. Spread the walnuts on a baking sheet and bake until browned and dry, about 20 minutes. Let cool completely.

For the peanuts: In a small bowl, whisk together the oil and chili powder. Add the peanuts and toss to coat evenly. Spread the peanuts on a baking sheet, sprinkle with salt, and bake until browned and dry, about 20 minutes. Let cool completely.

Store in airtight containers. They will keep for a few days at room temperature or a few months in the freezer. (To refresh after freezing, bake for a few minutes, then cool before serving.)

Makes 4 cups (1 cup each)

Spicy Steamed Vegetable Dumplings

Serve these dumplings with tamari, Ginger-Soy Dipping Sauce (page 306), or Spicy Peanut Sauce (page 305). Wonton or dumpling wrappers and hoisin sauce can be found in well-stocked supermarkets and Asian grocery stores.

6 ounces extra-firm tofu, crumbled

One 8-ounce can water chestnuts, drained and rinsed

1/2 cup fresh bean sprouts, chopped

1 garlic clove, minced

2 teaspoons peeled and minced fresh ginger

1 tablespoon hoisin sauce

1 teaspoon cornstarch

1 teaspoon dry sherry

1/4 teaspoon salt

24 wonton or dumpling wrappers

2 tablespoons peanut oil

2 teaspoons tamari or other soy sauce

1/2 cup water

Chiffonade of romaine lettuce for serving

1 In a food processor, combine the tofu, water chestnuts, bean sprouts, garlic, and ginger and process until fairly smooth, but with a little texture remaining. Transfer the mixture to a medium-size bowl and add the hoisin sauce, cornstarch, sherry, and salt, mixing well.

2 Place 1 wonton wrapper on a work surface and spoon 2 to 3 teaspoons of the filling mixture onto the center of the wrapper. Fold the wrapper in half to form a triangle. Moisten the edges of the wrapper with a little water to seal. Then pull the opposite corners toward the center, moisten the inside of one corner with water, and press onto the opposite corner to seal. Repeat with the remaining wrappers and filling mixture.

3 Heat the oil in a large nonstick skillet over medium-high heat. Working in batches, place the dumplings in the skillet, without crowding them, and cook until golden, about 3 minutes. Stir in the tamari and then the water. Return all the dumplings to the skillet, cover, reduce the heat to medium, and steam the dumplings for 5 minutes.

4 Place the dumplings on small plates lined with lettuce and serve at once, with individual bowls of your favorite dipping sauce.

Serves 6

Baba Ganoush Roll-Ups

The Middle Eastern–style eggplant puree called baba ganoush is a popular multipurpose spread that is especially good slathered on lavash or other flatbread, rolled up, and cut into bite-size pieces. Arranged on a tray, they make an easy and elegant party hors d'oeuvre that will disappear quickly.

1 large eggplant (about 2 pounds)

2 garlic cloves, quartered lengthwise

1/3 cup tahini (sesame paste)

Juice of 1 lemon

3/4 teaspoon salt

Cayenne

1/4 cup regular or soy yogurt

2 tablespoons minced fresh parsley
   leaves

2 to 3 lavash or other flatbreads

1 Preheat the oven to 350 degrees F. Cut the eggplant lengthwise in half and place cut side down on a lightly oiled baking sheet. Cut 4 deep gashes in each eggplant half and insert the garlic pieces. Bake the eggplant until soft, about 40 minutes. Allow to cool.

2 Scoop out the eggplant flesh and the garlic and place in a food processor. Add the tahini, lemon juice, salt, and cayenne to taste and pulse until well combined. Transfer to a medium-size bowl and stir in the yogurt and parsley.

3 Spread the eggplant mixture on a piece of lavash, leaving a 1/2-inch border all around, and roll up. Cut crosswise into 2-inch pieces and stand on end on a serving platter. Repeat with the remaining lavash until the eggplant mixture is used up, and serve.

Serves 4 to 6

note: The roll-ups can be refrigerated in an airtight container until ready to use. They will keep well for a few hours but are best served shortly after they are sliced. You can make the puree in advance and refrigerate it, then assemble and slice the roll-ups close to serving time, or assemble the rolls ahead, wrap tightly, and refrigerate, then cut into slices just before serving.

Oven-Baked Potato Chips

Hand-crafted potato chips elevate this common snack to tasty new heights. Serve with drinks prior to a casual meal or give new meaning to the old "chip-and-dip" standby by arranging the chips on a silver platter, surrounding a small bowl of your favorite dip. Apply the dip like caviar with a tiny spoon.

2 large or 3 small Yukon Gold potatoes (about 1 pound)

Salt

1 Preheat the oven to 425 degrees F. Using a sharp knife or a mandoline or other vegetable slicer, cut the potatoes into paper-thin slices. Place the potato slices in a bowl of cold water for about 5 minutes to remove some of the starch. Drain and dry very well, using a dish towel or salad spinner.

2 Spread the potato slices on a lightly oiled baking sheet, making sure they do not overlap. Sprinkle with salt and bake, turning once, until lightly browned and crisp, about 10 minutes on each side. Although they will hold up for a while, the chips taste best shortly after baking.

Serves 8

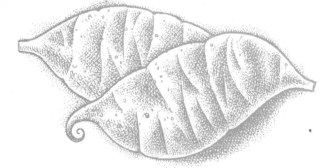

Chipotle-Avocado Dip

The vibrant flavors of the Southwest combine in this versatile dip made with creamy avocados and smoky chipotle chiles in adobo sauce. Fresh garlic and lime juice add even more depth. While this is great as a dip served with cut-up vegetables, tortilla chips, or crackers, it also makes a good spread to use in wrap sandwiches.

3 ripe avocados, peeled, pitted, and
    coarsely chopped
Juice of 1 lime
$1/3$ cup canned chipotle chiles in adobo
    sauce
2 garlic cloves, minced

Place the avocados, lime juice, chiles, with their sauce, and garlic in a food processor or blender. Process until smooth, then transfer to a bowl. Cover and chill until ready to serve. This dip is best served within a few hours after it is made.

Serves 6

Meatless "Meat and Potato" Appetizers

Hors d'oeuvres and other tasty nibbles are usually reserved for parties and other social gatherings. These flavorful, often fussy little creations help to make a party special. Substantial appetizers and canapés are sometimes referred to as "heavy hors d'oeuvres" by caterers and others in the business. Although this expression is unappetizing at best, it certainly gets the point across that carrot sticks are not on the menu.

By serving hearty vegetarian appetizers, you can dispel the carrot stick myth and serve "heavy" hors d'oeuvres that are healthy and delicious. Choices abound among various ethnic cuisines. Consider a Spanish tapas buffet, a Chinese dim sum table, or a Middle Eastern *mezze* with dolmas, hummus, and baba ganoush. An Indian selection could include an assortment of pakoras and samosas with various chutneys. A hearty Mediterranean menu will always win approval. Serve vegetable tarts, veggie roll-ups on flatbread, or perhaps crostini or bruschetta topped with mushroom duxelles or red pepper–walnut pâté.

I love to see the looks of surprise and delight on guests' faces when they arrive at a vegetarian party expecting little more than crudités, only to find themselves surrounded by opulent full-flavored dishes designed for "meat and potatoes" people. If you want the food at your next party to be memorable, consider serving some "heavy" vegetarian hors d'oeuvres.

Texas Caviar

The down-home goodness of black-eyed peas is celebrated in this hearty spread. Serve it as you would any caviar—with toast points, crackers, or toasted French or Italian bread rounds. Although iced vodka is often served with regular caviar, I prefer to wash down this "caviar" with a cold beer.

1¹/₂ cups cooked black-eyed peas or one
  15-ounce can, drained and rinsed

1 garlic clove, minced

1 scallion, minced

3 tablespoons minced fresh parsley
  leaves

1¹/₂ tablespoons olive oil

2 teaspoons cider vinegar

¹/₂ teaspoon Dijon mustard

Splash of Tabasco sauce

¹/₈ teaspoon sugar

Salt and freshly ground black pepper

1 Place the black-eyed peas, garlic, and scallion in a food processor and pulse until coarsely chopped; do not overprocess. Transfer to a bowl.

2 Stir in the parsley, oil, vinegar, mustard, Tabasco, and sugar. Season to taste with salt and pepper and stir until well combined. Cover and chill before serving.

Serves 4

Red Pepper—Walnut Pâté

The rich texture and flavor of this pâté will satisfy the heartiest of appetites. It's great spooned into a hollowed-out raw red bell pepper and served with crackers or cut-up vegetables, or used as a spread for crostini or bruschetta.

2 large red bell peppers

2 tablespoons olive oil

1 small yellow onion, finely minced

1 garlic clove, minced

1 cup chopped walnuts

2 tablespoons minced fresh parsley
 leaves

Salt and freshly ground black pepper

1 Roast the peppers over an open flame or under the broiler, turning frequently, until the skin is blackened on all sides. Place in a paper bag, seal the bag, and let steam for 5 minutes. Remove from the bag and scrape the charred skin from the peppers. Remove the stems and seeds, coarsely chop the peppers, and set aside.

2 Heat the oil in a medium-size skillet over medium heat. Add the onion and garlic and cook until softened, about 5 minutes. Remove from the heat.

3 In a food processor, combine the onion mixture, the reserved roasted peppers, the walnuts, parsley, and salt and pepper to taste and process until smooth. Transfer to a bowl, cover, and chill before serving.

Serves 4 to 6

Three-Stripe Vegetable Pâté

Layers of mushroom, spinach, and tomato combine with creamy cannellini beans in this hearty but elegant pâté. Serve it whole on a buffet table, or sliced and plated for a seated meal.

4 ounces spinach, tough stems removed and washed well

3 cups cooked cannellini beans or two 15-ounce cans, drained and rinsed

2 tablespoons regular or soy milk

1/2 teaspoon salt

1/4 teaspoon freshly ground black pepper

Pinch of ground nutmeg

1 cup chopped mushrooms

1 garlic clove, minced

2 tablespoons dry white wine

1/2 teaspoon dried thyme

2 tablespoons tomato sauce

1/2 teaspoon dried basil

Fresh basil leaves (optional) and cherry tomatoes for garnish

1 Lightly steam or boil the spinach until tender. Drain well, squeezing out the excess liquid. Finely chop and set aside.

2 Process the beans in a food processor until smooth. Add the milk, salt, and pepper and process to mix well. Divide the bean mixture evenly among three bowls.

3 Lightly oil a 4 x 8-inch loaf pan or pâté mold. Combine the spinach, nutmeg, and the bean mixture from one of the bowls in the food processor and puree. Taste and adjust the seasonings. Spoon the spinach mixture into the prepared pan, smoothing the top.

4 Place the mushrooms, garlic, wine, and thyme in a small saucepan and simmer over low heat until the mushrooms and garlic are soft, about 5 minutes. Drain well.

5 Fold the mushroom mixture into the second bowl of bean mixture and blend well. Carefully spread the mushroom mixture over the spinach layer, being careful not to disturb the bottom layer. Smooth the top.

6 Add the tomato sauce and basil to the remaining bean mixture and blend well. Carefully spread the tomato mixture over the mushroom layer, being careful not to disturb it. Cover and refrigerate overnight.

7 To serve, unmold the pâté onto a plate and garnish with basil leaves, if using, and cherry tomatoes.

note: The appeal of this pâté is in the attractive presentation of three distinct layers. For that reason, it is important to use a narrow, deep pan—no more than 4 inches wide.

Serves 8

Country-Style Lentil Pâté

Cooked lentils combined with sunflower seeds form the basis of a coarse, vegetarian-style country pâté. It can be made several days ahead of time for no-fuss entertaining. Serve with French bread rounds or crackers.

2 tablespoons olive oil

1 medium-size yellow onion, coarsely grated

1 garlic clove, minced

1 tablespoon brandy

1 teaspoon sweet paprika

1 teaspoon dried thyme

1/2 teaspoon salt

1/8 teaspoon cayenne

2 cups cooked lentils, drained well

1/2 cup shelled sunflower seeds

2 tablespoons chopped fresh parsley leaves

2 tablespoons all-purpose flour

1 Preheat the oven to 375 degrees F. Generously oil an 8 x 4-inch loaf pan.

2 Heat the oil in a small skillet over medium heat. Add the onion and garlic and cook, stirring, until softened, about 5 minutes. Stir in the brandy, paprika, thyme, salt, and cayenne and cook for 2 minutes longer. Set aside.

3 In a food processor, combine the lentils, sunflower seeds, and parsley and pulse to mix. Add the onion mixture and process until blended but not pureed; leave some texture. Transfer the mixture to a bowl and stir in the flour, blending well. Taste to adjust the seasonings, then spoon into the prepared pan.

4 Bake until firm, about 30 minutes. Serve warm or cool.

Serves 6

Soup's On

Soups are among the most comforting of foods, especially thick, rich chowders, hearty bean soups, and creamy bisques. Each bowl has stick-to-your-ribs goodness in every spoonful. Many naturally vegetarian soups are as satisfying as those with meat, thanks to a variety of protein-rich beans, legumes, and grains. Potatoes also play an important role in many vegetable-based soups, adding substance, taste, and texture to a variety of simmering kettles.

Soups can be lush and lavish or humble and homey, but they never fail to satisfy. Sometimes nothing but a bowl of soup will do. It can lift your spirits, revitalize your energy, and soothe your soul. Added to its list of virtues is the fact that soup is usually economical and simple to make. Most soups keep well, taste even better reheated, are loaded with nutrients, and can be very filling. No wonder they're adored by so many people all over the world.

Whether it is enjoyed as a first course or served as the main course, a soup should complement the rest of the meal in its taste and texture. For example, when soup makes the meal, choose a substantial bean soup or chowder. As part of a larger meal, a lighter, more brothy soup may be best. With recipes such as *Home-Style Noodle Soup*, *Louisiana Vegetable Gumbo*, and *Mushroom Barley Soup*, this chapter is bound to have the soup-of-the-day you crave most any time.

Many of the recipes call for vegetable stock or water. Using a rich vegetable stock, like the one on page 36, will give your soups more depth. If you use water, the soup will have a thinner flavor and additional vegetables and seasonings may be added. As an alternative to homemade vegetable stock, canned or powdered vegetable broth may be used. Since these products vary greatly in taste, be especially careful to monitor how much salt you use.

Vegetable Stock

Home-Style Noodle Soup

Faux Pho

Tuscan Bread Soup

Minestrone with Tiny "Meatballs"

Oyster Mushroom Chowder

Mushroom Barley Soup

Sea Vegetable Bisque

Vichyssoise Frappé

Gutsy Gazpacho

Three Sisters Corn Chowder

Baked Five-Onion Soup

Roasted Carrot and Potato Soup

Hot Potato Soup

Two-Potato Three-Bean Soup

Lentil Soup with Potatoes and Chard

Thick as Pea Soup

Cabbage and Potato Soup

Black Bean Soup with Sherry

Creamy White Bean Soup

Louisiana Vegetable Gumbo

Ravishing Red Bean Gumbo

Warming Winter Vegetable Soup

Creamy Peanut Soup

Chestnut Soup

Vegetable Stock

⌇⌇⌇

This rich, full-bodied stock tastes similar to a light chicken stock and can be used in any soup recipe to enrich the flavor. Additional vegetables such as leeks or mushrooms can be added, but stay away from anything too assertive, such as cabbage, beets, or broccoli. For an even richer stock, roast the vegetables before adding them to the stockpot.

1 tablespoon olive oil

1 large yellow onion, left unpeeled, quartered

1 large carrot, coarsely chopped

1 celery stalk (including leaves), coarsely chopped

2 quarts water

3 large all-purpose potatoes

3 garlic cloves, left unpeeled, crushed

1/2 cup coarsely chopped fresh parsley leaves

2 bay leaves

1/2 teaspoon black peppercorns

1 teaspoon salt

1 Heat the oil in a stockpot over medium heat. Add the onion, carrot, and celery, cover, and cook, stirring a few times, until softened, about 5 minutes. Remove the lid and stir in the water.

2 Thoroughly scrub the potatoes and peel them thickly. Add the potato peels to the stock; reserve the potatoes for another use. Add the garlic, parsley, bay leaves, peppercorns, and salt. Bring to a boil, then reduce the heat to low and simmer for $1^1/2$ hours.

3 Strain the stock through a sieve into a large bowl or pot, pressing against the solids with the back of a spoon. The stock can be used now, cooled and refrigerated for up to 3 or 4 days, or portioned and frozen for up to a month.

Makes about 6 cups

Stocking Up on Vegetable Stock

The foundation of any good soup is a good stock and, naturally, the soups in this book call for vegetable stock. If you want a particularly rich vegetable stock, first roast vegetables such as onions, carrots, celery, garlic, and squash until they caramelize. After adding the roasted vegetables to the stockpot, deglaze the roasting pan with white wine and add that to the pot. You can also include onion skins and potato peelings to add depth of flavor and color to the stock.

Allow the stock to simmer for up to 2 hours, then strain it, pressing against the solids with the back of a spoon to extract all the liquid; discard the solids. The resulting stock will have a full rich flavor, making it suitable as the basis for soups and sauces. Vegetable stock can be stored in the refrigerator for several days, if kept in a tightly covered container. Before using it, however, bring the stock to a boil and taste it to check the flavor. Since vegetable stock freezes well, it is also convenient to portion it into small containers and freeze it for future use.

For those occasions where there's no time to make your own stock, keep a supply of store-bought stock on hand. As the taste and quality differ significantly among brands, experiment until you find one you like. Good-quality commercial vegetable stocks made without additives are available at natural food stores, where you can also find powdered vegetable bases. Some brands are high in sodium, so read the labels carefully.

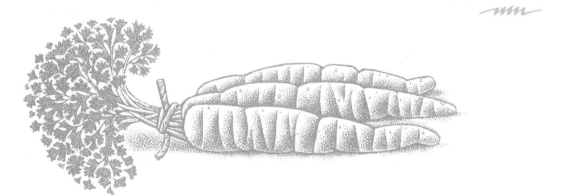

Home-Style Noodle Soup

To many of us, our mother's homemade noodle soup is among our most comforting memories—a steaming bowl of rich broth and tender noodles that made us feel better no matter what. This version, made with vegetable stock, is every bit as satisfying as the soup I remember.

1 tablespoon olive oil

1 large onion, chopped

2 medium-size carrots, chopped

1 celery stalk, diced

6 cups vegetable stock (page 36)

Pinch of turmeric

Salt and freshly ground black pepper

6 ounces egg noodles or fettuccine,
   broken into thirds

1 tablespoon minced fresh parsley leaves

1 In a large saucepan, heat the oil over medium heat. Add the onion, carrots, and celery, cover, and cook, stirring a few times, until softened, about 5 minutes. Add the stock, turmeric, and salt and pepper to taste. Bring to a boil, then reduce the heat to low and simmer, uncovered, until the vegetables are tender, about 30 minutes. About 10 minutes before the vegetables are done, add the noodles to the soup and cook until tender.

2 Stir the parsley into the soup, taste to adjust the seasonings, and simmer for 5 minutes to blend the flavors before ladling into bowls.

Serves 4 to 6

Faux Pho

～✐～

Pho is a rich Vietnamese noodle soup traditionally made with beef. This meatless version, enriched with dark miso paste, is made with seitan, or "wheat-meat." Rice sticks (dried rice noodles) and hoisin sauce are available in well-stocked supermarkets and Asian grocery stores.

---

8 ounces rice sticks

1 tablespoon peanut oil

4 ounces seitan, cut into thin strips

$1/4$ cup hoisin sauce

2 tablespoons fresh lime juice

6 cups water

1 small red onion, chopped

1 hot green chile, seeded and minced

2 cloves

2 star anise

1 cinnamon stick

1 tablespoon peeled and chopped fresh
   ginger

2 tablespoons tamari or other soy sauce

3 tablespoons dark miso paste

2 tablespoons minced fresh cilantro
   leaves

1 bunch scallions, thinly sliced

1 cup fresh bean sprouts

1 Soften the noodles in warm water to cover for 30 minutes. Drain and set aside.

2 Heat the oil in a large skillet over medium-high heat. Add the seitan strips and brown, turning once, on both sides. Reduce the heat to medium-low, stir in the hoisin sauce and I tablespoon of the lime juice, and simmer for I minute. Remove from the heat and set aside.

3 Bring the water to a boil in a large saucepan over high heat. Add the onion, chile, cloves, anise, cinnamon stick, ginger, and soy sauce, reduce the heat to low, and simmer for 15 minutes to make a stock. Strain the stock and return it to the pan.

4 Stir in the remaining I tablespoon lime juice. Transfer $1/2$ cup of the hot liquid to a small bowl, add the miso paste, and stir to blend well. Stir the blended miso paste into the soup, along with the reserved seitan and noodles, and simmer for 5 minutes to heat through; do not let boil.

5 Divide the soup among individual bowls and garnish with the cilantro, scallions, and bean sprouts. Serve at once.

Serves 4 to 6

Tuscan Bread Soup

Hearty bean soups such as this one are particularly popular in Tuscan cooking. For an alternative presentation, omit the slices of bread and serve the soup in individual hollowed-out small round loaves of artisanal bread.

1 tablespoon olive oil

1 large onion, minced

1 celery stalk, minced

1 large garlic clove, minced

One 14.5-ounce can diced tomatoes, with their juices

6 cups vegetable stock (page 36)

1 teaspoon minced fresh oregano leaves or ¹/₂ teaspoon dried

2 tablespoons minced fresh parsley leaves

¹/₄ teaspoon red pepper flakes

Salt and freshly ground black pepper

1¹/₂ cups cooked cannellini beans or one 15-ounce can, drained and rinsed

Six ¹/₂-inch-thick slices Italian bread

Freshly grated Parmesan cheese or soy Parmesan or extra virgin olive oil

1 Heat the oil in a large saucepan over medium heat. Add the onion and celery, cover, and cook, stirring a few times, until softened, about 5 minutes. Add the garlic and cook for 30 seconds. Add the tomatoes, stock, oregano, parsley, red pepper flakes, and salt and pepper to taste and bring to a boil. Reduce the heat to low and simmer for 30 minutes.

2 Add the beans and simmer for 10 minutes longer.

3 Place a slice of bread in the bottom of each bowl. Ladle the soup into the bowls, sprinkle with grated cheese or drizzle with extra virgin olive oil, and serve at once.

Serves 6

Minestrone with Tiny "Meatballs"

In my family, minestrone with meatballs was called "wedding soup," I presume because it was often served at weddings. But don't wait for a wedding to try it—it's great anytime. I find thawed veggie burgers to be the easiest way to make mini "meatballs." The texture holds together well, they're readily available, and they brown up nicely.

2 tablespoons olive oil

1 small yellow onion, minced

2 small carrots, chopped

1 celery stalk, finely chopped

2 large garlic cloves, minced

One 14.5-ounce can diced tomatoes, with their juices

6 cups vegetable stock (page 36), or more if needed

Salt and freshly ground black pepper

4 frozen vegetarian burgers, thawed

1 tablespoon freshly grated Parmesan cheese or soy Parmesan

1 tablespoon minced fresh parsley leaves

1 small zucchini, ends trimmed, halved lengthwise, and cut crosswise into $1/4$-inch-thick slices

$1^1/_2$ cups cooked chickpeas or one 15-ounce can, drained and rinsed

$1/2$ cup orzo or other tiny pasta

2 tablespoons minced fresh basil leaves (optional)

1 Heat I tablespoon of the oil in a large saucepan over medium heat. Add the onion, carrots, celery, and garlic and cook, stirring, until soft, about 10 minutes. Add the tomatoes, stock, and salt and pepper to taste. Bring to a boil, reduce the heat to medium-low, and simmer, partially covered, for 20 minutes.

2 While the soup is simmering, break up the thawed veggie burgers and place in a medium-size bowl. Add the Parmesan and parsley, blending well. Using your hands, shape the mixture into I-inch balls. Heat the remaining I tablespoon oil in a large skillet over medium heat. Add the balls and cook until browned on all sides, 5 to 7 minutes total. Set aside.

3 Add the zucchini and chickpeas to the soup and cook for another I5 minutes, adding more stock if necessary. Add the pasta and cook until just tender, 5 to 10 minutes longer. Stir in the basil, if using, and taste to adjust the seasonings.

4 To serve, divide the "meatballs" among the soup bowls and ladle the soup over them.

Serves 6

Oyster Mushroom Chowder

~~~

Creamy oyster mushrooms have a slight "seafood" taste and a texture similar to that of oysters. Kelp flakes, or ground kelp, are available in shaker containers in natural food stores. Sprinkled on the chowder, they make a lovely garnish while adding a nutritious taste of the sea.

2 tablespoons olive oil

1 small yellow onion, chopped

1 celery stalk, chopped

1 large all-purpose potato, peeled and
   diced

4 cups vegetable stock (page 36)

3/4 teaspoon minced fresh thyme leaves
   or 1/4 teaspoon plus a pinch dried

1/2 teaspoon salt, or more to taste

1/8 teaspoon cayenne

1 1/2 cups regular or soy milk

2 tablespoons cornstarch, dissolved in
   1/4 cup water

8 ounces oyster mushrooms

1/4 teaspoon Old Bay seasoning

Kelp flakes (optional)

1 Heat I tablespoon of the oil in a large saucepan over medium heat. Add the onion and celery, cover, and cook, stirring a few times, until softened, about 5 minutes. Add the potato, stock, thyme, salt, and cayenne and bring to a boil. Reduce the heat to low, partially cover, and simmer until the potato is soft, I5 to 20 minutes.

2 Transfer I cup of the mixture to a food processor or blender and process until smooth. Return the mixture to the soup and stir in the milk. Heat to a simmer, add the cornstarch mixture, and boil, stirring, for I minute, or until thickened.

3 Meanwhile, slice or quarter any larger mushrooms; leave smaller ones whole or halve them. Heat the remaining I tablespoon oil in a medium-size skillet. Add the mushrooms, sprinkle with the Old Bay seasoning, and cook for I minute.

4 Add the mushrooms to the soup and serve, garnished with kelp flakes, if desired.

Serves 4 to 6

Mushroom Barley Soup

Barley adds stick-to-your-ribs goodness to this warming winter soup that is enjoyed throughout Eastern Europe. Regular white mushrooms allow the subtle nuttiness of the barley to come through. Dry vermouth can be substituted for the white wine to add a more sophisticated flavor.

---

1 tablespoon olive oil

2 leeks, white part only, washed well and
   chopped

1 celery stalk (including leaves), chopped

1 cup barley

5 cups vegetable stock (page 36) or
   water

2 tablespoons dry white wine

1 bay leaf

8 ounces white button mushrooms, sliced

2 tablespoons minced fresh parsley
   leaves

1 tablespoon minced fresh thyme leaves
   or 1¹/₂ teaspoons dried

Salt and freshly ground black pepper

1 Heat the oil in a large saucepan over medium heat. Add the leeks and celery, cover, and cook, stirring a few times, until softened, about 5 minutes. Add the barley, stock, wine, and bay leaf, cover, and simmer for 15 minutes.

2 Stir in the mushrooms, parsley, and thyme. Season with salt and pepper to taste and cook, uncovered, until the barley is tender, about 10 minutes longer. Remove and discard the bay leaf before serving.

Serves 4

Sea Vegetable Bisque

With three different varieties of sea vegetable, this soup is a powerhouse of minerals and vitamins, including iron, potassium, magnesium, iodine, and B vitamins. For the best quality, buy only certified organic sea vegetables and miso paste, available at natural food stores. Use a pair of scissors to snip the nori into thin strips.

1 tablespoon olive oil

1 small yellow onion, chopped

1 celery stalk, chopped

1 large all-purpose potato, peeled and
   diced

4 cups vegetable stock (page 36) or
   water

One 2-inch square kombu sea vegetable

Salt

$1/8$ teaspoon cayenne

1 ounce dulse sea vegetable, chopped

1 cup regular or soy milk

1 tablespoon mellow white miso paste,
   dissolved in $1/4$ cup warm water

$1/4$ teaspoon Old Bay seasoning

Thin nori strips for garnish

1 Heat the oil in a large saucepan over medium heat. Add the onion and celery, cover, and cook, stirring a few times, until softened, about 5 minutes. Add the potato, stock, kombu, salt to taste, and cayenne. Bring to a boil, then reduce the heat to medium-low and simmer until the potato is very soft, about 20 minutes. Remove the kombu and stir in the dulse.

2 Strain the soup through a colander, reserving the broth. Transfer the solids plus I cup of the broth to a food processor or blender. Process until smooth. Return the mixture to the pan and stir in the remaining broth, the milk, dissolved miso, and Old Bay seasoning. Warm the soup over low heat, being careful not to let it boil.

3 To serve, ladle into bowls and garnish with thin strips of nori.

Serves 4 to 6

Magnificent Miso

Miso soup is the Japanese answer to "Mom's chicken soup." Miso is a fermented soybean paste that is said to strengthen the immune system and provide other health benefits. It is high in protein and rich in enzymes and other nutrients. Highly concentrated, with a salty flavor, miso paste makes a nutritious soup when simply diluted with hot water. Miso can also be used to enrich sauces, stews, and other dishes. It is available in a variety of colors and flavors, depending on the grain or bean the soybean paste is combined with, such as barley, chickpeas, or rice. The lighter-colored miso pastes, made with rice or chickpeas, have a milder almost sweet flavor and work best in salad dressings and light soups and sauces. The darker misos, often made with barley, have a more assertive flavor and should be used to flavor gravies and stews. Miso can be found in natural food stores and Asian markets.

Vichyssoise Frappé

The classic chilled potato soup gets a makeover in this updated presentation that is a great conversation starter when served as the first course of a special dinner. For a more classic presentation, omit the final "froth" and serve in soup bowls instead of goblets. I prefer Yukon Gold potatoes for extra flavor.

---

1 tablespoon olive oil

1 leek, white part only, washed well and
   chopped

3 or 4 large Yukon Gold or other all-
   purpose potatoes (about 1$1/2$ pounds),
   peeled and chopped

3 cups vegetable stock (page 36)

1 cup regular or soy milk, or more if
   necessary

$1/2$ teaspoon salt, or more to taste

$1/8$ teaspoon cayenne

Snipped fresh chives, plus 8 to 12 whole
   chives for garnish

1 Heat the oil in a large saucepan over medium heat. Add the leek, cover, and cook, stirring a few times, until softened, about 5 minutes. Add the potatoes and stock and simmer until the potatoes are soft, 20 to 30 minutes.

2 Process the soup in a food processor or blender, in batches if necessary, until smooth. Transfer to a bowl. Stir in the milk, salt, and cayenne. Cover and refrigerate for at least several hours, or overnight. If the chilled soup is too thick, add more milk and adjust the seasonings.

3 Just before serving, process the soup in a blender or food processor for several seconds, until frothy. Pour into stemmed goblets, sprinkle with snipped chives, and garnish with 2 whole chives placed upright in each goblet, leaning against the rim of the glass.

Serves 4 to 6

Gutsy Gazpacho

Minced jalapeño chiles, along with a healthy dose of Tabasco, add a kick to the classic chilled vegetable soup. Naturally, if a tamer soup is preferred, you can omit the chiles and Tabasco from it, but be sure to set them out on the table for guests to add as desired. If this soup is to be part of a summer buffet table, keep it chilled by adding a tray of ice cubes made with tomato juice.

---

3 large ripe tomatoes, peeled, seeded, and chopped

1 small yellow bell pepper, seeded and chopped

1 small red onion, chopped

1 small cucumber, peeled, seeded, and chopped

2 garlic cloves, finely minced

1 or 2 jalapeño chiles, to your taste, seeded and minced

4 cups tomato juice

2 tablespoons fresh lemon juice

1 tablespoon balsamic vinegar

1 tablespoon olive oil

1/2 teaspoon salt

1/4 teaspoon Tabasco sauce, or to taste

1/4 cup minced scallions

1/4 cup minced fresh parsley leaves

1 In a large bowl, combine the tomatoes, bell pepper, onion, cucumber, garlic, and chiles. Stir in the tomato juice, lemon juice, vinegar, and oil. Add the salt and Tabasco. Cover the bowl and refrigerate for at least 2 hours, or overnight, to blend the flavors. Check the seasonings again before serving.

2 To serve, ladle the soup into bowls and garnish with the minced scallions and parsley.

Serves 6

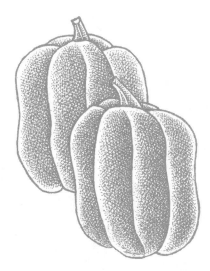

Three Sisters Corn Chowder

In this satisfying chowder, the subtle sweetness of the corn, squash, and beans—called the "three sisters" by the Iroquois—harmonizes well, just as good sisters should.

1 tablespoon olive oil

1 small yellow onion, chopped

1 small butternut squash, peeled, halved, seeded, and cut into 1/4-inch dice

1 medium-size all-purpose potato, peeled and diced

2 1/2 cups vegetable stock (page 36)

1 1/2 cups cooked pinto beans or one 15-ounce can, drained and rinsed

2 3/4 cups fresh or frozen corn kernels

2 cups regular or soy milk

Salt and freshly ground black pepper

1   Heat the oil in a large saucepan over medium heat. Add the onion, cover, and cook, stirring a few times, until softened, about 5 minutes. Add the squash and potato, stir in the stock, and bring to a boil. Reduce the heat to low, cover, and cook until the vegetables are tender, 20 to 30 minutes.

2   Add the beans and 2 1/2 cups of the corn and cook, uncovered, for 15 minutes longer to thicken the soup and blend the flavors. Stir in the milk and simmer for about 5 minutes. Remove from the heat.

3   Transfer about 2 cups of the soup to a food processor or blender and process until smooth. Stir the puree back into the chowder and season to taste with salt and pepper.

4   Ladle the soup into bowls and garnish with the remaining 1/4 cup corn kernels.

Serves 4 to 6

Baked Five-Onion Soup

mm

Classic French onion soup is made with one kind of onion, but I enjoy the subtle flavor differences of a number of the members of the onion family. And where better than an onion soup to bring the whole family together? Some people add wine to their onion soup, but I prefer the depth a little brandy gives to it. Of course, you can omit the alcohol altogether if you prefer, and add a splash of tamari soy sauce instead. Vegetarian Worcestershire sauce, made without anchovies, is available in natural food stores. Like the brandy, it adds a layer of complexity, but if you can't find it, the soup will still taste fine.

---

2 tablespoons olive oil

1 small yellow onion, thinly sliced

1 small red onion, thinly sliced

1 leek, white part only, washed well and
  chopped

2 shallots, minced

$1/3$ cup brandy

6 cups vegetable stock (page 36) or
  water

2 scallions, minced

1 tablespoon vegetarian Worcestershire
  sauce

Salt and freshly ground black pepper

Four to six $1/2$-inch-thick slices French or
  Italian bread

4 to 6 slices Fontina cheese or soy
  mozzarella

1 Heat the oil in a large saucepan over medium heat. Add the yellow and red onions, leek, and shallots, cover, and cook, stirring occasionally, until softened, about 10 minutes. Remove the lid, add the brandy, and stir until the alcohol cooks off, about 5 minutes.

2 Add the stock, scallions, and Worcestershire, bring the soup to a boil, and season with salt and pepper to taste. Reduce the heat to low, cover, and simmer for 30 minutes.

3 Preheat the broiler. Ladle the soup into flameproof soup crocks, top each with a slice of bread and cheese, and run under the broiler until the cheese melts (see Note). Serve at once.

Serves 4 to 6

note: If you don't have soup crocks, place the bread on a baking sheet, top each slice with cheese, and run under the broiler to melt the cheese and toast the bread. Ladle the soup into bowls, top with the bread, and serve at once.

Roasted Carrot and Potato Soup

This soup can also be made using leftover roasted vegetables. On a night when you're planning to serve roasted vegetables, simply add a few extra to use in the soup the following day. The caramelization of the roasted vegetables is what gives the soup an especially rich flavor.

---

3 medium-size carrots, coarsely chopped

2 large all-purpose potatoes, peeled and sliced

1 small yellow onion, coarsely chopped

1 tablespoon olive oil

1 teaspoon minced fresh thyme leaves or 1/2 teaspoon dried

Salt and freshly ground black pepper

4 cups vegetable stock (page 36) or water

Fresh thyme sprigs for garnish (optional)

1 Preheat the oven to 375 degrees F. Place the carrots, potatoes, and onion in a lightly oiled baking dish. Drizzle with the oil and season with the thyme and salt and pepper to taste. Cover tightly with a lid or a sheet of aluminum foil and roast for 30 minutes to soften.

2 Uncover the vegetables and roast, stirring once, for about 30 minutes longer to brown them slightly.

3 Transfer the roasted vegetables to a large saucepan. Add the stock and bring to a boil. Reduce the heat to low and simmer for 15 minutes.

4 In batches, process the soup in a food processor or blender until smooth. Return the soup to the saucepan and heat over medium heat. Taste to adjust the seasonings.

5 To serve, ladle into soup bowls and garnish each with a sprig of fresh thyme, if using.

Serves 6

Hot Potato Soup

In addition to being temperature hot, this rich potato soup is spicy hot as well, thanks to the chile paste, available in Asian markets. It's a great pantry ingredient to keep on hand to add heat and flavor to stir-fries, soups, and sauces.

1 tablespoon olive oil

2 leeks, white part only, washed well and chopped

4 cups vegetable stock (page 36) or water

3 large Yukon Gold or other all-purpose potatoes (about 1 1/2 pounds), peeled and diced

1 cup regular or soy milk

1 tablespoon minced fresh parsley leaves

Salt and freshly ground black pepper

1 1/2 to 3 teaspoons Asian chile paste, to your taste, for serving

1 Heat the oil in a large saucepan over medium heat. Add the leeks, cover, and cook, stirring a few times, until softened, about 5 minutes. Add the stock and potatoes and bring to a boil. Reduce the heat to low and simmer until the potatoes are soft, about 20 minutes.

2 Press the potato mixture through a sieve into a large bowl. Stir in the milk, parsley, and salt and pepper to taste. Return the soup to the saucepan and simmer for 5 minutes over low heat to heat through and blend the flavors.

3 To serve, ladle the soup into bowls and swirl $1/4$ to $1/2$ teaspoon chile paste into each bowl, according to taste.

Serves 6

Two-Potato Three-Bean Soup

~~~

To make a quick version of this soup, use canned beans (one 15-ounce can each), adding them during the last 15 to 20 minutes of cooking. Feel free to vary the types of beans used, and include some green beans too if you like.

1/2 cup dried chickpeas, rinsed, picked over, and soaked overnight in water to cover generously

1/2 cup dried kidney beans, rinsed, picked over, and soaked overnight in water to cover generously

1/2 cup dried white beans, rinsed, picked over, and soaked overnight in water to cover generously

2 tablespoons olive oil

1 medium-size yellow onion, diced

1 celery stalk, diced

1 medium-size all-purpose potato, peeled and diced

1 medium-size sweet potato, peeled and diced

6 cups vegetable stock (page 36) or water

2 bay leaves

1 teaspoon salt

1/8 teaspoon freshly ground black pepper

1/2 teaspoon Tabasco sauce, or to taste

2 tablespoons minced fresh parsley leaves

1 Drain the chickpeas, place in a large pot of water, and bring to a boil. Reduce the heat to low and cook, covered, for 30 minutes.

2 Drain the kidney beans and white beans, add to the pot, and cook until all the beans are just soft, 1 to 1 1/2 hours longer. Drain and set aside.

3 Heat the oil in a large saucepan over medium heat. Add the onion, celery, and both potatoes, cover, and cook, stirring a few times, until the vegetables soften slightly and give off some of their liquid, about 5 minutes. Add the stock, bay leaves, salt, and pepper and bring to a boil. Reduce the heat to low, stir in the reserved beans, cover, and simmer until the vegetables are tender and the soup has thickened slightly, about 45 minutes.

4 Add the Tabasco and parsley and taste to adjust the seasonings. Remove and discard the bay leaves, ladle the soup into bowls, and serve.

Serves 6

Lentil Soup with Potatoes and Chard

Potatoes and Swiss chard give texture and flavor to this hearty lentil soup, making it an ideal one-dish meal. I like to serve it with a rustic loaf of crusty bread.

2 tablespoons olive oil

1 medium-size yellow onion, chopped

1 small carrot, chopped

1/3 cup minced celery

2 garlic cloves, minced

2 medium-size all-purpose potatoes,
   peeled and diced

1 1/2 cups dried brown lentils, rinsed and
   picked over

6 cups vegetable stock (page 36) or
   water

1/4 cup minced fresh parsley leaves

2 bay leaves

1 teaspoon salt

1/8 teaspoon freshly ground black pepper

Leaves from 1 small bunch Swiss chard
   (about 6 cups)

1 Heat the oil in a large saucepan over medium heat. Add the onion, carrot, celery, and garlic, cover, and cook, stirring a few times, until softened, about 5 minutes. Add the potatoes, lentils, stock, parsley, bay leaves, salt, and pepper and bring to a boil. Reduce the heat to low, cover, and simmer, stirring occasionally, until the lentils are tender, 30 to 40 minutes. Add more water if the soup becomes too thick. Remove and discard the bay leaves.

2 Meanwhile, in a large pot of boiling salted water, cook the chard until tender, about 5 minutes. Drain, rinse under cold water to cool, and coarsely chop.

3 Stir the chard into the soup and simmer for 5 minutes longer. Adjust the seasonings and serve.

Serves 6

Thick as Pea Soup

Liquid Smoke and soy bacon bits, available in most supermarkets, add a smoky flavor to this wholesome soup without the need for the traditional ham hock. I sometimes add a little chopped cabbage to the soup along with the peas.

2 tablespoons olive oil

1 medium-size yellow onion, chopped

1 medium-size carrot, chopped

1 celery stalk, chopped

6 cups vegetable stock (page 36) or
   water

1 small all-purpose potato, peeled and
   diced

1 pound dried green split peas, rinsed
   and picked over

1 bay leaf

1 teaspoon salt

1/8 teaspoon freshly ground black pepper

Splash of Liquid Smoke (optional)

Soy bacon bits for garnish

1 Heat the oil in a large saucepan over medium heat. Add the onion, carrot, and celery, cover, and cook, stirring a few times, until softened, about 5 minutes. Add the stock, potato, split peas, bay leaf, salt, and pepper and bring to a boil. Reduce the heat to low, cover, and simmer until the vegetables are soft and the soup has thickened, about 45 minutes. If the consistency becomes too thick, add more water.

2 Stir in the Liquid Smoke, if using, and taste to adjust the seasonings. Remove and discard the bay leaf.

3 To serve, ladle the soup into bowls and garnish with soy bacon bits, if using.

Serves 6

Cabbage and Potato Soup

This soup made frequent appearances at my house when I was growing up, enjoyed as a main course with crusty Italian bread. It tasted so good, I never realized my mom was making this economical soup to help pinch pennies for the family budget. She used regular cabbage and white potatoes, but I prefer the flavor of Savoy cabbage and Yukon Gold potatoes. Peel the potatoes or leave them unpeeled, as you prefer.

1 tablespoon olive oil

1 medium-size yellow onion, minced

1 small head Savoy cabbage, cored and shredded

2 garlic cloves, minced

2 large Yukon Gold or other all-purpose potatoes (about 1 pound), diced

One 14.5-ounce can diced tomatoes, with their juices

6 cups vegetable stock (page 36) or water

1 teaspoon minced fresh savory leaves or 1/2 teaspoon dried

Salt and freshly ground black pepper

1 1/2 cups cooked cannellini beans or one 15-ounce can, drained and rinsed

2 tablespoons chopped fresh parsley leaves for garnish

1 Heat the oil in a large saucepan over medium heat. Add the onion, cabbage, and garlic, cover, and cook, stirring a few times, until softened, about 5 minutes. Stir in the potatoes, tomatoes, stock, savory, and salt and pepper to taste. Bring to a boil, then reduce the heat to low and simmer until the vegetables are soft, about 40 minutes.

2 Add the beans and cook for another 10 minutes. Adjust the seasonings.

3 Ladle the soup into bowls and garnish with the parsley.

Serves 6

Black Bean Soup with Sherry

⁓⁓⁓

In addition to making beans more digestible, soaking them cuts down on cooking time—so if you don't have time to soak the beans, the soup will take twice as long to cook. I like to puree half this soup for a texture variation, but you can puree all of it for a smooth soup, or omit that step altogether if you prefer a chunky texture.

1¹/₂ cups dried black beans, rinsed, picked over, and soaked overnight in water to cover generously

2 quarts water

2 bay leaves

1 tablespoon olive oil

1 large yellow onion, chopped

1 small red or green bell pepper, seeded and minced

3 or 4 garlic cloves, to your taste, minced

One 14.5-ounce can crushed tomatoes

1 teaspoon dried oregano

1 teaspoon salt

¹/₈ teaspoon cayenne

2 tablespoons minced fresh parsley leaves

¹/₄ cup dry sherry, or more to taste

1 teaspoon Tabasco sauce, or to taste

Sour cream or tofu sour cream for garnish (optional)

1 Drain the beans, place in a large saucepan with the water and bay leaves, and bring to a boil. Reduce the heat to low, cover, and simmer until the beans are soft, about 1¹/₂ hours, skimming off the foam that rises to the top.

2 Meanwhile, heat the oil in a medium-size skillet over medium heat. Add the onion, bell pepper, and garlic, cover, and cook, stirring a few times, until softened, about 5 minutes.

3 Add the sautéed vegetables to the beans, along with the tomatoes, oregano, salt, and cayenne. Simmer until the vegetables are soft, about 30 minutes.

4 Puree about half of the soup in a blender or food processor and return it to the pan. Add more water if the soup is too thick. Simmer the soup for about 15 minutes longer to blend the flavors. About 5 minutes before the end of the cooking time, stir in the parsley, sherry, and Tabasco. Taste to adjust the seasonings.

5 Ladle the soup into bowls and garnish each serving with sour cream, if desired.

Serves 6

Creamy White Bean Soup

Buttery white beans and creamy potatoes make a smooth and sultry soup. The secret to the great texture of this soup is pureeing a portion of it. The soup also lends itself well to the flavors of different herbs. I use tarragon here, but sage, thyme, or basil would also be a good choice.

2 tablespoons olive oil

1 large onion, diced

1 celery stalk, diced

1 large all-purpose potato, peeled and
  diced

1 pound dried white beans, rinsed, picked
  over, soaked overight in water to cover
  generously, and drained

6 cups vegetable stock (page 36) or
  water

2 bay leaves

2 teaspoons minced fresh tarragon
  leaves or 1 teaspoon dried

Salt and freshly ground black pepper

Minced fresh parsley leaves for garnish

1 Heat the oil in a large saucepan over medium heat. Add the onion and celery, cover, and cook, stirring a few times, until softened, about 5 minutes. Add the potato, beans, stock, and bay leaves and bring to a boil. Reduce the heat to low and simmer, partially covered, until the beans are soft, $1^1/_2$ to 2 hours. If the soup becomes too thick, add more water. Remove and discard the bay leaves. Stir in the tarragon and season to taste with salt and pepper.

2 Transfer 2 cups of the soup to a blender or food processor and process until smooth. Stir back into the soup and taste to adjust the seasonings.

3 Ladle the soup into bowls, sprinkle with parsley, and serve.

Serves 6

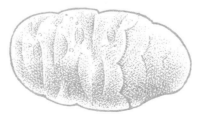

Louisiana Vegetable Gumbo

Gumbo is one of the great comfort foods to come out of Louisiana. This spicy, rich concoction is actually more of a stew than a soup, but it is really in a class by itself. The word "gumbo" means "okra," and there is plenty of it in this recipe. The amount of rice served with the gumbo should be dictated by personal preference. Filé powder is made from ground sassafras leaves; it is available in well-stocked supermarkets and specialty grocers.

1 tablespoon olive oil

1 large onion, diced

1 medium-size green bell pepper, seeded and diced

$1/2$ cup chopped celery

2 garlic cloves, minced

6 cups vegetable stock (page 36) or water

One 14.5-ounce can diced tomatoes, with their juices

$1^1/2$ cups sliced fresh or frozen okra

1 small zucchini, ends trimmed and sliced

1 teaspoon dried thyme

1 teaspoon filé powder

$3/4$ teaspoon salt

$1/8$ teaspoon freshly ground black pepper

Tabasco sauce

2 to 3 cups hot cooked long-grain rice

1 Heat the oil in a large saucepan over medium heat. Add the onion, bell pepper, celery, and garlic, cover, and cook, stirring a few times, until softened, about 5 minutes. Add the stock, tomatoes, okra, zucchini, thyme, filé powder, salt, pepper, and Tabasco to taste. Simmer, partially covered, over low heat, stirring occasionally, for 30 to 40 minutes. Taste to adjust the seasonings.

2 To serve, spoon about $1/2$ cup of the cooked rice into each soup bowl and ladle the hot gumbo over the top.

Serves 4 to 6

Ravishing Red Bean Gumbo

For those who like the rich taste of gumbo but don't like okra, here's a delicious non-okra gumbo made rich and vibrantly colorful with red beans, red onion, and red bell pepper.

1 tablespoon olive oil

1 large red onion, diced

1 large red bell pepper, seeded and diced

$1/2$ cup chopped celery

2 garlic cloves, minced

6 cups vegetable stock (page 36) or water

One 14.5-ounce can diced tomatoes, with their juices

1 teaspoon filé powder (available in well-stocked supermarkets and specialty grocers)

1 teaspoon dried thyme

1 teaspoon salt

$1/8$ teaspoon cayenne

$1^1/2$ cups cooked dark red kidney beans or other red beans or one 15-ounce can, drained and rinsed

2 to 3 cups hot cooked long-grain rice

Tabasco sauce for serving

1 Heat the oil in a large saucepan over medium heat. Add the onion, bell pepper, celery, and garlic, cover, and cook, stirring a few times, until softened, about 5 minutes. Add the stock, tomatoes, filé powder, thyme, salt, and cayenne, partially cover, and simmer over medium-low heat, stirring occasionally, until the vegetables are soft and the liquid has reduced somewhat, 30 to 40 minutes.

2 Add the kidney beans and simmer, uncovered, for 10 minutes longer, to heat through. Taste to adjust the seasonings.

3 To serve, spoon $1/2$ cup rice into each soup bowl and ladle the hot gumbo on top. Pass a bottle of Tabasco at the table.

Serves 4 to 6

Warming Winter Vegetable Soup

This soup relies on root vegetables like carrots and parsnips to give it a subtle sweetness. Spinach and kidney beans add a vibrant color contrast, along with great taste and nutrition. I like to use unpeeled potatoes, but you can peel them if you prefer.

1 tablespoon olive oil

1 medium-size yellow onion, chopped

2 medium-size carrots, halved lengthwise
and cut crosswise into 1/4-inch-thick
slices

1 celery stalk, minced

3 small red potatoes, diced

1 small parsnip, peeled and chopped

1 large garlic clove, minced

6 cups vegetable stock (page 36)

4 ounces spinach, thick stems removed,
washed well, and chopped

1 1/2 cups cooked dark red kidney beans
or one 15-ounce can, drained and
rinsed

2 tablespoons chopped fresh parsley
leaves

Salt and freshly ground black pepper

1   Heat the oil in a large saucepan over medium heat. Add the onion, carrots, and celery, cover, and cook, stirring a few times, until softened, about 5 minutes. Add the potatoes, parsnip, and garlic and cook, covered, for 5 minutes. Add the stock, increase the heat to high, and bring to a boil. Reduce the heat to low and simmer, partially covered, until the vegetables are tender, 30 to 40 minutes.

2   Add the spinach, beans, and parsley and season with salt and pepper to taste. Simmer, uncovered, for 10 minutes to blend the flavors before serving.

Serves 4 to 6

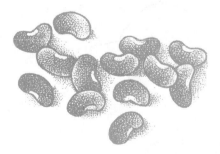

Creamy Peanut Soup

In the United States, peanuts are often relegated to snack food or the better half of a PBJ. In Africa, however, where they are known as groundnuts, peanuts are a nutritious mainstay, often used in soups and stews. This creamy and comforting soup is inspired by the spicy groundnut dishes of Africa.

1 tablespoon olive oil

1 small yellow onion, chopped

1 small all-purpose potato, chopped

1 small red bell pepper, seeded and
    chopped

1 small hot chile, seeded and chopped

5 cups vegetable stock (page 36) or
    water

$1/2$ cup creamy natural peanut butter

Salt and freshly ground black pepper

$1/4$ cup unsalted roasted peanuts,
    chopped

1 Heat the oil in a large saucepan over medium heat. Add the onion, potato, bell pepper, and chile, cover, and cook, stirring a few times, until softened, about 5 minutes. Add the stock and bring to a boil. Reduce the heat to low and simmer until the vegetables are tender, 20 to 30 minutes.

2 Process the soup in a blender or food processer, in batches, until smooth. Return all but I cup of the soup to the saucepan and return to a simmer.

3 Meanwhile, combine the peanut butter and the reserved cup of soup in the blender or processor and process until smooth. Stir the peanut butter mixture into the soup, season to taste with salt and pepper, and simmer for 10 minutes to blend the flavors.

4 To serve, ladle the soup into bowls and sprinkle with the chopped peanuts.

Serves 4 to 6

Chestnut Soup

Although peeling chestnuts takes time, if you love chestnuts, it's worth the effort. Once they are peeled, the recipe goes together quickly, resulting in a rich and creamy soup.

1 pound chestnuts

1 tablespoon olive oil

1 medium-size yellow onion, minced

$^1/_3$ cup finely minced celery

2 cups vegetable stock (page 36)

1$^3/_4$ cups regular or soy milk

$^3/_4$ teaspoon salt

$^1/_8$ teaspoon cayenne

$^1/_8$ teaspoon ground nutmeg

1 Using a sharp knife, cut an X in the flat side of each chestnut. Place them in a large saucepan with enough water to cover and bring to a boil. Reduce the heat to medium-low and simmer for 5 minutes (the shells and skin will now be easier to remove). Drain the chestnuts and, when they are cool enough to handle, use a sharp knife to peel away the outer shells and inner skins. Set aside.

2 Heat the oil in a large saucepan over medium heat. Add the onion and celery, cover, and cook, stirring a few times, until softened, about 5 minutes. Add all but 4 of the chestnuts and the stock and bring to a boil. Reduce the heat to low and simmer, uncovered, for 15 minutes.

3 Transfer the mixture to a food processor and add 1 cup of the milk. Process until smooth. Return the mixture to the saucepan and add the salt, cayenne, and nutmeg. Stir in the remaining $^3/_4$ cup milk and simmer over low heat for 10 minutes; do not boil. Taste to adjust the seasonings.

4 Meanwhile, coarsely chop the reserved 4 chestnuts. When the soup is hot, ladle it into bowls and garnish with the chopped chestnuts.

Serves 4

CHAPTER THREE

Salad Days

In all probability, salads are not the first thing that comes to mind when you think about "meat and potatoes" foods. Still, there are many delicious and satisfying salads that can be classified as comfort food. (Think chef's salad, macaroni salad, and, of course, potato salad.)

This chapter contains nearly a dozen variations on potato salad—that favorite side dish that's almost too rich to be called a salad. There are healthful versions that taste indulgent, such as a variation on the classic Niçoise salad—a blend of potatoes, green beans, and other vegetables without the traditional tuna—or *Gado Gado*, a spicy Indonesian potato salad. There's also *German Hot Potato Salad*, *Pesto Potato Salad*, and even *Sweet Potato and Pea Salad*.

In addition to potato salads, you will find a great selection of slaws, pasta and grain salads, and other vibrantly flavorful cold dishes, many of which can be meals in themselves. Others make perfect "sides" to accompany a variety of entrées.

In the summer, you can rely on main-dish salads to help you beat the heat. They can be made ahead of time or put together quickly at the last minute. Generous mounds of crisp, cool greens combined with whole grains, beans, vegetables, and flavorful dressings provide nourishing and satisfying meals without heating up the kitchen. Main-dish salads are also a great way to use up leftovers. Cold rice or other grains can be transformed into a hearty main-dish entrée by adding chopped vegetables, canned beans, and a light vinaigrette. Or combine leftover pasta with an Asian sesame or peanut sauce for a cold noodle salad.

A few simple rules will insure great salads. Foremost is to use only the freshest of ingredients. Wash and dry all greens thoroughly. Use high-quality ingredients in your dressings, such as extra virgin olive oil, and add the dressing a little at a time to lightly coat the salad rather than drench it. And finally, some salads—such as slaws and marinated salads—are meant to be dressed ahead of time, while others, such as those of leafy greens, are best when dressed at the last minute.

Purple Potato Salad

Roasted New Potato Salad with Peas,
    Pine Nuts, and Mint

Tomato-Potato Salad

Provençal Potato Salad

German Hot Potato Salad

Pesto Potato Salad

Niçoise-Style Salad

Gado Gado (Indonesian Potato Salad)

Three-Bean Salad with New Potatoes

Sweet Potato and Pea Salad

Tried and True Tabbouleh

Couscous Tabbouleh

Moroccan Couscous Salad

Caribbean Couscous Salad

Cold Noodle Salad with Spicy Sesame Sauce

Tuscan Summer Pasta Salad

Orange-and-Sesame-Tossed Penne Salad with
    Red Beans and Watercress

Call It Macaroni Salad

Madras Rice Salad with Mangoes and
    Peanuts

"Hoppin' John" Rice Salad

Spicy Southwestern Rice Salad

Baby Spinach Salad with Smoked Tofu and
    Crispy Slivered Shallots

Wheat-Meat and Romaine Salad with Red
    Potatoes

Soy Good Chef's Salad

Vibrant Vegetable Slaw

Creamy Caraway Cabbage Slaw

Carrot-Apple-Jicama Slaw

Purple Potato Salad

Small purple potatoes are turning up in supermarkets everywhere. Here, red onion, purple cabbage, and red beets are in keeping with the salad's purple-reddish color theme. Bright green peas and tarragon add an attractive color accent and a touch of sweetness.

1½ pounds small purple potatoes

1 small red onion, chopped

1 small red beet, peeled and shredded

½ cup shredded purple cabbage

½ cup frozen baby peas, thawed

1 garlic clove, minced

3 tablespoons tarragon vinegar

½ cup extra virgin olive oil

½ teaspoon salt

1 tablespoon minced fresh tarragon
   leaves

1 Place the potatoes in a large saucepan with salted cold water to cover and bring to a boil. Reduce the heat to medium-low, cover, and simmer until the potatoes are tender, 25 to 30 minutes. Drain well and allow to cool slightly.

2 Halve or quarter the potatoes and place in a large bowl. Add the onion, beet, cabbage, and peas and toss well. Set aside.

3 In a small bowl, whisk together the garlic, vinegar, oil, and salt. Pour the dressing over the potatoes, add the tarragon, and toss gently to combine. Chill for at least 1 hour before serving.

4 Taste and adjust the seasonings if necessary before serving chilled or at room temperature. This salad is best served on the same day it is prepared.

Serves 4

Roasted New Potato Salad with Peas, Pine Nuts, and Mint

R oasting the potatoes and onion gives them a rich depth of flavor, while peas and mint add a fresh-tasting sparkle to this potato salad.

2 pounds new potatoes

1/2 cup olive oil

Salt and freshly ground black pepper

1/4 cup pine nuts

2 shallots, chopped

1/4 cup chopped fresh mint leaves, plus mint sprigs for garnish

3 tablespoons white wine vinegar

1 cup frozen peas, thawed

1 Preheat the oven to 425 degrees F. Halve or quarter the potatoes and place in a medium-size bowl. Add I tablespoon of the oil, season with salt and pepper, and toss to coat the potatoes with the oil. Transfer to a baking sheet and bake, turning once, until tender and golden brown, about 30 minutes. About 2 minutes before removing the potatoes from the oven, add the pine nuts to the baking sheet to toast lightly. Remove from the oven and allow to cool.

2 In a food processor, combine the shallots, chopped mint, and vinegar and process until the shallots and mint are finely minced. Add the remaining 7 tablespoons oil and salt and pepper to taste. Process until well combined.

3 Place the potatoes and pine nuts in a serving bowl, add the peas, and pour on the dressing. Toss gently to coat evenly. Garnish with mint sprigs and serve at room temperature or chilled. This salad is best served the day it is made.

Serves 4 to 6

Potato Salad for the Twenty-First Century

When we think of potato salad, many of us imagine that 1950s version: chunks of boiled white potatoes combined in a large ceramic bowl with diced celery and minced onion, coated in an eggy mayonnaise with a touch of pickle relish or mustard, and garnished with sliced hard-cooked eggs and a sprinkling of paprika. Many of us grew up piling mounds of the white stuff onto our Melamine picnic plates without giving a thought to calories or cholesterol. However, in today's health-conscious society, potato salad is often banished from the cookout menu because of its high fat and cholesterol content. We've also been warned of the dangers of food poisoning from eating foods that contain eggs when left unrefrigerated under the hot summer sun. For these reasons, some people may hesitate to prepare the familiar side dish.

Perhaps it's time to let the picnickers of other nations show us the way to healthier potato salads. There are many varieties to choose from, since nearly every potato-growing country in the world has its own potato salad. In India, chunks of potatoes are tossed in a fragrant cilantro sauce. In African countries where yams are plentiful, they make delicious yam salads. Peruvian potato salad is spiced with ground chiles. All are made without a speck of mayonnaise. Italian potato salad is redolent of fresh basil and fruity olive oil. Perhaps the world's most elegant potato salad is the French Niçoise salad, made with its namesake tiny black olives, new potatoes, tender *haricots verts* (thin green beans), capers, and a light vinaigrette. The traditional version also includes tuna, but even without it, this salad can be a meal in itself, served on fresh mixed greens along with a loaf of crusty French bread.

One of the best ways to lighten up potato salad is to take a cue from the European versions and use a light olive oil dressing in place of mayonnaise. Other appealing innovations include using ingredients such as shallots and fresh herbs, and the unexpected addition of fruits or vegetables, such as apples and beets. Since the skin is the most nutritious part of the potato, consider using tender new red potatoes and leaving the skin on.

Although the classic version of potato salad still thrives, you can make a healthier version of it by using eggless mayonnaise made with soy (see page 309). Simply prepare your traditional potato salad recipe and substitute the soy mayo for the regular kind. Your potato salad will still be creamy, but lower in fat and cholesterol-free.

Tomato-Potato Salad

Fresh herbs, cherry tomatoes, and yellow bell pepper add vibrancy to this colorful potato salad, while sunflower seeds lend a bit of crunch.

1¹/₂ pounds small new potatoes

2 cups halved cherry tomatoes

¹/₂ large yellow bell pepper, seeded and diced

1 tablespoon minced fresh dill

1 tablespoon minced fresh parsley leaves

¹/₂ cup extra virgin olive oil

1 garlic clove, minced

¹/₄ cup fresh lemon juice

Salt and freshly ground black pepper

2 tablespoons shelled sunflower seeds

1 Place the potatoes in a large saucepan with salted cold water to cover and bring to a boil. Reduce the heat to medium-low, cover, and simmer until the potatoes are tender but still firm, 20 to 25 minutes. Drain well and let cool. (Do not peel.)

2 Slice the potatoes or cut into quarters, and place in a large bowl. Add the tomatoes, bell pepper, dill, and parsley and set aside.

3 In a small bowl, whisk together the oil, garlic, lemon juice, and salt and pepper to taste. Pour the dressing over the potato salad, add the sunflower seeds, and toss gently to coat. Taste to adjust the seasonings before serving. This salad is best served at room temperature, on the day it is made.

Serves 4 to 6

Provençal Potato Salad

Colorful peppers, sun-dried tomatoes, and flavorful olives and capers add a touch of the French countryside to this bold potato salad.

1 small red bell pepper

1 small yellow bell pepper

1¹/₂ pounds small waxy white potatoes

¹/₄ cup Niçoise olives, pitted

2 tablespoons chopped oil-packed sun-dried tomatoes

¹/₃ cup extra virgin olive oil

3 tablespoons white wine vinegar

1 teaspoon Dijon mustard

1 tablespoon capers, drained

2 tablespoons minced fresh chives

Salt and freshly ground black pepper

1 Roast the peppers over an open flame or under the broiler, turning often, until charred and blackened on all sides. Place in a paper or plastic bag, seal the bag, and let steam for 10 minutes. Peel, halve, core, and seed the peppers, scraping off the blackened bits. Cut the peppers into 1-inch squares and set aside.

2 Place the potatoes in a large saucepan with salted cold water to cover and bring to a boil. Reduce the heat to medium-low, cover, and simmer until the potatoes are tender, 25 to 30 minutes. Drain and let cool slightly.

3 Peel the potatoes and cut into 1-inch chunks. Transfer to a medium-size bowl and add the reserved peppers, olives, and sun-dried tomatoes. Toss gently until combined.

4 In a small bowl, whisk together the oil, vinegar, mustard, capers, and chives. Add the dressing to the potato mixture and toss gently until well coated. Season to taste with salt and pepper. Serve warm or chilled. This salad is best served within 24 hours.

Serves 4 to 6

German Hot Potato Salad

mmm

Vegetarian bacon and olive oil replace the traditional bacon and bacon grease for a healthful adaptation of an Old World favorite. For a more buttery taste, use Yukon Gold potatoes. For a sweeter flavor (and added color), use unpeeled new red potatoes.

---

1 1/2 pounds waxy white potatoes

1/3 cup olive oil

3 strips vegetarian bacon

1/4 cup chopped yellow onion

1/4 cup chopped celery

1/4 cup white wine vinegar

1/4 cup water

1 teaspoon sugar

1/8 teaspoon sweet paprika

1 dill pickle, chopped

Salt and freshly ground black pepper

2 tablespoons minced fresh parsley leaves

2 tablespoons minced fresh chives

1 Place the potatoes in a large saucepan with salted cold water to cover and bring to a boil. Reduce the heat to medium-low, cover, and simmer until the potatoes are tender, 30 to 45 minutes, depending on the size. Drain and allow to cool slightly.

2 While the potatoes are cooking, heat the oil in a large skillet over medium heat. Add the bacon and cook, turning several times, until crisp and browned on both sides. Remove the bacon from the pan and drain on paper towels.

3 Add the onion and celery to the skillet, cover, and cook, stirring a few times, until softened, about 5 minutes. Stir in the vinegar, water, sugar, and paprika and bring to a boil, then reduce the heat to very low to keep warm.

4 When the potatoes are cool enough to handle, peel them and cut into 1/4-inch-thick slices. Add to the skillet with the dressing. Crumble the reserved bacon and add it to the potatoes, along with the chopped pickle and salt and pepper to taste. Increase the heat to medium and stir gently until the salad is heated through. Transfer to a bowl, sprinkle with the parsley and chives, and serve warm.

Serves 4 to 6

Pesto Potato Salad

Pesto and potatoes are a winning combination—the intoxicating flavors of basil and garlic match well with the creamy sweetness of the new potatoes. Celery, scallions, and pine nuts add a bit of crunch.

2 pounds small red potatoes

2 tablespoons pine nuts

1/2 cup chopped celery

3 scallions, minced

1/3 cup pesto, homemade (page 313) or
   store-bought

1 tablespoon white wine vinegar

1/3 cup extra virgin olive oil

Salt and freshly ground black pepper

1 Place the potatoes in a large saucepan with salted cold water to cover and bring to a boil. Reduce the heat to medium-low, cover, and simmer until just tender, 25 to 30 minutes.

2 Meanwhile, place the pine nuts in a single layer in a small dry skillet and toast over medium heat, stirring frequently, until golden, about 3 minutes. Allow to cool slightly.

3 When the potatoes are cooked, drain and rinse under cold running water until cool enough to handle. Quarter the potatoes and place in a large bowl. Add the celery and scallions and set aside.

4 In a small bowl, combine the pesto, vinegar, and oil. Blend well, then pour over the potato salad and toss gently to coat evenly. Season to taste with salt and pepper, sprinkle on the pine nuts, and serve. This salad will keep for 1 to 2 days in the refrigerator.

Serves 4 to 6

Niçoise-Style Salad

F lavorful Niçoise olives team up with potatoes, green beans, and a vinaigrette dressing for a delicious salad inspired by the French country classic. Chickpeas are used in place of the traditional tuna for added substance.

$1^1/_2$ pounds waxy white potatoes

6 ounces green beans, ends trimmed, steamed just until tender, and cut into 1-inch lengths

2 tablespoons minced scallions

1 cup halved cherry tomatoes

2 tablespoons Niçoise olives, pitted

1 cup cooked or canned chickpeas, drained and rinsed if canned

$^1/_2$ cup olive oil

$^1/_4$ cup white wine vinegar

1 tablespoon Dijon mustard

2 garlic cloves, minced

2 tablespoons minced fresh parsley leaves

1 tablespoon minced fresh basil leaves

1 tablespoon minced fresh chervil leaves

Salt and freshly ground black pepper

Salad greens, torn into bite-size pieces, for serving

1 Place the potatoes in a large saucepan with salted cold water to cover and bring to a boil. Reduce the heat to medium-low, cover, and simmer until the potatoes are tender, 30 to 45 minutes, depending on the size. Drain and allow to cool slightly.

2 Peel the potatoes and cut into $^1/_4$-inch-thick slices. Transfer to a large bowl. Add the green beans, scallions, tomatoes, olives, and chickpeas and toss to mix. Set aside.

3 In a small bowl, whisk together the oil, vinegar, mustard, garlic, parsley, basil, chervil, and salt and pepper to taste. Pour over the salad and toss gently until thoroughly coated. Serve on a bed of torn salad greens. This salad is best served at room temperature shortly after assembly; if you wish, the various components of the salad can be prepared in advance.

Serves 4 to 6

Gado Gado (Indonesian Potato Salad)

~m~

Despite what many people think, Americans have not cornered the market on potato salad. Case in point is the Indonesian potato salad called gado gado, a flavorful blend of potatoes, vegetables, and bean sprouts, spiked with chile paste and other Asian seasonings. I like to add tempeh, which is Indonesian in origin, for extra substance.

---

4 ounces tempeh (optional)

1¹/₂ pounds Yukon Gold or other all-purpose potatoes

2 or 3 scallions, to your taste, chopped

1 cup frozen peas, thawed

¹/₂ cup grated carrots

1 cup fresh bean sprouts

¹/₃ cup toasted sesame oil

3 tablespoons rice vinegar

2 teaspoons tamari or other soy sauce

1 teaspoon light brown sugar

¹/₂ teaspoon Asian chile paste, or to taste

3 tablespoons chopped peanuts

3 cups shredded romaine lettuce

1 If using tempeh, place it in a small saucepan with water to cover and bring to a boil. Reduce the heat to low and simmer for 10 minutes. Drain the tempeh, pat dry, and allow to cool, then finely chop and set aside.

2 Cut the potatoes into 1-inch chunks and place in a large saucepan with cold salted water to cover. Bring to a boil, reduce the heat to medium-low, and simmer until the potatoes are tender, about 20 minutes. Drain and rinse under cold running water, then place in a large bowl. Add the scallions, peas, carrot, tempeh, if using, and bean sprouts.

3 In a small bowl, whisk together the oil, vinegar, tamari, brown sugar, and chile paste. Pour the dressing over the salad, add the peanuts, and toss well to coat evenly. Serve on a bed of shredded romaine. This salad is best served shortly after it is made.

Serves 4 to 6

Three-Bean Salad with New Potatoes

Two picnic favorites—three-bean salad and potato salad—combine for a flavorful dish that's substantial enough to be an al fresco entrée when served on a bed of lettuce with warm crusty bread. To round out the meal even further, you could begin with a soup and end with a rich dessert.

1½ pounds new white or red potatoes

1½ cups cooked dark red kidney beans or one 15-ounce can, drained and rinsed

1½ cups cooked chickpeas or one 15-ounce can, drained and rinsed

6 ounces green beans, ends trimmed, steamed just until tender, and cut into 1-inch lengths

4 scallions, minced

½ cup olive oil

¼ cup cider vinegar

½ teaspoon sugar

2 garlic cloves, finely minced

¼ teaspoon red pepper flakes

¼ teaspoon dry mustard

Salt and freshly ground black pepper

¼ cup minced fresh parsley leaves

1 Place the potatoes in a large saucepan with salted cold water to cover and bring to a boil. Reduce the heat to medium-low, cover, and simmer until the potatoes are tender, 30 to 45 minutes, depending on the size. Drain and allow to cool.

2 Halve or quarter the potatoes, depending on size, and place in a large bowl. Add the kidney beans, chickpeas, green beans, and scallions and set aside.

3 In a small bowl, whisk together the oil, vinegar, sugar, garlic, red pepper flakes, mustard, and salt and pepper to taste. Pour the dressing over the salad, add the parsley, and toss gently to coat evenly with the dressing. Chill the salad in the refrigerator for at least 1 hour before serving to allow the flavors to blend. This salad can be refrigerated for up to 2 days.

Serves 4 to 6

Sweet Potato and Pea Salad

If you like sweet potatoes as much as I do, you'll love this salad. Their bright orange color combined with the green peas is a sight to behold, and the flavor is satisfying and delicious. It's become one of my favorite ways to enjoy sweet potatoes.

4 sweet potatoes (about 2 pounds)

1 cup frozen baby peas, thawed

3 scallions, minced

2 tablespoons chopped fresh parsley
    leaves

$1/2$ cup extra virgin olive oil

$1/4$ cup fresh lemon juice

$1/2$ teaspoon light brown sugar

Salt

1 Place the sweet potatoes in a large saucepan with salted water to cover and bring to a boil. Reduce the heat to medium and simmer until the potatoes are tender but still firm, 30 to 45 minutes, depending on the size. Drain and rinse under cold running water, then peel and cut into $1/2$-inch chunks.

2 Place the potato chunks in a large bowl and add the peas, scallions, and parsley.

3 In a small bowl, whisk together the oil, lemon juice, brown sugar, and salt to taste. Pour the dressing over the potato mixture and toss gently to coat evenly. Serve chilled or at room temperature. This salad is best served within 24 hours.

Serves 4 to 6

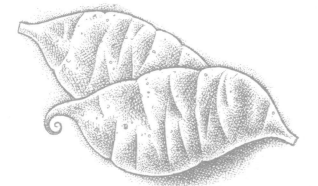

Tried and True Tabbouleh

~~~

This classic Middle Eastern bulgur salad is made even more hearty and healthful with the addition of chickpeas. An abundance of fresh parsley along with mint gives it the fresh taste for which it is known. Serve with hummus and pita bread for a satisfying Middle Eastern–inspired meal.

2 cups water

Salt

1 cup fine- or medium-grade bulgur

2 large ripe tomatoes, peeled, seeded, and chopped

1 bunch scallions, chopped

1/2 cup cooked or canned chickpeas, drained and rinsed if canned

Leaves from 1 bunch fresh parsley, minced (about 1 cup)

1/4 cup chopped fresh mint leaves

1/3 cup olive oil

3 tablespoons fresh lemon juice

1 small head romaine lettuce, cut crosswise into chiffonade strips

1 Bring the water to a boil in a medium-size saucepan. Salt the water lightly, then stir in the bulgur, cover, turn off the heat, and let sit until the bulgur softens and absorbs most of the water, about 25 minutes.

2 Drain the bulgur in a strainer and press out any remaining water. Place in a large bowl and add the tomatoes, scallions, chickpeas, parsley, and mint.

3 In a small bowl, whisk together the oil, lemon juice, and salt to taste. Pour the dressing over the salad and toss well to combine. Cover and refrigerate for at least 1 hour, and up to 4 hours.

4 To serve, arrange the lettuce on a serving platter. Mound the tabbouleh on top of the lettuce and serve.

Serves 4 to 6

Couscous Tabbouleh

~~~

Bulgur is used to make traditional tabbouleh, but couscous can be used to make a lighter variation. Orange juice and raisins lend a hint of sweetness, and a variety of vegetables including red onion and red bell pepper add color and texture.

---

2 cups water

Salt

1 cup instant couscous

1/2 small red onion, finely minced

1/2 small red bell pepper, seeded and chopped

1/2 small cucumber, peeled, seeded, and chopped

1/4 cup chopped almonds, roasted (page 9)

1/3 cup golden raisins

Leaves from 1 bunch fresh parsley, minced (about 1 cup)

1/4 cup olive oil

1/4 cup fresh orange juice

1 tablespoon fresh lemon juice

Cayenne

Butter lettuce leaves for serving

1 Bring the water to a boil in a medium-size saucepan. Salt the water, add the couscous, cover, and remove from the heat. Let sit until the water is absorbed, about 10 minutes.

2 Transfer the couscous to a medium bowl and add the onion, bell pepper, cucumber, almonds, raisins, and parsley.

3 In a small bowl, whisk together the oil, orange juice, lemon juice, and salt and cayenne to taste. Pour the dressing over the salad and toss well to combine. Cover and refrigerate for at least 1 hour before serving. This salad is best served the day it is made, so it still has its bright flavor.

4 To serve, arrange a bed of lettuce leaves on a platter and place the tabbouleh on top.

Serves 4

Moroccan Couscous Salad

Couscous is a mainstay in Moroccan cuisine, so it's only natural to create a couscous salad featuring Moroccan seasonings such as cumin, coriander, and cinnamon. The distinctive bite of fiery harissa sauce, a spicy condiment made with chiles, garlic, and fragrant spices, also identifies the salad as Moroccan-inspired. Harissa sauce is available at Middle Eastern and specialty food shops. If you can't find it, add a minced chile or some Asian chile paste to provide a touch of heat.

2 cups vegetable stock (page 36)

1 cup instant couscous

$1/3$ cup golden raisins

1 medium-size carrot, grated

4 scallions, minced

1 teaspoon harissa sauce, or more to taste

3 tablespoons olive oil

1 small red bell pepper, seeded and cut into $1/4$-inch dice

$1/2$ teaspoon ground cumin

$1/2$ teaspoon ground coriander

$1/4$ teaspoon ground cinnamon

$1/2$ teaspoon salt

1 cup cooked or canned chickpeas, drained and rinsed if canned

$1/4$ cup slivered almonds, toasted (page 9)

3 tablespoons fresh lemon juice

1 Bring the stock to a boil in a medium-size saucepan. Stir in the couscous and raisins, cover, remove from the heat, and let stand for 10 minutes.

2 Stir the carrot, scallions, and harissa into the couscous and set aside.

3 Heat the oil in a large skillet over medium heat. Add the bell pepper, cumin, coriander, cinnamon, and salt and cook, stirring frequently, until the spices are fragrant, about 2 minutes. Remove from the heat.

4 In a large bowl, combine the couscous mixture, bell pepper mixture, chickpeas, almonds, and lemon juice and toss to blend. Adjust the seasonings. Serve the salad chilled or at room temperature. This salad will keep for a day or two in the refrigerator, but, if making it ahead, don't add the almonds until just before serving, or they will lose their crunchiness.

Serves 4

Caribbean Couscous Salad

Although it looks like a grain, couscous is actually made from semolina and therefore more akin to pasta. Whatever you call it, it's delicious, nourishing, and easy to use. It also makes a great base for a salad. I think it works especially well with the tropical flavors of the Caribbean.

2 cups apple juice

1 cup water

Salt

1¹/₂ cups instant couscous

1 small yellow bell pepper, seeded and cut into ¹/₄-inch dice

1 cup frozen peas, thawed

1 cup cooked or canned dark red kidney beans, drained and rinsed if canned

3 scallions, minced

¹/₄ cup chopped pitted dates

¹/₃ cup extra virgin olive oil

3 tablespoons fresh lime juice

1 teaspoon light brown sugar

¹/₂ teaspoon ground cumin

¹/₂ teaspoon ground allspice

¹/₈ teaspoon cayenne

¹/₂ cup chopped pecans, roasted (page 9)

¹/₄ cup unsweetened flaked coconut

1 Combine the apple juice, water, and a pinch of salt in a medium-size saucepan and bring to a boil. Stir in the couscous, cover, remove from the heat, and let stand for 10 minutes.

2 Meanwhile, in a large bowl, combine the bell pepper, peas, kidney beans, scallions, and dates. Set aside.

3 In a small bowl, whisk together the oil, lime juice, brown sugar, cumin, allspice, cayenne, and salt to taste.

4 Add the couscous to the vegetable mixture, pour on the dressing, and toss to combine well. Sprinkle with the pecans and coconut and serve. This salad will keep in the refrigerator for a day or two, but if you are making it ahead, do not add the pecans and coconut until ready to serve.

Serves 4

Cold Noodle Salad with Spicy Sesame Sauce

Cold noodle salads are popular throughout Asia. This one, rich with tahini and chile paste, is especially flavorful. Soba are Japanese buckwheat noodles, available in Asian and specialty markets, as well as some natural food stores. If necessary, you can substitute another type of Asian noodle, or linguine.

8 ounces soba noodles

2 tablespoons toasted sesame oil

1 small red bell pepper, seeded and cut into thin strips

1 medium-size cucumber, peeled, halved lengthwise, seeded, and thinly sliced

1/4 cup minced scallions

One 8-ounce can sliced water chestnuts, drained and rinsed

1/4 cup tahini (sesame paste)

1 garlic clove, minced

3 tablespoons tamari or other soy sauce

2 tablespoons water

1 teaspoon Asian chile paste, or more to taste

1 Cook the noodles according to the package directions. Drain and rinse under cold running water.

2 In a medium-size bowl, toss the noodles with I tablespoon of the oil. Add the bell pepper, cucumber, scallions, and water chestnuts. Set aside.

3 In a small bowl, combine the tahini, garlic, the remaining I tablespoon oil, the tamari, water, and chile paste, stirring well to blend. Add the sauce to the noodles and vegetables and toss gently to coat evenly. Cover and refrigerate for an hour or two to allow the flavors to blend.

4 Serve cool or at room temperature, but not directly from the refrigerator. This salad is best served within I to 2 days.

Serves 4

Tuscan Summer Pasta Salad

This hearty pasta salad, imbued with the flavors of Tuscany, combines fresh summer produce with pantry ingredients. The artichoke hearts and olives add piquancy and the grated fennel lends a faintly licorice taste, while the cannellini beans provide protein and substance.

---

12 ounces tricolor rotini

1/2 cup extra virgin olive oil

1 small yellow bell pepper, seeded and chopped

1 cup cherry tomatoes, halved

1/4 cup chopped red onion

1/4 cup grated fennel bulb

One 9-ounce jar marinated artichoke hearts, drained and chopped

1 1/2 cups cooked cannellini beans or one 15-ounce can, drained and rinsed

1/3 cup Gaeta olives, pitted

1/4 cup minced fresh parsley leaves

3 tablespoons balsamic vinegar

1/4 cup pesto, homemade (page 313) or store-bought

Salt and freshly ground black pepper

Salad greens for serving

1 Cook the pasta in a large pot of boiling salted water, stirring occasionally, until *al dente*, 8 to 10 minutes. Drain and rinse under cold running water. Place in a large bowl and toss with 1 tablespoon of the oil.

2 Add the bell pepper, tomatoes, onion, fennel, artichoke hearts, beans, olives, and parsley to the pasta and toss. Set aside.

3 In a small bowl, whisk together the remaining 7 tablespoons oil, the vinegar, pesto, and salt and pepper to taste. Add the dressing to the pasta salad and toss gently to coat evenly. Taste to adjust the seasonings if necessary.

4 Divide the salad greens among individual plates, top with the pasta salad, and serve. You can prepare the salad several hours in advance, but add the dressing just prior to serving so the ingredients don't become soggy.

Serves 4 to 6

Salad Days

Here are some tips for creating easy and delicious main-dish salads:

- Use pantry items such as canned chickpeas, artichoke hearts, and roasted red bell peppers to add extra flavor, color, and nutrition.

- Incorporate both raw and cooked vegetables for textural contrast.

- Sprinkle salads with your favorite nuts or seeds to add crunch and boost protein and essential fatty acids.

- Toss thawed frozen peas into a salad for color and texture.

- Make a large quantity of salad dressing and keep it in the refrigerator. It's better for you than commercial dressings, it's less expensive, and it tastes better too.

- Incorporate some sort of fruit or other surprise ingredient to add interest.

- Add a small amount of mesclun mix to your regular lettuce. Stretching the mesclun with other lettuces will save money, but your salad will have the look and taste of a sophisticated salad.

- Arrange salads with an eye for presentation, incorporating a variety of colorful vegetables and other ingredients in aesthetic ways.

- Serve salads on oversized plates, as they do in restaurants.

Orange-and-Sesame-Tossed Penne Salad with Red Beans and Watercress

∼ww∼

A fusion of Italian pasta and Asian seasonings combines with meaty kidney beans and peppery watercress in this lively salad. The deep burgundy color of the beans against the bright green watercress is especially appealing.

12 ounces penne pasta

1/4 cup plus 1 teaspoon toasted
   sesame oil

1 1/2 cups cooked dark red kidney beans
   or one 15-ounce can, drained and
   rinsed

2 scallions, finely chopped

Finely chopped zest and juice of
   1 orange

1 tablespoon rice vinegar

1 tablespoon minced fresh chives

1 tablespoon tamari or other soy sauce

2 teaspoons peeled and grated fresh
   ginger

Leaves from 2 bunches watercress,
   coarsely chopped

8 yellow or red cherry tomatoes
   (optional), halved

1 Cook the pasta in a large pot of salted boiling water until *al dente*, about 8 minutes. Drain and rinse under cold running water, then place in a large bowl and toss with I teaspoon of the oil.

2 Add the kidney beans and scallions to the pasta, toss, and set aside.

3 In a food processor, combine the orange zest and juice, rice vinegar, chives, tamari, ginger, and the remaining 1/4 cup oil and process until well blended. Pour the dressing over the pasta salad, add the watercress and tomatoes, if using, and toss gently to combine well. This salad is best served shortly after it is made. You can prepare the various components ahead of time, then combine when ready to serve.

Serves 4

Call It Macaroni Salad

Traditional macaroni salad is lightened with soy mayonnaise, which can be purchased at natural food stores or well-stocked supermarkets or made using the recipe on page 309.

12 ounces elbow macaroni

1 celery stalk, minced

3 tablespoons seeded and finely minced red bell pepper

3 tablespoons sweet pickle relish

2 tablespoons grated red onion

1 cup regular or soy mayonnaise

1½ teaspoons Dijon mustard

¼ cup regular or soy milk

1 tablespoon white wine vinegar

½ teaspoon salt

Sweet paprika for garnish

1 Cook the macaroni in a large pot of salted boiling water until *al dente*, about 8 minutes. Drain, rinse under cold running water, and transfer to a large bowl.

2 Add the celery, bell pepper, pickle relish, and onion to the macaroni, toss, and set aside.

3 In a small bowl, whisk together the mayonnaise, mustard, milk, vinegar, and salt. Add the dressing to the macaroni mixture and stir gently to coat evenly. Sprinkle with paprika, cover, and refrigerate to chill before serving. This will keep for a day or two in the refrigerator.

Serves 4 to 6

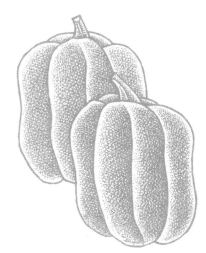

Madras Rice Salad with Mangoes and Peanuts

These days, many people ignore the familiar yellow spicy blend called Madras curry powder in favor of the more authentic garam masalas and other Indian spice blends. Still, I sometimes enjoy the particular flavor of this supermarket standby. I chose flaxseed oil for its nutritional benefit, but any flavorless oil can be used.

1/3 cup flaxseed oil

3 tablespoons fresh lime juice

2 teaspoons Madras curry powder

1 teaspoon light brown sugar

1/8 teaspoon cayenne

3 cups cold cooked basmati rice

1 small red bell pepper, seeded and cut into 1/2-inch dice

1 small red onion, chopped

1 large ripe mango, peeled, seeded, and cut into 1/2-inch dice

1/4 cup golden raisins

Salad greens for serving

Chopped unsalted roasted peanuts for garnish

1 In a small bowl, whisk together the oil, lime juice, curry powder, brown sugar, and cayenne. Set aside.

2 In a large bowl, combine the rice, bell pepper, onion, mango, and raisins. Add the dressing and toss gently to coat evenly.

3 To serve, line a platter or plates with salad greens, spoon the rice salad onto the greens, and garnish with chopped peanuts.

Serves 4 to 6

"Hoppin' John" Rice Salad

I nspired by the popular New Year's dish of the American South, this salad can be enjoyed at any time of year. Black-eyed peas, rice, and bits of sweet red onion are tossed in a spicy vinaigrette and garnished with sour cream.

1/3 cup extra virgin olive oil

3 tablespoons cider vinegar

1 tablespoon fresh lemon juice

2 garlic cloves, minced

1/2 teaspoon minced fresh thyme leaves

1/4 teaspoon Tabasco sauce

Salt and freshly ground black pepper

3 cups cold cooked long-grain white rice

1 1/2 cups cooked black-eyed peas or one
15-ounce can, drained and rinsed

1 small red onion, chopped

1 head butter lettuce, separated into
leaves

Sour cream or tofu sour cream

1 In a small bowl, whisk together the oil, vinegar, lemon juice, garlic, thyme, Tabasco, and salt and pepper to taste. Set aside.

2 In a large bowl, combine the rice, black-eyed peas, and onion. Add the dressing and toss to combine well.

3 Line four plates or a shallow serving bowl with the lettuce leaves and top with the rice salad. Top with a dollop of sour cream, grind a little fresh pepper on top, and serve.

Serves 4

Spicy Southwestern Rice Salad

Jicama, a popular ingredient in the Southwest, looks like a cross between a potato and a turnip, but it has a mild, sweet taste similar to an apple. It adds crunch to this spicy rice salad featuring pinto beans, cilantro, and hot chiles. If two serrano chiles have more heat than you'd like, use less or omit them altogether.

2 serrano chiles, seeded and minced

1 garlic clove, minced

1 teaspoon ground cumin

2 tablespoons white wine vinegar

2 tablespoons fresh lime juice

1/2 cup olive oil

Salt and freshly ground black pepper

3 cups cold cooked long-grain rice

1 small red onion, chopped

1 small jicama, peeled and shredded

1 small red bell pepper, seeded and chopped

1 1/2 cups cooked pinto beans or one 15-ounce can, drained and rinsed

2 tablespoons minced fresh cilantro leaves

1 In a small bowl, whisk together the chiles, garlic, cumin, vinegar, lime juice, oil, and salt and pepper to taste. Set aside.

2 In a large bowl, combine the rice, onion, jicama, bell pepper, beans, and cilantro. Add just enough of the dressing to coat (reserve any extra for another use) and stir gently to combine well. Taste and adjust the seasonings before serving. This salad will keep for a day or two in the refrigerator. Serve cool, but not refrigerator-cold, or at room temperature.

Serves 4 to 6

Baby Spinach Salad with Baked Tofu and Crispy Slivered Shallots

Look for baked tofu in the refrigerated cases of natural food stores and some supermarkets. This salad is best when made with garden-fresh, very ripe tomatoes. If tender baby spinach is unavailable, use regular spinach. Vegetarian Worcestershire sauce, made without anchovies, is available at natural food stores.

1/3 cup extra virgin olive oil

2 tablespoons white wine vinegar

1 tablespoon fresh lemon juice

1 teaspoon vegetarian Worcestershire sauce

1 teaspoon Dijon mustard

1/8 teaspoon Tabasco sauce

Salt and freshly ground black pepper

6 cups fresh baby spinach leaves

8 ounces baked tofu, cut into 1/2-inch-wide 1/4-inch-thick strips

One 9-ounce jar marinated artichoke hearts, drained

1/3 cup Kalamata olives, pitted

1 cup cherry tomatoes, halved

Crispy Slivered Shallots (recipe follows)

1 In a small bowl, whisk together the oil, vinegar, lemon juice, Worcestershire, mustard, Tabasco, and salt and pepper to taste. Set aside.

2 Divide the spinach among four serving plates. Arrange the tofu, artichoke hearts, olives, and cherry tomatoes on top of the spinach. Drizzle with the dressing, scatter the shallots over the top, and serve. The dressing can be made ahead if you like, but it should not be added to the salad until serving time.

Serves 4

Crispy Slivered Shallots

4 medium-size shallots, halved lengthwise

3 tablespoons olive oil

1 Cut the shallots into very thin slices and separate into individual slivers.

2 In a medium skillet, heat the oil over medium-high heat. Add the shallots and cook, stirring constantly, until crisp, about 5 minutes. Remove from the pan and drain on paper towels.

Makes about 1 cup

Wheat-Meat and Romaine Salad with Red Potatoes

This hearty main-dish salad is ideal for the "meat and potatoes" person at your house—delicious chunks of new potatoes and strips of seitan (wheat-meat) in a garlicky sherry vinaigrette over crisp romaine lettuce. If seitan is unavailable, substitute baked tofu, available at natural food stores and some supermarkets.

1 pound small red potatoes

1/2 cup olive oil

6 ounces seitan, cut into thin strips

Salt and freshly ground black pepper

3 garlic cloves, minced

1/4 cup sherry vinegar

1/2 teaspoon minced fresh oregano
    leaves or 1/4 teaspoon dried

1/4 cup chopped shallots

1 small head romaine lettuce, torn into
    bite-size pieces

1 tablespoon torn fresh basil leaves

8 cherry tomatoes, halved

1 Place the potatoes in a large saucepan with salted cold water to cover and bring to boil. Reduce the heat to medium-low, cover, and simmer until tender, 25 to 30 minutes. Drain and set aside.

2 Heat 1 tablespoon of the oil in a large skillet over medium-high heat. Add the seitan and cook, stirring, until browned on both sides, about 5 minutes. Season with salt and pepper and set aside to cool.

3 In a small bowl, whisk together the remaining 7 tablespoons oil, the garlic, vinegar, oregano, and salt and pepper to taste. Set aside.

4 In a large bowl, combine the potatoes and seitan with the shallots, romaine, basil, and tomatoes. Add the dressing and toss gently to coat evenly. This salad is best served at room temperature.

Serves 4 to 6

Soy Good Chef's Salad

Thanks to the ingenuity of a few pioneering food companies, vegetarians can now enjoy a variety of meatless "cold cuts," making a vegetarian chef's salad not only possible but deliciously probable. Now available in most well-stocked supermarkets, vegetarian ham, turkey, and bacon, as well as soy cheese, provide familiar family favorites to help ease the transition to a vegetarian diet.

1 large head Boston or butter lettuce, separated into leaves

4 slices soy cheese, cut into 1/2-inch-wide strips

4 slices vegetarian turkey, cut into 1/2-inch-wide strips

4 slices vegetarian ham, cut into 1/2-inch-wide strips

2 medium-size ripe tomatoes, cut into eighths

2 strips vegetarian bacon, cooked and chopped, or 1/4 cup soy bacon bits

1/2 cup extra virgin olive oil

3 tablespoons balsamic vinegar

1 garlic clove, minced

1/4 teaspoon dry mustard

1/2 teaspoon salt

1/8 teaspoon freshly ground black pepper

4 black olives, pitted

1 Tear the lettuce into bite-size pieces and divide among four individual plates. Divide the soy cheese, vegetarian turkey, and ham among the salads, arranging them on top of the lettuce. Divide the tomato wedges among the salads, placing them in between the ham and cheese slices. Sprinkle the bacon over the salads.

2 In a small bowl, whisk together the oil, vinegar, garlic, mustard, salt, and pepper.

3 Drizzle the dressing over the salads, top each salad with an olive, and serve.

Serves 4

Vibrant Vegetable Slaw

Two kinds of cabbage go into this crunchy slaw, with a touch of radish to give it bite, and a creamy soy-based dressing to keep it healthful. Slaws are a great way to enjoy more raw vegetables and a perfect accompaniment to sandwiches as well as veggie burgers and hotdogs.

³/₄ cup regular or soy mayonnaise
  (page 309)

¹/₄ cup regular or soy milk

1 teaspoon sugar or a natural sweetener
  (page 330)

2 tablespoons fresh lemon juice

¹/₄ teaspoon celery salt

1 teaspoon Dijon mustard

¹/₈ teaspoon Tabasco sauce

1 small head green cabbage, cored and
  shredded (about 4 cups)

¹/₂ small head purple cabbage, cored and
  shredded (about 2 cups)

1 small carrot, grated

3 or 4 red radishes, to your taste,
  trimmed and shredded

2 tablespoons minced scallions

2 tablespoons minced fresh parsley
  leaves

Salt and freshly ground black pepper

1 In a blender or small bowl, combine the mayonnaise, milk, sugar, lemon juice, celery salt, mustard, and Tabasco and blend or whisk until well combined. Set aside.

2 In a large bowl, combine the cabbages, carrot, radishes, scallions, and parsley and toss well. Add the dressing and stir to combine well. Season with salt and pepper to taste. Cover and refrigerate for several hours before serving chilled. This slaw is best the day it is made.

Serves 6 to 8

Creamy Caraway Cabbage Slaw

Cabbage and caraway are a natural combination, and grated apple and raisins make sweet additions to this crisp coleslaw.

1 small head green cabbage, cored and shredded

1 small carrot, grated

1 large Granny Smith apple, left unpeeled, cored, chopped, and tossed with 1 teaspoon fresh lemon juice

2 tablespoons golden raisins

1 tablespoon caraway seeds

$^2/_3$ cup regular or soy mayonnaise (page 309)

$^1/_4$ cup regular or soy milk

2 tablespoons fresh lemon juice

1 teaspoon sugar or a natural sweetener (page 330)

$^3/_4$ teaspoon salt

$^1/_4$ teaspoon freshly ground black pepper

1 In a large bowl, combine the cabbage, carrot, apple, raisins, and caraway seeds. Set aside.

2 In a small bowl, combine the mayonnaise, milk, lemon juice, sugar, salt, and pepper and stir until well blended. Add the sauce to the slaw and toss until thoroughly combined. Serve at once or refrigerate, covered, to serve chilled. This slaw is best the day it is made.

Serves 6

Carrot-Apple-Jicama Slaw

J icama, which can be eaten raw or cooked, tastes like a cross between apples and water chestnuts. It will keep for two to three weeks in the refrigerator.

2 large carrots

1 large jicama, halved lengthwise and
    peeled

1 Granny Smith apple, peeled and cored

2 tablespoons fresh lime juice

1 tablespoon fresh lemon juice

1/4 cup extra virgin olive oil

2 tablespoons fresh orange juice

1/2 teaspoon sugar or a natural
    sweetener (page 330)

1/2 teaspoon salt

1/8 teaspoon Tabasco sauce

2 tablespoons minced fresh cilantro
    leaves

1 Using a hand grater, mandoline or other vegetable slicer, or food processor fitted with the shredding attachment, shred the carrots, jicama, and apple. Place in a large bowl, add the lime and lemon juices, and toss to combine. Set aside.

2 In a small bowl, combine the oil, orange juice, sugar, salt, and Tabasco. Pour the dressing over the slaw, add the cilantro, and toss to combine well. Chill well before serving. This slaw is best the day it is made.

Serves 6

Simmering Stews

Nothing says good old-fashioned comfort food quite like a pot of stew simmering on the stove. Even the meat lovers in your house will enjoy these rich and flavorful stews chock-full of fresh vegetables, beans, potatoes, herbs, and spices.

One of the many pluses to meatless stews is a shorter cooking time. Since these stews don't need to simmer for several hours to tenderize tough cuts of meat, most can be ready within an hour, all the time they need to bring out the rich flavors of the vegetables. Like most stews, these benefit from being made ahead and reheated so that the flavors intensify. Vegetable stews can contain as few as two or three main ingredients or up to a dozen. The vegetables may be added all at once or at different times, according to how long each one takes to cook. The main differences between stews and soups are that stews have less liquid and their ingredients are generally cut into larger pieces. Stews can be thickened in a number of ways. My favorite method is to puree a cup or two of the cooked stew in a blender or food processor and then stir it back into the pot. This enriches the flavor while adding body to the stew. You can also thicken stews with a cornstarch-and-water mixture, added near the end of the cooking time.

Cooking a pot of stew the night before can be the answer to the "no time to cook" dinnertime dilemma. With a quick reheat, dinner is served—one that tastes like you've been cooking it all day. Serve over rice or noodles or with a loaf of crusty bread for a complete one-dish meal.

These savory stews hail from all over the world. From *Basque-Style Fava Bean Stew* and *African Groundnut Stew* to *Glorious Goulash*, a pot of stew translates to great eating anywhere.

Vegetarian Brunswick Stew

Jammin' Vegetable Jambalaya

Vegetarian Burgoo

Home-Style Seitan Stew

Tempeh Cacciatore

Glorious Goulash

Soy Stroganoff

Thai Tofu Curry with Potatoes and Pineapple

Winter Vegetable Stew with Potato Gnocchi

My Wild Irish Stew

Campari-Scented Vegetable Stew with
   Fennel and Orange Zest

Vegetable Tagine

Spicy African Sweet Potato Stew

African Groundnut Stew

Basque-Style Fava Bean Stew

Kale and Cannellini Bean Stew

Mexican Corn, Tomatillo, and Red Bean Stew

Indian Chickpea and Potato Stew

Spiced Lentil-Coconut Stew

Red Beans Bourguignon

Chili con Frijoles

"Meaty" Eggplant-Portobello Chili

Vegetarian Brunswick Stew

This fresh interpretation of a Southern favorite tastes even better the day after it's made. It is especially good served with corn bread or over biscuits. Crumbled tofu or TVP (textured vegetable protein) may be used instead of vegetarian burger crumbles. Liquid Smoke is a hickory flavoring that adds a pleasant smoked nuance to the stew; it can be found in the supermarket. Vegetarian Worcestershire sauce, made without anchovies, is available in natural food stores.

1 tablespoon olive oil

1 package vegetarian sausage links, cut into 1/2-inch pieces

1 medium-size yellow onion, finely chopped

1 celery stalk, minced

1 large all-purpose potato, peeled and diced

2 garlic cloves, minced

1 1/2 teaspoons peeled and grated fresh ginger

3 1/2 cups vegetable stock (page 36) or water

One 14.5-ounce can diced tomatoes, with their juices

One 16-ounce package frozen succotash

3 tablespoons vegetarian Worcestershire sauce or tamari or other soy sauce

1/2 teaspoon Tabasco sauce

2 teaspoons prepared mustard

1 teaspoon light brown sugar

1/2 teaspoon ground allspice

Salt and freshly ground black pepper

One 12-ounce package frozen vegetarian burger crumbles

1/2 teaspoon Liquid Smoke

1 Heat the oil in a large pot over medium heat. Add the vegetarian sausage and cook, stirring a few times, until browned on all sides, about 5 minutes. Remove the sausage from the pan and set aside.

2 Add the onion, celery, potato, garlic, and ginger to the oil remaining in the pot. Add 1/4 cup of the stock, cover, and cook, stirring a few times, until the vegetables are softened, about 5 minutes. Add the remaining 3 1/4 cups stock, then stir in the tomatoes, succotash, Worcestershire, Tabasco, mustard, brown sugar, allspice, and salt and pepper to taste and bring to a boil. Reduce the heat to low and simmer uncovered, stirring occasionally, until the vegetables are very tender, 45 to 50 minutes. During the last 10 minutes of cooking, add the reserved sausage, vegetarian burger crumbles, and Liquid Smoke. Serve hot.

Serves 4 to 6

Jammin' Vegetable Jambalaya

Kidney beans and vegetarian sausage links are used to make a meatless version of the Louisiana classic. Serve over hot cooked rice, and be sure to put a bottle of Tabasco on the table for those who want to add a little extra.

1½ tablespoons olive oil

1 large yellow onion, chopped

1 celery stalk, chopped

1 large red bell pepper, seeded and
    chopped

2 garlic cloves, minced

One 28-ounce can diced tomatoes, with
    their juices

1½ teaspoons minced fresh thyme
    leaves

½ teaspoon minced fresh marjoram
    leaves

1 teaspoon Tabasco sauce

1 teaspoon salt

2 cups water

8 ounces vegetarian sausage links, cut
    into 1-inch pieces

1½ cups cooked dark red kidney beans
    or one 15-ounce can, drained and
    rinsed

1 tablespoon chopped fresh parsley
    leaves

Hot cooked long-grain rice

1 Heat I tablespoon of the oil in a large saucepan over medium heat. Add the onion, celery, bell pepper, and garlic, cover, and cook, stirring a few times, until softened, about 5 minutes. Stir in the tomatoes, thyme, marjoram, Tabasco, salt, and water, cover, and simmer until the vegetables are tender, about 30 minutes.

2 Meanwhile, heat the remaining $1\frac{1}{2}$ teaspoons oil in a medium-size skillet over medium-high heat. Add the vegetarian sausage and cook, stirring occasionally, until browned all over, about 5 minutes.

3 Add the sausage to the tomato mixture, along with the beans and parsley. Cook, uncovered, for I0 minutes, stirring occasionally, to heat though, adding more water if the jambalaya becomes too dry. Serve hot over rice.

Serves 4

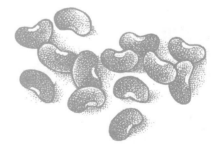

Vegetarian Burgoo

This hearty vegetable stew is inspired by the classic Kentucky burgoo, which, in addition to a plethora of vegetables, traditionally contains whatever meat is available. In this version, I use vegetarian sausage and chickpeas, but feel free to use tempeh, firm tofu, or other beans. Fresh-baked corn bread is a natural accompaniment.

1 tablespoon olive oil

8 ounces vegetarian sausage links, cut into bite-size pieces

1 medium-size yellow onion, chopped

1 medium-size green bell pepper, seeded and chopped

1 pound all-purpose potatoes, peeled and diced

2 cups cored and shredded Savoy cabbage

1 small butternut squash, peeled, seeded, and diced

1 medium-size turnip, peeled and diced

One 14.5-ounce can diced tomatoes, with their juices

3 cups vegetable stock (page 36) or water

2 tablespoons tamari or other soy sauce

2 bay leaves

Salt and freshly ground black pepper

2 teaspoons minced fresh oregano leaves or 1 teaspoon dried

$1/2$ teaspoon red pepper flakes

3 cups cooked chickpeas or two 15-ounce cans, drained and rinsed

1 Heat the oil in a large pot over medium heat. Add the sausage and cook, stirring occasionally, until browned all over, about 5 minutes. Remove from the pot and set aside.

2 Add the onion to the pot, cover, and cook, stirring a few times, until softened, about 5 minutes. Add the bell pepper, cover, and cook, stirring a few times, until tender, about 5 minutes. Stir in the potatoes, cabbage, squash, turnip, tomatoes, stock, tamari, bay leaves, and salt and pepper to taste. Cover and simmer until the vegetables are tender, about 45 minutes. Add the oregano, red pepper flakes, and chickpeas and cook, uncovered, for 10 minutes to blend the flavors and reduce the liquid slightly. Remove and discard the bay leaves. Stir in the reserved vegetarian sausage, heat through, and serve.

Serves 6

Home-Style Seitan Stew

mm

Chock-full of chunks of tender fresh vegetables, this stew has all the flavor of the rich, brothy stews of my childhood; seitan is a natural choice to replace the beef in the original. The dish can be ready to eat in less than an hour. As with most stews, the flavor improves when reheated, so make it ahead of time if you can. Serve over freshly cooked noodles.

2 tablespoons olive oil

1 pound seitan (see page 127), cut into
    1-inch cubes

Salt and freshly ground black pepper

1 large yellow onion, chopped

1 large red bell pepper, seeded and cut
    into 1-inch squares

2 garlic cloves, minced

2 teaspoons chopped fresh thyme leaves
    or 1 teaspoon dried

1 teaspoon chopped fresh oregano
    leaves or 1/2 teaspoon dried

1 bay leaf

1/4 cup all-purpose flour

One 14.5-ounce can diced tomatoes, with
    their juices

8 ounces green beans, ends trimmed and
    cut into 1-inch pieces

2 cups vegetable stock (page 36) or
    water

1/2 cup dry white wine

1 Heat 1 tablespoon of the oil in a large nonstick skillet over medium-high heat. Add the seitan and cook, stirring occasionally, until browned on all sides, about 5 minutes. Season with salt and pepper, remove from the pan, and set aside.

2 Heat the remaining 1 tablespoon oil in a large saucepan over medium heat. Add the onion, bell pepper, garlic, thyme, oregano, and bay leaf, cover, and cook, stirring a few times, until the vegetables are softened, about 5 minutes. Add the flour and cook, stirring constantly, for about 1 minute to remove the raw taste from the flour. Stir in the tomatoes, green beans, stock, and wine and bring to a boil. Reduce the heat to low and simmer, uncovered, stirring occasionally, for 20 minutes. Season to taste with salt and pepper.

3 Add the reserved seitan and simmer for 10 minutes, or until heated through. Serve hot.

Serves 4 to 6

Tempeh Cacciatore

Inspired by the popular Italian chicken dish, this "hunter's-style" tempeh stew, made with tomatoes, white wine, and fresh herbs, is best served over a sturdy Italian pasta such as pappardelle or fettuccine.

12 ounces tempeh

2 tablespoons olive oil

$^1/_2$ cup dry white wine

1 medium-size yellow onion, chopped

1 medium-size carrot, thinly sliced

1 celery stalk, chopped

1 medium-size red bell pepper, seeded
  and chopped

1 large garlic clove, chopped

2 tablespoons tomato paste, blended
  with 1 cup hot water

One 14.5-ounce can diced tomatoes, with
  their juices

1 teaspoon minced fresh oregano leaves
  or $^1/_2$ teaspoon dried

2 bay leaves

Salt and freshly ground black pepper

1 Place the tempeh in a medium-size saucepan with water to cover and bring to a boil. Reduce the heat to low and simmer for 10 minutes. Drain the tempeh and pat dry. Cut into 1-inch pieces.

2 Heat 1 tablespoon of the oil in a medium-size skillet over medium heat. Add the tempeh and cook, stirring occasionally, until golden brown, about 5 minutes. Remove from the skillet with a slotted spoon and drain on paper towels. Deglaze the pan with the wine, stirring to scrape up any browned bits on the bottom. Simmer until the wine reduces by half, then remove the skillet from the heat and set aside.

3 Heat the remaining 1 tablespoon oil in a large saucepan over medium heat. Add the onion, carrot, celery, bell pepper, and garlic, then stir in the diluted tomato paste, cover, and cook until the vegetables soften, about 10 minutes. Stir in the diced tomatoes, oregano, and bay leaves, season to taste with salt and pepper, and simmer, uncovered, for 20 minutes to blend the flavors.

4 Add the tempeh and reduced wine and simmer for 15 minutes longer to blend the flavors. Add more water if the cacciatore seems dry. Remove and discard the bay leaves before serving.

Serves 4

Glorious Goulash

Tempeh stands up well to the sauerkraut in this robust stew, which is best served over noodles. A crisp white wine or cold beer would complement the dish nicely.

1 pound tempeh, cut into 1/2-inch-wide strips

2 tablespoons olive oil

1 medium-size yellow onion, chopped

1 medium-size carrot, thinly sliced

2 garlic cloves, minced

2 tablespoons tomato paste

1/2 cup dry white wine

1 tablespoon sweet paprika

1 teaspoon caraway seeds

2 cups fresh or canned sauerkraut, rinsed and drained well

1 1/2 cups vegetable stock (page 36) or water, or more if needed

1/2 cup sour cream or tofu sour cream

Salt and freshly ground black pepper

2 tablespoons minced fresh parsley leaves

1 Place the tempeh in a medium-size saucepan with water to cover and bring to a boil. Reduce the heat to low and simmer for 10 minutes. Drain the tempeh and pat dry.

2 Heat the oil in a large saucepan over medium heat. Add the tempeh and cook, stirring occasionally, until browned all over, 5 to 7 minutes. Remove the tempeh with a slotted spoon and set aside. Add the onion and carrot, cover, and cook, stirring a few times, until softened, about 5 minutes. Add the garlic and cook for 1 minute longer.

3 Stir in the tomato paste, wine, paprika, caraway seeds, tempeh, and sauerkraut. Add the stock and bring to a boil. Reduce the heat to low, cover, and simmer until the vegetables are soft and the flavors have developed, about 30 minutes. If the goulash seems dry, add more stock or water.

4 Just before serving, remove from the heat and whisk in the sour cream, stirring to blend. Season to taste with salt and pepper and serve sprinkled with the parsley.

Serves 4

Soy Stroganoff

G reen beans are also delicious prepared stroganoff-style—consider adding some cooked beans to the pan when you add the tofu for additional color, texture, and flavor.

2 tablespoons olive oil

1 pound extra-firm tofu, cut into ¹/₂-inch
   cubes

1 large yellow onion, chopped

8 ounces white button mushrooms, sliced
   or quartered, depending on size

1 tablespoon sweet paprika

2 tablespoons all-purpose flour

1 tablespoon tomato paste

¹/₄ cup dry white wine

1¹/₂ cups vegetable stock (page 36) or
   water

Salt and freshly ground black pepper

¹/₂ cup sour cream or tofu sour cream,
   plus more for serving if desired

Hot cooked noodles

1 Heat I tablespoon of the oil in a large skillet over medium heat. Add the tofu and cook, stirring occasionally, until golden brown on all sides, about 7 minutes. Remove from the skillet with a slotted spoon and set aside.

2 Add the remaining I tablespoon oil and the onion to the skillet, cover, and cook, stirring a few times, until the onion is softened, about 5 minutes. Add the mushrooms and cook until they release their juices, I to 2 minutes. Stir in the paprika and flour and cook, stirring constantly, for I minute to remove the raw taste from the flour. Add the tomato paste and wine, stirring until smooth. Add the stock and bring to a boil. Reduce the heat to low, season to taste with salt and pepper, and simmer for 20 minutes.

3 Remove from the heat and slowly whisk in the sour cream, blending well. Add the tofu and simmer for 5 minutes over very low heat to heat through.

4 Serve over the hot noodles and top with additional sour cream, if desired.

Serves 4

Roots: Cooking with the Vegetable Underground

Root vegetables such as carrots, parsnips, and turnips, as well as their subterranean colleagues onions and potatoes, are especially suited to slow-simmering stews, although their talents don't end there. Besides working their flavorful magic in a simmering stewpot, these members of the vegetable underground—roots, bulbs, and tubers—are adept in other culinary areas.

Onions, for example, are the foundation of countless savory recipes. Untold numbers of soups, sauces, and sautés begin with the cooking of an onion. Imagine how lackluster our meals would be without them.

Potatoes are among our most-beloved comfort foods, whether mashed, baked, boiled, or fried. Carrots can be absolute culinary chameleons. Grated raw in a salad, pureed to star in its own soup, or featured in stews or stir-fries, the carrot can be found posing as a side dish, entrée, juice, or even dessert.

Dig a little deeper into the underground vegetable community and you'll discover the beet, radish, celery root (celeriac), parsnip, turnip, and rutabaga. Beets are delicious boiled, roasted, or pickled, served hot or cold, in soups or as a side, or in salads. In addition to the small red orb that graces our salads, other radish varieties include the large white Japanese daikon and the tiny mild French breakfast radish.

Celery root is an aromatic knobby root that tastes somewhat similar to celery and can be eaten raw or cooked. It is used in salads, soups, and stews. Parsnips, which look like white carrots, are just as sweet, but with a creamy, more potato-like texture. Turnips don't usually win popularity contests, but they can be quite tasty when prepared with a touch of sweetness or as part of a root vegetable medley. Rutabagas taste similar to turnips, and, like them, benefit from a slightly sweet preparation, although they are also good mashed or used in a medley.

Consider going back to your roots and experience the delicious world of root vegetables.

Thai Tofu Curry with Potatoes and Pineapple

‑‑‑‑‑

This sublime dish was inspired by Thai Massaman curry, which is named for the Muslim people in southern Thailand. It derives its delicate sweetness from pineapple and coconut milk, as well as cardamom, cinnamon, and other fragrant spices. Thai bird chiles, galangal, and lemongrass are all available at Asian markets. Galangal is a relative of ginger that has a more pungent, peppery flavor than regular ginger. Slender Thai bird chiles are responsible for packing the punch in many hot Thai dishes, but a serrano can be used in their place here. When using fresh lemongrass, be sure to remove the tough outer layers of the stalk to reveal the tender inner core, the part used in cooking. As the name implies, lemongrass adds a delicate, lemony flavor to dishes, without the acidity of lemon juice.

Serve this stew over jasmine rice. To add extra flavor to the tofu, sauté it in a small amount of oil until golden brown on all sides before adding to the stew.

---

2 shallots, chopped

1 garlic clove, minced

1 Thai bird or serrano chile, seeded and minced

1 teaspoon peeled and minced fresh galangal or ginger

1 teaspoon trimmed and minced fresh lemongrass

1 tablespoon tamari or other soy sauce

1 teaspoon light brown sugar

1/2 teaspoon ground cardamom

1/2 teaspoon ground coriander

1/4 teaspoon turmeric

1　In a food processor, combine the shallots, garlic, chile, galangal, lemongrass, tamari, and brown sugar and process until smooth. Add the cardamom, turmeric, cumin, cinnamon, and I tablespoon of the oil and process to form a paste. Blend in the water. Set aside.

2　Heat the remaining I tablespoon oil in a large pot over medium heat. Add the onion, cover, and cook, stirring a few times, until softened, about 5 minutes. Add the potatoes and spice mixture and cook for 2 to 3 minutes longer. Stir in the stock, cover, and simmer until the vegetables are soft, 20 to 30 minutes.

1/8 teaspoon ground cumin

1/8 teaspoon ground cinnamon

2 tablespoons peanut oil

1/2 cup water

1 medium-size yellow onion, coarsely
chopped

2 large all-purpose potatoes, peeled and
cut into 1-inch chunks

1 1/2 cups vegetable stock (page 36) or
water

1 pound extra-firm tofu, cut into 1-inch
chunks

1 cup pineapple chunks (fresh or canned)

1 cup unsweetened coconut milk

3 Stir in the tofu, pineapple, and coconut milk and simmer for 5 minutes longer to heat through. Serve hot.

Serves 4

Winter Vegetable Stew with Potato Gnocchi

This comforting cold-weather stew is so colorful and fresh tasting it may remind you of spring-time even in the dead of winter. Make your own gnocchi (page 235), or buy packaged gnocchi at well-stocked supermarkets or Italian specialty shops.

1 tablespoon olive oil

1 large yellow onion, chopped

1 large carrot, sliced

1 celery stalk, chopped

1 large potato, peeled and diced

1 small parsnip, peeled, halved
    lengthwise, and sliced crosswise

1 small red bell pepper, seeded and diced

2 garlic cloves, minced

1/2 cup dry white wine

2 cups vegetable stock (page 36) or
    water, or more if needed

1 bay leaf

1/2 teaspoon minced fresh marjoram
    leaves or 1/4 teaspoon dried

1/2 teaspoon minced fresh basil leaves or
    1/4 teaspoon dried

Salt and freshly ground black pepper

1 cup frozen peas

11/2 cups cooked chickpeas or one
    15-ounce can, drained and rinsed

2 tablespoons minced fresh parsley leaves

2 tablespoons pesto, homemade
    (page 313) or store-bought

8 ounces potato gnocchi (see headnote),
    cooked and still hot

1 Heat the oil in a large pot over medium heat. Add the onion, carrot, and celery, cover, and cook, stirring a few times, until softened, about 5 minutes. Stir in the potato, parsnip, bell pepper, and garlic and cook, uncovered, for 2 minutes. Add the wine, stock, bay leaf, marjoram, basil, and salt and pepper to taste. Bring to a boil, then reduce the heat to low, cover, and cook, stirring occasionally, until the vegetables are tender, 20 to 30 minutes.

2 Add the peas, chickpeas, and parsley, then stir in the pesto and more stock if the stew is too dry. Simmer for 10 minutes longer. Remove the bay leaf. Serve topped with the gnocchi.

Serves 4

My Wild Irish Stew

I sometimes serve this stew on Saint Patrick's Day, over spinach noodles accompanied by Irish soda bread. Since Saint Patrick himself wasn't Irish, I don't think he'd mind that this stew isn't exactly authentic, since it uses beans in place of the traditional meat. You can peel the potatoes if you like, but I usually leave them unpeeled for added nutrition.

1 tablespoon olive oil

1 small yellow onion, chopped

1 celery stalk, cut into 1/4-inch-thick

  slices

5 small waxy white potatoes, quartered

1 pound baby carrots

2 garlic cloves, minced

3 cups vegetable stock (page 36) or

  water

1/4 cup dry red wine (optional)

2 bay leaves

1/4 cup tamari or other soy sauce

8 ounces white button mushrooms,

  quartered

1 cup chopped kale

1 teaspoon dried thyme

Salt and freshly ground black pepper

1 tablespoon cornstarch, dissolved in

  2 tablespoons water

1 1/2 cups cooked chickpeas or cannellini

  beans or one 15-ounce can, drained

  and rinsed

Minced fresh parsley leaves for garnish

1 Heat the oil in a large pot over medium heat. Add the onion and celery, cover, and cook, stirring a few times, until softened, about 5 minutes. Add the potatoes, carrots, garlic, stock, wine, if using, and bay leaves. Bring to a boil, then reduce the heat to low, cover, and simmer for 15 minutes.

2 Add the tamari, mushrooms, kale, thyme, and salt and pepper to taste and cook until the vegetables are tender, about 15 minutes.

3 Stir in the cornstarch mixture, bring to a boil, and cook, stirring, for 1 minute, or until the stew is thickened. Add the beans, reduce the heat, and simmer gently until heated through, about 10 minutes longer. Serve sprinkled with parsley.

Serves 6

Campari-Scented Vegetable Stew with Fennel and Orange Zest

~~~

A romatic fennel and orange zest combined with Campari create an intensely flavored, sophisticated stew. If Gaeta olives are unavailable, substitute any imported brine-cured black olive. This stew is equally good served over rice or noodles or accompanied by warm crusty bread.

---

1 large fennel bulb

2 tablespoons olive oil

1 medium-size yellow onion, chopped

1 large garlic clove, minced

1/2 teaspoon chopped fresh marjoram
leaves or 1/4 teaspoon dried

1/2 teaspoon chopped fresh basil leaves
or 1/4 teaspoon dried

Salt and freshly ground black pepper

1 tablespoon all-purpose flour

2 cups vegetable stock (page 36) or
water

1/2 cup Campari

1 tablespoon grated orange zest

One 9-ounce package frozen artichoke
hearts, cooked according to package
instructions, drained, and sliced

1 1/2 cups cooked chickpeas or one
15-ounce can, drained and rinsed

1/4 cup Gaeta olives, pitted

1 Remove the fennel tops and reserve for another use, or discard. Using a sharp knife, remove the core at the base of the fennel bulb, trim the base, and separate the layers. Cut the fennel into 1/2-inch pieces; set aside.

2 Heat the oil in a large skillet over medium heat. Add the onion, cover, and cook, stirring a few times, until softened, about 5 minutes. Add the fennel, garlic, marjoram, basil, and salt and pepper to taste and stir for about 30 seconds. Sprinkle with the flour and cook, stirring constantly, for I to 2 minutes to remove the raw flour taste, watching carefully so the flour does not brown.

3 Blend in the stock and Campari, bring to a boil, and boil until the liquid is reduced by about half. Reduce the heat to low, add the orange zest, cover, and simmer until the vegetables are tender, about 20 minutes.

4 Add the artichoke hearts, chickpeas, and olives and cook for I0 minutes longer to blend the flavors, adding more water if necessary. Adjust the seasonings and serve.

Serves 4

Vegetable Tagine

This fragrant Moroccan stew is named for the earthenware pot in which it is traditionally cooked. While I use chickpeas in this recipe, it is also delicious made with seitan, tempeh, or even eggplant. I especially enjoy it served over couscous with a bowl of harissa sauce on the side, so guests can enjoy it as spicy or mild as they like. Lemon zest and juice are used here instead of the traditional preserved lemon, but you can use that instead, if you prefer; look for preserved lemons at Middle Eastern markets (you will need the chopped peel of 1 preserved lemon for this recipe).

1 tablespoon olive oil

1 medium-size yellow onion, chopped

1 small red bell pepper, seeded and
  chopped

2 garlic cloves, minced

1 teaspoon peeled and minced fresh
  ginger

1/2 teaspoon ground cumin

1/2 teaspoon ground cinnamon

1/2 teaspoon turmeric

1/2 teaspoon sweet paprika

One 14.5-ounce can diced tomatoes,
  with their juices

1 teaspoon chopped lemon zest

1 tablespoon fresh lemon juice

Salt and freshly ground black pepper

1 1/2 cups vegetable stock (page 36) or
  water

1/2 cup golden raisins

1 1/2 cups cooked chickpeas or one
  15-ounce can, drained and rinsed

1/3 cup pitted oil-cured black olives

2 tablespoons minced fresh cilantro or
  parsley leaves

1 Heat the oil in a large saucepan over medium heat. Add the onion and bell pepper, cover, and cook, stirring a few times, until softened, about 5 minutes. Add the garlic, ginger, cumin, cinnamon, turmeric, paprika, tomatoes, lemon zest and juice, and salt and pepper to taste. Stir in the stock and raisins and bring to a boil. Reduce the heat to low, cover, and simmer for 30 minutes, or until the vegetables are soft and the stew is thickened.

2 Add the chickpeas, olives, and cilantro and cook, uncovered, for 10 minutes longer, adding a little water if necessary. Taste to adjust the seasonings and serve.

Serves 4 to 6

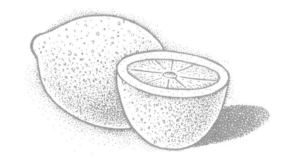

Spicy African Sweet Potato Stew

Yams are traditional in African cooking, but yams and sweet potatoes are more or less interchangeable. If you can find real yams, use them; otherwise, the more readily available sweet potatoes are perfect in this stew. For a less spicy stew, substitute mild chiles for the hot ones, or eliminate the chiles altogether. This stew is delicious served over basmati rice.

1 tablespoon olive oil

1 medium-size yellow onion, chopped

1 small red or yellow bell pepper, seeded and chopped

2 garlic cloves, minced

1 1/2 pounds sweet potatoes or yams, peeled and cut into 1/2-inch chunks

2 hot chiles, seeded and chopped

One 14.5-ounce can diced tomatoes, with their juices

1/2 teaspoon light brown sugar

1 teaspoon chili powder

1/4 teaspoon ground allspice

2 cups vegetable stock (page 36) or water

Salt and freshly ground black pepper

1 1/2 cups cooked dark red kidney beans or one 15-ounce can, drained and rinsed

1 Heat the oil in a large saucepan over medium heat. Add the onion, bell pepper, garlic, sweet potatoes, and chiles and cook, stirring, until the vegetables soften, about 10 minutes.

2 Add the tomatoes, brown sugar, chili powder, allspice, stock, and salt and pepper to taste and bring to a boil. Reduce the heat to low, cover, and simmer until the vegetables are tender, about 20 minutes.

3 Stir in the kidney beans and cook, uncovered, for 10 minutes longer. Taste to adjust the seasonings. For a thicker stew, you can puree up to 2 cups of the stew in a blender or food processor, then stir the puree back into the stew and allow it to heat through before serving.

Serves 4 to 6

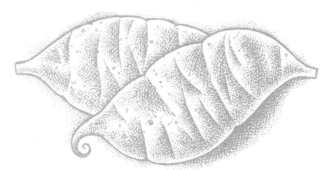

African Groundnut Stew

In Africa, peanuts are called groundnuts. Here they are featured in a colorful and spicy stew that includes winter squash and black-eyed peas. Rice is a natural accompaniment.

1 tablespoon olive oil

1 medium-size yellow onion, diced

2 garlic cloves, minced

1 or 2 hot or mild chiles, to your taste, seeded and chopped

1 1/2 teaspoons peeled and grated fresh ginger

1/2 tablespoon light brown sugar

3/4 teaspoon ground cinnamon

1/4 teaspoon ground cumin

1 1/2 pounds winter squash, such as butternut or Buttercup, seeded, peeled, and cut into bite-size cubes (about 3 1/2 cups)

1 1/2 cups water

1/4 cup creamy natural peanut butter

Salt and freshly ground black pepper

1 1/2 cups cooked black-eyed peas or one 15-ounce can (see Note), drained and rinsed

1/2 cup chopped unsalted roasted peanuts

1 Heat the oil in a large saucepan over medium heat. Add the onion, cover, and cook, stirring a few times, until softened, about 5 minutes. Stir in the garlic, chiles, ginger, brown sugar, cinnamon, and cumin and cook for I minute. Add the squash and stir to coat with the spices. Add I 1/4 cups of the water and salt and pepper to taste. Bring to a boil, then reduce the heat to low.

2 Put the peanut butter in a small bowl and slowly add the remaining 1/4 cup water, stirring until smooth.

3 Stir the peanut butter mixture into the stew, cover, and simmer until the vegetables are tender, about 30 minutes. About 10 minutes before the end of the cooking time, add the black-eyed peas and peanuts and simmer until heated through. Before serving, taste to adjust the seasonings.

note: Many people feel frozen black-eyed peas are preferable to canned because they have a fresher flavor. I've used both with good results, and usually it is availability that determines which one I use (dried is also another option, if you have the time).

Serves 6

Basque-Style Fava Bean Stew

This rustic stew was inspired by Marie Lange, my friend Lisa's mother. While fresh fava beans are best, they can be difficult to find and are time-consuming to prepare. For this recipe, you need to start with at least three pounds of fresh fava beans, which will need to be shelled, blanched briefly in boiling water, and their tough outer skins removed. Canned, frozen, or dried favas—or even lima beans—can be used instead. A loaf of warm crusty artisanal bread is an ideal accompaniment.

2 tablespoons olive oil

1 celery stalk, chopped

1 small yellow onion, chopped

1 small red bell pepper, seeded and cut into 1/2-inch dice

1 large garlic clove, minced

4 small new red or white potatoes, quartered

One 14.5-ounce can diced tomatoes, with their juices

1 Heat the oil in a large pot over medium heat. Add the celery and onion, cover, and cook, stirring a few times, until softened, about 5 minutes. Add the bell pepper, garlic, potatoes, tomatoes, wine, bay leaves, thyme, oregano, turmeric, and red pepper flakes. Stir in the stock and bring to boil. Reduce the heat to low, season with salt and pepper to taste, cover, and simmer for 30 minutes, or until the vegetables are just tender and the stew is beginning to thicken.

$^1/_3$ cup dry white wine

2 bay leaves

1 teaspoon minced fresh thyme leaves or
  $^1/_2$ teaspoon dried

1 teaspoon minced fresh oregano leaves
  or $^1/_2$ teaspoon dried

$^1/_4$ teaspoon turmeric

$^1/_8$ teaspoon red pepper flakes

$1^1/_2$ cups vegetable stock (page 36) or
  water

Salt and freshly ground black pepper

2 cups cooked fava beans (see headnote)

One 9-ounce package frozen artichoke
  hearts, cooked according to package
  directions and drained

2 tablespoons minced fresh parsley
  leaves

2 Add the fava beans, artichokes, and parsley and simmer for 15 minutes longer, adding more water if the
stew is too thick. Remove and discard the bay leaves
before serving.

Serves 4 to 6

Kale and Cannellini Bean Stew

Other dark greens such as escarole or chard may be used instead of kale, if you prefer. For added color, you could substitute sweet potatoes for the white potatoes. While this stew can be served over rice or noodles, I prefer it alone in bowls accompanied by warm bread or focaccia. Before chopping the kale, be sure to cut out the tough center stems.

1 tablespoon olive oil

1 large yellow onion, chopped

2 garlic cloves, minced

2 cups vegetable stock (page 36) or
   water

2 tablespoons dry white wine

2 large all-purpose potatoes, peeled and
   diced

2 bay leaves

1/2 teaspoon red pepper flakes

Salt and freshly ground black pepper

8 cups chopped kale (1 bunch)

3 cups cooked cannellini beans or two
   15-ounce cans, drained and rinsed

1 Heat the oil in a large pot over medium heat. Add the onion and garlic, cover, and cook, stirring a few times, until softened, about 5 minutes. Add the stock, wine, potatoes, bay leaves, red pepper flakes, and salt and pepper to taste. Cover and simmer, stirring occasionally, until the potatoes are soft, about 20 minutes.

2 Add the kale and simmer until tender, about 10 minutes. Stir in the beans and simmer until heated through, about 5 minutes. Taste to adjust the seasonings, remove and discard the bay leaves, and serve.

Serves 4 to 6

Mexican Corn, Tomatillo, and Red Bean Stew

This colorful chili-like stew can be served over rice or noodles or accompanied with corn bread. Tomatillos look like small green tomatoes with papery husks. If you can't find fresh ones, substitute green tomatoes, or use canned tomatillos.

1 tablespoon olive oil

1 medium-size yellow onion, diced

2 garlic cloves, minced

3 tomatillos, husks removed, rinsed, and
    chopped

2 jalapeño chiles, seeded and chopped

One 14.5-ounce can crushed tomatoes

2 tablespoons chili powder

1 teaspoon ground cumin

1 teaspoon dried oregano

1 teaspoon salt

$1/2$ teaspoon freshly ground black pepper

3 cups water

2 cups fresh or frozen corn kernels

3 cups cooked dark red kidney beans or
    two 15-ounce cans, drained and rinsed

2 tablespoons chopped fresh cilantro
    leaves

1 In a large pot, heat the oil over medium heat. Add the onion and garlic, cover, and cook, stirring a few times, until softened, about 5 minutes. Add the tomatillos and chiles and cook until softened, about 2 minutes. Stir in the tomatoes, chili powder, cumin, oregano, salt, and pepper. Add the water and bring to a boil. Reduce the heat to low and simmer for 30 minutes, or until the vegetables are tender and the flavors blended.

2 Stir in the corn, kidney beans, and cilantro and taste to adjust the seasonings. Simmer for 10 minutes longer, and serve.

Serves 4 to 6

Indian Chickpea and Potato Stew

Chickpeas are used frequently in Indian cooking, especially to add protein to many traditional vegetarian dishes. In this stew, chickpeas and potatoes are complemented by fragrant Indian spices and hot chiles. Serve over basmati rice.

2 tablespoons olive oil

1 large yellow onion, chopped

1 teaspoon minced garlic

1 pound waxy white potatoes, peeled and
 diced (about 3 cups)

1 or 2 jalapeño chiles, to your taste,
 seeded and minced

One 28-ounce can diced tomatoes, with
 their juices

1 tablespoon tamari or other soy sauce

$1/2$ teaspoon minced fresh thyme leaves
 or $1/4$ teaspoon dried

$1/2$ teaspoon ground fennel

$1/4$ teaspoon ground cumin

$1/4$ teaspoon cayenne

1 cup water, or more if needed

Salt and freshly ground black pepper

$1 1/2$ cups cooked chickpeas or one
 15-ounce can, drained and rinsed

1 Heat the oil in a large saucepan over medium heat. Add the onion, garlic, potatoes, and jalapeño. Cover and cook until the vegetables begin to soften, about 5 minutes. Reduce the heat to low, add the tomatoes, tamari, thyme, fennel, cumin, cayenne, and water, and season with salt and pepper to taste. Cover and cook until the vegetables are tender, about 20 minutes, adding more water if necessary.

2 Add the chickpeas and simmer for another 10 minutes to blend the flavors before serving.

Serves 4 to 6

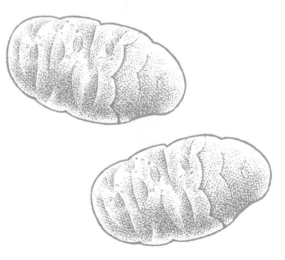

Spiced Lentil-Coconut Stew

Among the colorful assortment of lentils available—from bright orange to dusky green—I find the brown ones to be the "meatiest" of the bunch. Lentils are frequently used in Indian cooking, where they readily absorb the flavors of the fragrant spices. Make plenty of basmati rice to accompany this stew.

1 tablespoon olive oil

1 small yellow onion, chopped

1 small carrot, thinly sliced on a diagonal

2 garlic cloves, minced

1 small hot chile, seeded and minced

1 teaspoon peeled and minced fresh
   ginger

1/2 teaspoon ground cardamom

1/2 teaspoon dry mustard

1/4 teaspoon ground allspice

1/8 teaspoon turmeric

3 cups vegetable stock (page 36) or
   water

11/2 cups dried brown lentils, picked over
   and rinsed

1 large waxy white potato, peeled and
   diced

2 cups chopped well-washed spinach

1 cup unsweetened coconut milk

Salt and freshly ground black pepper

1 Heat the oil in a large saucepan over medium heat. Add the onion, carrot, garlic, chile, and ginger, cover, and cook, stirring occasionally, until softened, about 10 minutes. Stir in the cardamom, mustard, allspice, and turmeric and cook, stirring, for 30 seconds.

2 Pour in the stock, add the lentils and potato, and bring to a boil. Reduce the heat to low, cover, and cook until the lentils and vegetables are soft, about 45 minutes. About 10 minutes before the end of the cooking time, stir in the spinach, coconut milk, and salt and pepper to taste; add more stock if the stew is too dry. Serve hot.

Serves 6

Red Beans Bourguignon

The Burgundy region of France is the inspiration for this hearty bean dish. Serve it over noodles with crusty French bread and a glass of, what else, Burgundy wine.

8 ounces pearl onions

1 tablespoon olive oil

8 ounces white button mushrooms, quartered

8 ounces baby carrots

2 garlic cloves, minced

2 tablespoons tomato paste

2 teaspoons minced fresh thyme leaves or 1 teaspoon dried

2 bay leaves

1 1/2 cups vegetable stock (page 36) or water

2 cups dry red wine

3 cups cooked dark red kidney beans or two 15-ounce cans, drained and rinsed

Salt and freshly ground black pepper

1 1/2 tablespoons cornstarch, dissolved in 2 tablespoons water

1 Blanch the onions in a saucepan of boiling water for 2 minutes, then drain (this makes the onions easier to peel). Remove the root ends and peel. Set aside.

2 Heat the oil in a large saucepan over medium heat. Add the mushrooms and cook until they release their juices, about 2 minutes. Remove with a slotted spoon and set aside. Add the blanched onions, the carrots, and garlic to the pan and cook until softened, about 5 minutes. Stir in the tomato paste, thyme, bay leaves, and stock and bring to a boil, then reduce the heat to low, cover, and simmer until the vegetables are tender, about 30 minutes.

3 Add the wine, beans, and salt and pepper to taste. Return to a boil, then reduce the heat to low, add the mushrooms, and simmer, uncovered, 10 minutes more.

4 Add the cornstarch mixture, bring to a boil, and boil, stirring, for I minute, or until thickened. Remove and discard the bay leaves, and serve.

Serves 4

Chili con Frijoles

No "carne" in this chili—just "mucho frijoles," and lots of vegetables and chili spices. As with most chilis and stews, the flavor deepens if reheated the day after it is cooked, so plan to make this in advance. Serve accompanied with shredded cheese, sour cream, or other favorite chili garnishes. I especially like it over rice, topped with diced avocado.

1 tablespoon olive oil

1 large red onion, diced

1 large red bell pepper, seeded and diced

2 garlic cloves, minced

One 14.5-ounce can diced tomatoes, with their juices

1/4 cup tomato paste

3 tablespoons chili powder

1 teaspoon ground cumin

1/2 teaspoon dried oregano

1 teaspoon salt

1/2 teaspoon freshly ground black pepper

2 1/2 cups water

1 1/2 cups cooked dark red kidney beans or one 15-ounce can, drained and rinsed

1 1/2 cups cooked light red kidney beans or one 15-ounce can, drained and rinsed

1 1/2 cups cooked pinto beans or one 15-ounce can, drained and rinsed

1 Heat the oil in a large saucepan over medium heat. Add the onion, bell pepper, and garlic, cover, and cook, stirring a few times, until softened, about 5 minutes. Stir in the tomatoes, tomato paste, chili powder, cumin, oregano, salt, pepper, and water and bring to a boil. Reduce the heat to low and simmer, stirring occasionally, until the vegetables are just tender and the chile is beginning to thicken, about 20 minutes.

2 Stir in the beans and simmer for 15 to 20 minutes longer. Taste to adjust the seasonings, adding more water, if necessary. Ladle the chili into bowls and serve with your favorite accompaniments.

Serves 6

"Meaty" Eggplant-Portobello Chili

E ggplant and portobello mushrooms join forces to add a meaty texture to this very vegetarian chili. Serve over rice or noodles and accompany with a bowl of salsa and perhaps some cold Mexican beer, such as Corona or Dos Equis. If you like an extra kick of heat in your chili, add the jalapeños.

---

1 tablespoon olive oil

1 large yellow onion, chopped

1 large eggplant, peeled and chopped

3 large portobello mushrooms, stems trimmed and chopped

2 jalapeño chiles (optional), seeded and finely minced

2 large garlic cloves, minced

2 tablespoons tomato paste

One 28-ounce can crushed tomatoes

3 tablespoons chili powder

1 teaspoon dried marjoram

1 cup water

Salt and freshly ground black pepper

1   Heat the oil in a large saucepan over medium heat. Add the onion, cover, and cook, stiring a few times, until softened, about 5 minutes. Stir in the eggplant, mushrooms, chiles, if using, and garlic, cover, and cook until all the vegetables are tender, about 10 minutes.

2   Stir in the tomato paste, tomatoes, chili powder, marjoram, water, and salt and pepper to taste. Simmer, uncovered, over medium-low heat, stirring occasionally, until the chili thickens, about 30 minutes. Taste to adjust the seasonings and serve hot.

Serves 6

Steaks, Vegetarian Style

M any "meat and potatoes" people who consider going vegetarian lament giving up steaks, feeling those tastes and textures can't be duplicated with vegetables. Although they might enjoy a vegetarian lasagna or chili, they may be skeptical about the idea of a vegetarian steak.

I won't try to tell you that grilled tofu can taste like filet mignon. It's not going to happen. Nor is a portobello mushroom sautéed in Marsala wine going to fool anyone into thinking it's veal. But that is not the point. What can happen is that, like many of us "meat and potatoes" vegetarians, you can enjoy much of what it is you like about grilled or sautéed meat dishes—such as the preparation method, the texture, or the sauce—without the meat.

There's no reason why eliminating meat from your diet should mean eliminating great taste or the familiar flavors you grew up with and still enjoy. With these vegetarian recipes for steaks and cutlets, you can savor the aroma of a port wine sauce or an Indian tandoori, or dig into the down-home goodness of barbecue sauce, simmering with meaty slices of tempeh. Try tofu—the *other* other white meat—in a variety of delicious preparations such as lemony *Tofu and Mushroom Piccata, Crispy Stuffed "Fillets" of Soy with Spicy Ginger Sauce*, and *Shiitake-Stuffed Tofu Steaks with Hoisin Glaze*.

In addition to tofu, the "steaks" and cutlets called for in this chapter include tempeh, which is made from compressed soybeans, and seitan, a "meat" made from wheat, as well as meaty vegetables such as eggplant and mushrooms.

Homemade Seitan (Wheat-Meat)

Seitan Medallions and Button Mushrooms
   with a Brandy Reduction Sauce

Grilled Seitan with Nouveau Béarnaise Sauce

Wine-Braised Wheat-Meat Roulades

Mushroom-Stuffed Seitan Rolls with
   Basil Pesto

Ersatz Sauerbraten

Seitan and Shallots Marsala

Tandoori-Inspired Tempeh

Bronzed Tempeh with Broccoli and Spicy
   Peanut Sauce

Barbecued Tempeh

Pan-Seared Tempeh with Spicy Tomato Sauce

Almond-Crusted Tempeh Cutlets with
   Strawberry-Mango Salsa

Tamari-Seared Tofu with Asian Salsa Verde

Tofu and Mushroom Piccata

Tofu with Jerk-Spiced Barbecue Sauce

Crispy Stuffed "Fillets" of Soy with Spicy
   Ginger Sauce

Shiitake-Stuffed Tofu Steaks with Hoisin Glaze

Yuba-Wrapped Marinated Tofu with Mushroom
   Duxelles

Chicken-Fried "Steak"

Savory Soy Scrapple

Grilled Portobello Mushrooms with Garlic and
   Herb-Infused Olive Oil

Ginger-Sesame-Glazed Portobello
   Steaks over Sesame-Wasabi Mashers

Chipotle-Glazed Portobello Fajitas

Great Stuffed Mushrooms

Eggplant Teriyaki

Eggplant Braciole with Tomato
   Concassé

Spinach-and-Tofu-Stuffed Eggplant
   Roulades

Vegetable Towers with Red Wine
   Sauce

Vegetable Lover's Mixed Grill

Marinated Vegetables en Brochette

Homemade Seitan (Wheat-Meat)

Making homemade seitan, also called wheat gluten or "wheat-meat," can be a bit tricky at first, but once you get the hang of it, it's as easy as kneading bread. It's best to make a large amount at one time and freeze some, so you always have it on hand. If you don't have time to make your own from scratch, look for Seitan Quick Mix, a packaged mix that enables you to make fresh seitan in a fraction of the time. Precooked seitan is also available in natural food stores and Asian markets, but it is often seasoned with a marinade that may conflict with the flavors in your recipe, so choose carefully.

12 cups whole wheat flour (about
    4 pounds)

About 3¹/₂ quarts water

1 medium-size yellow onion, quartered

1 garlic clove, crushed

One 2-inch square kombu sea vegetable
    (optional)

¹/₂ cup tamari or other soy sauce

1 Place the flour in a large bowl and stir in about 5 cups of the water to form a soft, kneadable dough, adding more water as needed. Knead the dough in the bowl for about 5 minutes, then add enough water to cover the dough and let rest for 15 minutes.

2 Meanwhile, place the onion, garlic, kombu, if using, and tamari in a large pot with 2 quarts water and bring to a boil over high heat. Reduce the heat to low and keep at a simmer.

3 Place the bowl containing the dough and water in the sink and knead until the water turns milky white—that is the starch coming out. Drain off the milky water, cover the dough with fresh water, and knead again until the soaking water again becomes milky white. Repeat the process until the kneading water remains almost clear. The resulting ball of glutinous dough is raw seitan. (Note: For recipes calling for raw seitan, prepare the seitan only to this point.)

continued

4 Bring the pot of gently simmering liquid almost to a boil. Divide the seitan into 3 equal pieces and add to the pot. Simmer for 1 hour; *do not boil*. The longer and more slowly the seitan cooks, the denser the final texture will be. When cooked, the seitan will feel firm to the touch.

5 Remove the seitan from the pot and place on a baking sheet to cool. The seitan is now ready to use in recipes.

note: Seitan keeps well refrigerated with its cooking liquid in a tightly covered bowl for 3 to 4 days or in the freezer (still in its cooking liquid) for several weeks. The cooking liquid can be used as a base for soups, sauces, and gravies.

Makes three 1-pound pieces

Seitan Medallions and Button Mushrooms with a Brandy Reduction Sauce

The fragrant sauce for this special-occasion entrée is made with brandy enhanced by the flavor of fresh ginger. I like the visual appeal of whole small button mushrooms, but if the large ones are all you can find, slice them and use them—the taste will be the same.

1 tablespoon olive oil

1 pound seitan (page 127), cut into
 $^1/_2$-inch-thick slices

4 ounces small white button mushrooms,
 stems trimmed off near caps

1 teaspoon peeled and minced fresh
 ginger

$^1/_2$ cup brandy

1 cup vegetable stock (page 36)

Salt and freshly ground black pepper

1 Heat the oil in a large skillet over medium-high heat. Add the seitan and brown on both sides, about 5 minutes total. Remove from the skillet and set aside.

2 Add the mushrooms, ginger, and brandy to the skillet and simmer until the alcohol cooks off, about 1 minute. Remove the mushrooms from the skillet with a slotted spoon and set aside. Add the stock to the skillet, increase the heat to high, and reduce the liquid by half.

3 Return the seitan and mushrooms to the sauce, season with salt and pepper, and simmer for 2 minutes to heat through. Arrange the seitan on a serving platter, spoon the sauce and mushrooms on top, and serve.

Serves 4

Grilled Seitan with Nouveau Béarnaise Sauce

Infused with the flavors of tarragon, shallots, and white wine, this interpretation of the classic béarnaise sauce is the perfect complement to grilled seitan steaks. The sauce also tastes great on grilled vegetables.

1 pound seitan (page 127), cut into
   1/2-inch-thick slices

1 tablespoon olive oil

Salt and freshly ground black pepper

1/2 cup dry white wine

1/4 cup minced shallots

2 tablespoons minced fresh tarragon
   leaves or 1 tablespoon dried

1 cup regular or soy mayonnaise
   (page 309)

2 teaspoons fresh lemon juice

1 teaspoon Dijon mustard

Pinch of cayenne

Pinch of turmeric

1 Preheat the grill. Rub the seitan on both sides with 1 tablespoon of the oil and season with salt and pepper. Grill the seitan, turning once, until browned on both sides. Keep warm.

2 Meanwhile, place the wine, shallots, and tarragon in a small skillet over medium-high heat and simmer until the liquid reduces by half. Transfer to a food processor or blender, add the mayonnaise, lemon juice, mustard, cayenne, turmeric, and salt to taste, and process until smooth. Taste to adjust the seasonings.

3 Divide the sauce among individual serving plates. Top with the grilled seitan and serve at once.

Serves 4

Wine-Braised Wheat-Meat Roulades

~mm~

The key to making these roulades is to slice the seitan as thin as possible. The filling flavors the roulades from the inside, while the rich sauce permeates them from the outside.

---

1 pound seitan (page 127), cut into 6 to 8
  very thin slices about 3 x 6 inches

1 cup dry red wine

2 tablespoons plus 1 teaspoon olive oil

1 large garlic clove, minced

1/2 teaspoon dried thyme

Salt and freshly ground black pepper

1 large carrot, cut lengthwise into
  1/4-inch-thick strips (you will need 6 to
  8 strips)

1/2 medium-size red bell pepper, seeded
  and cut into 1/4-inch-wide strips (you
  will need 6 to 8 strips)

8 ounces spinach, thick stems removed
  and washed well

1 1/4 cups vegetable stock (page 36)

1 Place the seitan in a shallow bowl and add the wine, 2 teaspoons of the oil, the garlic, thyme, and salt and pepper to taste. Cover and marinate in the refrigerator for 1 hour, turning once. Meanwhile, lightly steam the carrot strips until crisp-tender. Set aside.

2 Heat 2 teaspoons of the oil in a small skillet and stir-fry the red pepper strips until crisp-tender. Set aside.

3 Remove the seitan from the marinade, reserving the marinade. Lay the seitan pieces out on a work surface, lining them up next to each other. Arrange a layer of spinach leaves on each piece of seitan, then place a carrot strip across one end of each seitan piece. Place a pepper strip alongside the carrot and season with salt and pepper. Roll up tightly, starting at the edge with the carrot and pepper strips, and tie each roulade at 1-inch intervals with kitchen twine.

4 Heat the remaining 1 tablespoon oil in a large skillet over medium-high heat. Add the roulades and cook, turning carefully, until browned all over, about 5 minutes. Pour in the stock and reserved marinade and bring to a boil. Reduce the heat to low and simmer, uncovered, for 15 minutes. Transfer the roulades to a serving platter and cover to keep warm.

5 Bring the cooking liquid to a boil and reduce by half. Remove the twine from the roulades and serve with the sauce.

Serves 4

Mushroom-Stuffed Seitan Rolls with Basil Pesto

Fragrant basil pesto accents these seitan rolls stuffed with portobello mushrooms. Unlike similar recipes made with flank steak, which requires lengthy simmering to become tender, naturally tender seitan only needs to be simmered long enough to absorb the surrounding flavors.

1 pound seitan (page 127), cut into six to
   eight ¹/₄-inch-thick slices

3 tablespoons olive oil

1 large garlic clove, minced

1 teaspoon minced fresh basil leaves

Salt and freshly ground black pepper

1 large portobello mushroom cap, cut
   into ¹/₄-inch-wide strips

4 scallions, split lengthwise in half

³/₄ cup vegetable stock (page 36)

¹/₂ cup Basil Pesto (page 313), thinned
   with a little hot water

1 Rub the seitan on both sides with I tablespoon of the oil, the garlic, basil, and salt and pepper to taste. Lay the slices out on a work surface.

2 Heat I tablespoon of the oil in a medium skillet over medium heat. Add the mushroom strips and scallions and cook, stirring, until softened, about 2 minutes. Remove from the heat.

3 Divide the scallions and mushrooms among the seitan pieces, arranging them on one long side of each piece. Roll up tightly, starting at the end with the scallions and mushrooms, and tie each roll securely at I-inch intervals with kitchen twine.

4 Heat the remaining I tablespoon oil in a large skillet over medium-high heat. Add the rolls and cook, turning carefully, until browned on all sides. Add the stock and bring to a boil. Reduce the heat to low and simmer, uncovered, for IO minutes.

5 Transfer the seitan rolls to a work surface or plate and remove the twine. Arrange on individual plates and surround each with a few spoonfuls of the pesto.

Serves 4

Ersatz Sauerbraten

The meat for traditional sauerbraten requires 3 to 4 days to absorb the flavors of the marinade. The wheat-meat slices in this vegetarian adaptation absorb the marinade in several hours (or overnight, if that fits your schedule better). Potatoes in some form—especially as dumplings or spaetzele—are traditional accompaniments, but boiled potatoes or potato pancakes would complement this hearty sweet-and-sour dish as well.

1 pound seitan (page 127), cut into
   $1/4$-inch-thick slices

1 large onion, coarsely chopped

2 garlic cloves, crushed

2 cups cider vinegar

1 cup water

$1/2$ cup dry red wine

4 black peppercorns

1 teaspoon caraway seeds

2 tablespoons firmly packed light brown
   sugar

1 bay leaf

2 tablespoons olive oil

Salt and freshly ground black pepper

1 tablespoon tomato paste

$1/2$ cup ground gingersnaps

$1/4$ cup golden raisins

$1/3$ cup sour cream or tofu sour cream
   (optional)

1 Place the seitan, onion, and garlic in a large bowl. Add the vinegar, water, wine, peppercorns, caraway seeds, brown sugar, and bay leaf, cover, and refrigerate for 2 to 3 hours, or overnight, turning the seitan a few times.

2 Remove the seitan from the marinade, reserving the marinade. Heat the oil in a large skillet over medium-high heat. Add the seitan and sear on both sides to brown. Season with salt and pepper and set the pan aside.

3 Strain the marinade through a fine-mesh strainer into a medium-size saucepan. Bring to a boil over high heat and boil to reduce by one-third. Reduce the heat to low, add the tomato paste, gingersnaps, and raisins, and stir until thickened. For a creamier sauce, stir in the sour cream.

4 Add $1/2$ cup of the sauce to the seitan and simmer until the seitan is hot. Transfer the seitan slices to a serving platter and top with the sauce. Serve at once.

Serves 4

Seitan and Shallots Marsala

I first got hooked on the flavor of Marsala wine when I began working in restaurants in the early 1980s. What I once used to flavor sautéed chicken and veal, I now use to make a rich sauce for vegetarian "meats."

---

3 tablespoons olive oil

4 shallots, quartered

1 cup vegetable stock (page 36)

1/2 cup dry Marsala wine

1 tablespoon tamari or other soy sauce

1 teaspoon minced fresh thyme leaves or
   1/2 teaspoon dried

1/2 teaspoon tomato paste

11/2 tablespoons cornstarch dissolved in
   2 tablespoons water

1 pound seitan (page 127), cut into
   1/4-inch-thick slices

Salt and freshly ground black pepper

1 Heat I tablespoon of the oil in a small skillet over medium heat. Add the shallots and cook, stirring, until soft and slightly caramelized, about 10 minutes. Transfer to a plate and set aside.

2 Add the stock, 1/4 cup of the Marsala, the tamari, thyme, and tomato paste to the skillet and heat almost to a boil. Whisk in the cornstarch mixture and boil, whisking, for I minute, or until the sauce is thickened. Set aside.

3 Heat the remaining 2 tablespoons oil in a large skillet over medium-high heat. Add the seitan and season with salt and pepper. Cook, turning once, until browned on both sides, 3 to 5 minutes total. Add the shallots and sauce and simmer for 5 minutes. Serve immediately.

Serves 4

Tandoori-Inspired Tempeh

Tandoori-style cooking is a northern Indian specialty, named for the clay oven in which the food is cooked after marinating in a creamy spice mixture. Firm-textured tempeh is an ideal match for a rich tandoori marinade.

1 pound tempeh, cut into 4 triangles

1 small yellow onion, chopped

3 garlic cloves, chopped

1 teaspoon peeled and minced fresh
  ginger

3/4 cup regular or soy yogurt

1 tablespoon fresh lemon juice

1 tablespoon olive oil

1 teaspoon ground coriander

1/2 teaspoon ground cumin

1/2 teaspoon turmeric

1/4 teaspoon ground cinnamon

1/4 teaspoon ground cardamom

1/2 teaspoon salt

1/8 teaspoon cayenne

Chopped fresh parsley leaves for garnish

1 Place the tempeh in a medium-size saucepan with water to cover and bring to a simmer. Cook for 10 minutes, then drain the tempeh and pat dry. Set aside.

2 In a food processor, combine the onion, garlic, and ginger and process until finely minced. Add the yogurt, lemon juice, oil, coriander, cumin, turmeric, cinnamon, cardamom, salt, and cayenne and process until smooth. Transfer to a shallow bowl and add the tempeh, turning to coat well. Cover and refrigerate for 2 to 3 hours.

3 Preheat the oven to 375 degrees F. Lightly oil a large shallow baking dish. Arrange the tempeh in the dish and pour the marinade over it.

4 Bake the tempeh, basting frequently with the marinade, until heated through, 20 to 30 minutes. Garnish with chopped parsley.

Serves 4

Bronzed Tempeh with Broccoli and Spicy Peanut Sauce

The tempeh takes its flavor and lovely bronze color from a flavorful tamari-based marinade in which it is also cooked. Tossed with bright green broccoli florets and creamy peanut sauce, it makes a feast for the senses. Serve on a bed of freshly cooked rice.

1 pound tempeh, cut into 4 pieces

2 garlic cloves, minced

3 scallions, chopped

1 tablespoon peeled and minced fresh ginger

2 tablespoons tamari or other soy sauce

1 tablespoon dry sherry

1 teaspoon sugar

1 tablespoon peanut oil

3 tablespoons creamy natural peanut butter

1 teaspoon Asian chile paste

1/4 cup water

2 cups broccoli florets, lightly steamed until crisp-tender

1/4 cup unsalted roasted peanuts

Hot cooked rice

1 Place the tempeh in a medium-size saucepan with water to cover, bring to a simmer, and cook for 10 minutes. Drain the tempeh and place in a shallow bowl.

2 In a small bowl, combine the garlic, scallions, ginger, tamari, sherry, and sugar. Pour over the tempeh and marinate for 1 hour in the refrigerator.

3 Heat the oil in a large skillet or wok over medium-high heat. Remove the tempeh from the marinade, reserving the marinade. Add the tempeh to the hot skillet and cook until lightly browned on both sides, about 2 minutes total. Remove with a slotted spoon and set aside.

4 Add the reserved marinade to the skillet and boil to reduce by one third. Stir in the peanut butter, chile paste, and water, blending well. Return the tempeh to the skillet, turning to coat it with the sauce. Stir in the broccoli and peanuts, tossing lightly to combine and heat through. Serve at once, over hot cooked rice.

Serves 4

Barbecued Tempeh

Barbecue sauce transforms virtuous tempeh into finger-licking comfort food. One of the benefits of homemade barbecue sauce is the ability to adjust the seasonings to suit your own taste. Use the recipe below as a guideline, altering the ingredients as you see fit. (In a pinch, bottled barbecue sauce may be used.)

---

1 pound tempeh, cut into $1/2$-inch-wide strips

2 tablespoons olive oil

1 small yellow onion, minced

1 garlic clove, minced

$1^1/_2$ teaspoons peeled and minced fresh ginger

One 14.5-ounce can crushed tomatoes

$1/_4$ cup unsulphured molasses

1 tablespoon Dijon mustard

3 tablespoons tamari or other soy sauce

1 tablespoon rice vinegar

$1/_8$ teaspoon cayenne

1 Place the tempeh in a medium-size saucepan with water to cover and bring to a simmer. Cook for 10 minutes, then drain the tempeh and pat dry. Set aside.

2 Heat the oil in a large skillet over medium heat. Add the tempeh and cook, turning, until browned on both sides, about 5 minutes total. Remove from the skillet with a slotted spoon and set aside.

3 Add the onion, garlic, and ginger to the skillet, cover, and cook, stirring a few times, until softened, about 5 minutes. Stir in the tomatoes, molasses, mustard, tamari, vinegar, and cayenne and bring to a boil. Reduce the heat to low and simmer, stirring occasionally, to thicken the sauce slightly and develop the flavors, about 15 minutes.

4 Return the tempeh to the sauce and cook for 10 minutes longer, then serve.

Serves 4

Pan-Seared Tempeh with Spicy Tomato Sauce

⌇⌇⌇

This spicy tomato sauce paired with golden brown slices of tempeh is great served over pasta. It can also be placed in a baking dish, topped with cheese, and baked "Parmesan-style." Extra-firm tofu can be used instead of the tempeh, if you prefer.

1 pound tempeh, halved and cut lengthwise into 1/4-inch-thick slices

2 tablespoons olive oil

2 garlic cloves, minced

1/2 teaspoon red pepper flakes, or to taste

One 28-ounce can crushed tomatoes

Salt and freshly ground black pepper

1 tablespoon minced fresh parsley leaves

1 teaspoon minced fresh marjoram leaves or 1/2 teaspoon dried

1 Place the tempeh in a medium-size saucepan with water to cover and bring to a simmer. Cook for 10 minutes, then drain the tempeh and pat dry. Set aside.

2 Heat 1 tablespoon of the oil in a large saucepan over low heat. Add the garlic and red pepper flakes and cook until fragrant, about 30 seconds. Add the tomatoes and salt and pepper to taste. Bring to a boil, then reduce the heat to low and cook, stirring occasionally, until slightly thickened, about 15 minutes. Stir in the parsley and marjoram and keep warm over low heat.

3 Heat the remaining 1 tablespoon oil in a large skillet over medium-high heat. Season the tempeh with salt and pepper, add to the skillet, and cook, turning once, until browned on both sides, about 2 minutes total. Add the tomato sauce and simmer for 5 minutes to blend the flavors, then serve.

Serves 4

Almond-Crusted Tempeh Cutlets with Strawberry-Mango Salsa

The creamy almond butter batter encasing the tempeh slices is coated with ground almonds that get fragrantly toasted when the tempeh is sautéed. The tangy salsa is an ideal accompaniment. Almond butter is available at natural food stores.

---

1 pound tempeh, halved and cut
   lengthwise into 1/4-inch-thick slices

1/4 cup almond butter

1 teaspoon tamari or other soy sauce

About 1/4 cup water

1 cup ground almonds

2 tablespoons peanut oil

Strawberry-Mango Salsa (page 317)

1 Place the tempeh in a medium-size saucepan with water to cover, bring to a simmer, and simmer for 10 minutes. Drain the tempeh, pat dry, and allow to cool.

2 In a shallow bowl, combine the almond butter, tamari, and enough water to make a smooth batter. Place the ground almonds on a plate. Dip the tempeh slices in the almond butter mixture, then coat evenly with the ground almonds, and set on a plate.

3 Heat the oil in a large skillet over medium heat. Add the tempeh slices and cook, turning once, until lightly browned on both sides, about 5 minutes total. Serve immediately, with the salsa.

Serves 4

The Tempeh Option

Tempeh is made from fermented soybeans that have been compressed into firm cakes. It has a distinctive nutty taste and meaty texture, and it readily absorbs the flavors of surrounding sauces and marinades. A popular meat alternative for vegetarian cooks, tempeh can be found in natural food stores and some supermarkets. As with all perishable foods, be sure to check the expiration date. Once opened, tempeh can be kept refrigerated, tightly wrapped, for up to 5 days or frozen for up to 3 months. It is a good idea to poach tempeh in simmering water for about 10 minutes before using in recipes to help mellow the flavor and make it more digestible.

Tamari-Seared Tofu with Asian Salsa Verde

~wn~

Searing the tofu with a splash of tamari turns it a lovely bronze shade while imparting loads of flavor. I like tofu prepared this way with no additional adornment, but the spicy Asian Salsa Verde does take it to the next level.

---

2 tablespoons peanut oil

1 pound extra-firm tofu, cut into

　1/2-inch-thick slices

Tamari or other soy sauce

Asian Salsa Verde (page 314)

1 Heat the oil in a large skillet over medium-high heat. Add the tofu slices and cook, turning once, until lightly browned on both sides, about 2 minutes total. While cooking, splash with a little tamari.

2 Serve with the salsa.

Serves 4

All About Tofu

Also known as bean curd, tofu is a cheese-like food made from cooked soybeans. The texture and taste of tofu can vary greatly from brand to brand, so it is a good idea to experiment until you find the ones you like best. Tofu is available in soft, firm, and extra-firm varieties. As a general rule, the softer tofu is best for sauces and the firmer kind works well in sautés and stir-fries. Fresh organic tofu is available in vacuum-packed tubs in the refrigerator sections of natural food stores and well-stocked supermarkets. Tofu is highly perishable, so check the expiration date before purchasing.

Japanese-style silken tofu, like regular tofu, is also available in soft, firm, and extra-firm varieties. It is usually found in aseptic containers that do not require refrigeration until opened. Silken tofu is used to make sauces, puddings, or anything where a creamy texture is desirable.

Tofu and Mushroom Piccata

This easy and elegant entrée is one of my favorite ways to prepare tofu. The fresh, clean taste of lemons permeates the tofu and mushrooms for a delicate yet bold flavor that goes well with potatoes or rice. Lightly sautéed spinach or steamed and sautéed green beans make a good accompaniment.

1 large lemon, peeled and white pith removed

1/2 cup all-purpose flour

1 pound extra-firm tofu, cut into 1/4-inch-thick slices

Salt and freshly ground black pepper

2 tablespoons olive oil

1/3 cup dry white wine

4 ounces white button mushrooms, thinly sliced

2 tablespoons capers, drained

2 tablespoons minced fresh parsley leaves

2 tablespoons butter or soy margarine (optional)

1 Preheat the oven to 275 degrees F. Cut the lemon into very thin rounds, discarding the seeds, and set aside.

2 Put the flour in a shallow bowl. Season the tofu with salt and pepper and dredge in the flour, tapping off any excess. Transfer the tofu slices to a platter and set aside.

3 Heat the oil in large skillet over medium-high heat. Add the tofu, in batches, and cook, turning once, until golden brown on both sides, about 2 minutes total. Place the tofu slices on a baking sheet and keep warm in the oven.

4 Deglaze the skillet with the wine, scraping up any browned bits from the bottom. Add the mushrooms and cook, stirring a few times, until slightly softened, about 2 minutes. Stir in the lemon slices, capers, and parsley and simmer until hot. Stir in the butter, if using, to enrich the sauce.

5 Arrange the tofu on a serving platter or individual plates. Pour the sauce over the tofu and serve at once.

Serves 4

Tofu with Jerk-Spiced Barbecue Sauce

~~~

Jerk spice seasonings add a tropical nuance to this barbecue sauce. Serve the sauce-drenched tofu over fragrant basmati rice and accompany with grilled plantains to continue the island theme. Omit the chile if you prefer less heat.

---

2 tablespoons olive oil

1 small yellow onion, finely chopped

1 hot chile, seeded and finely minced

2 garlic cloves, minced

1 teaspoon peeled and minced fresh
   ginger

One 6-ounce can tomato paste

2 tablespoons firmly packed light brown
   sugar

3 tablespoons tamari or other soy sauce

2 tablespoons fresh lemon juice

3/4 teaspoon ground allspice

1/2 teaspoon dried oregano

1/8 teaspoon ground nutmeg

1/8 teaspoon cayenne

1 teaspoon salt, plus more to taste

1 cup apple juice

1 pound extra-firm tofu, cut into
   1/2-inch-thick slices

Freshly ground black pepper

1 Heat I tablespoon of the oil in a medium-size sauce-pan over medium heat. Add the onion, cover, and cook, stirring a few times, until softened, about 5 minutes. Stir in the chile, garlic, ginger, tomato paste, brown sugar, tamari, lemon juice, allspice, oregano, nutmeg, cayenne, and salt, then pour in the apple juice and bring to a boil. Reduce the heat to low and simmer for 10 minutes to blend the flavors and thicken the sauce slightly.

2 Meanwhile, heat the remaining I tablespoon oil in a large skillet over medium heat. Add the tofu and cook, turning once, until golden brown on both sides, about 5 minutes total. Season with salt and pepper.

3 Add the barbecue sauce to the tofu and simmer for 10 minutes before serving.

Serves 4

Crispy Stuffed "Fillets" of Soy with Spicy Ginger Sauce

The delicate bean curd sheets and nori seaweed surround a fresh-tasting tofu stuffing made with crunchy water chestnuts and fragrant ginger, and the accompanying spicy ginger sauce amplifies the ginger in the stuffing. The outer layer fries up to a crisp golden brown in this "soy-stuffed soy," for an attractive presentation. Look for bean curd sheets (also called yuba) and other Asian ingredients in ethnic markets.

12 ounces extra-firm tofu, shredded

1/2 cup chopped canned water chestnuts

1/2 cup chopped white button mushrooms

3 tablespoons peeled and minced fresh ginger

3 scallions, minced

Salt and freshly ground black pepper

2 large bean curd sheets (yuba)

2 sheets nori seaweed

2 tablespoons olive oil

Spicy Ginger Sauce (page 307)

1 Preheat the oven to 350 degrees F. In a medium-size bowl, combine the shredded tofu, water chestnuts, mushrooms, ginger, and scallions. Season to taste with salt and pepper and set aside.

2 Place one of the bean curd sheets on a work surface. It should be soft and pliable; if it is brittle, soften it by moistening it with a small amount of water. Place a nori sheet on top of the bean curd sheet and spread half of the stuffing mixture evenly down the length of the nori. Fold the sides and ends of the bean curd sheet over the stuffing, gently forming an elongated rectangular shape. Moisten the edges with a small amount of water and press to seal. Set aside, seam side down. Repeat with the remaining bean curd sheet, nori, and stuffing.

continued

3 Heat the oil in a large skillet over medium-high heat, add the "fillets," and cook, turning once, until golden brown on both sides, 1 to 2 minutes per side. Transfer to a baking sheet and bake for 10 to 15 minutes, until heated through and crispy on the outside.

4 To serve, transfer the fillets to a cutting board and cut into 1-inch-thick slices; do not separate the slices. Using a metal spatula, transfer the fillets to a large platter, retaining their rectangular shape. Top with the sauce and serve at once.

Serves 4

Shiitake-Stuffed Tofu Steaks with Hoisin Glaze

~~~

The tofu absorbs flavor from both the garlic-and-ginger-infused shiitake stuffing and the sweet and sassy hoisin sauce that glazes the outside. When cutting the pockets in the tofu, be careful not to cut too close to the edges.

2 tablespoons peanut oil

4 ounces shiitake mushrooms, stems discarded and caps chopped

3 scallions, minced

1 garlic clove, minced

1 tablespoon peeled and minced fresh ginger

Salt and freshly ground black pepper

1 pound extra-firm tofu, cut into 4 equal slices

1/3 cup hoisin sauce

1 Heat 1 tablespoon of the oil in a small skillet over medium heat. Add the mushrooms, scallions, garlic, and ginger and cook, stirring, until softened, about 3 minutes. Season with salt and pepper to taste and set aside to cool.

2 Carefully cut a pocket in the side of each slice of tofu. Stuff the tofu with the mushroom mixture.

3 Heat the remaining 1 tablespoon oil in a large skillet over medium heat. Add the tofu and cook until golden brown on the first side. Turn and cook for 1 minute longer. Add the hoisin sauce to the pan, spooning it over the tofu to coat. Carefully turn the tofu over to be sure both sides are glazed with hoisin, and serve at once.

Serves 4

Yuba-Wrapped Marinated Tofu with Mushroom Duxelles

~~~

Bean curd sheets, or yuba, are a versatile ingredient in Asian cooking, often used as dumpling wrappers. Here yuba is used as a crispy outer wrapper for a flavorful tofu cutlet topped with mushroom duxelles, a classic French preparation of chopped mushrooms often used for stuffing. To complement the flavors inside the packets, serve them surrounded by a few spoonfuls of Marvelous Mushroom Sauce (page 303). Look for yuba in Japanese and other Asian markets.

---

1 pound extra-firm tofu, cut into 4 slices

1/4 cup tamari or other soy sauce

1/4 cup dry red wine

2 garlic cloves, minced

1/4 cup olive oil

8 ounces white button mushrooms, finely chopped

1 teaspoon minced fresh thyme leaves

Salt and freshly ground black pepper

2 bean curd sheets (yuba)

1 Place the tofu in a shallow bowl. Add the tamari, wine, and garlic, cover, and refrigerate for I hour.

2 Heat 2 teaspoons of the oil in a medium-size skillet over medium heat. Add the mushrooms and cook, stirring, until they release their juices. Reduce the heat to low and continue to cook, stirring occasionally, until the liquid evaporates and the mushrooms are dry; be careful not to burn them. Season with the thyme and salt and pepper to taste. Set aside to cool.

3 Preheat the oven to 350 degrees F. Remove the tofu from the marinade (discard the marinade) and place on a platter. Heat I tablespoon of the oil in a large skillet over medium heat. Add the tofu and cook, turning once, until lightly browned on both sides, about 2 minutes total. Return the tofu to the platter and allow to cool.

4 Cut the yuba sheets in half to make 4 pieces. Soften with a little water if necessary to make them pliable. Place a piece of tofu on the lower third of a yuba sheet and top with one-quarter of the mushroom mixture. Fold the sides over the tofu and roll up to enclose the tofu and mushrooms and create a flat parcel. Moisten the edges and press gently to seal. Repeat with the remaining yuba sheets, tofu, and mushroom mixture.

5 Heat the remaining 2 tablespoons plus I teaspoon oil in a large skillet over medium heat. Add the parcels and cook, turning once, until golden brown and crispy on both sides, about 2 minutes per side. Transfer to a baking sheet and bake until heated through, about I0 to I5 minutes. Serve hot.

Serves 4

Chicken-Fried "Steak"

If it's not steak and it's not chicken, what is it? It's tofu, and it's one hundred percent delicious. Karen Davis, president and founder of United Poultry Concerns, graciously allowed me to adapt this down-home country recipe from her cookbook, *Instead of Chicken, Instead of Turkey* (Book Publishing Company, 1999). Serve with Good Gravy (page 302) and mashed potatoes. Freezing the tofu before using it gives it a firmer texture.

1 pound extra-firm tofu

2 tablespoons tamari or other soy sauce

Salt and freshly ground black pepper

1/4 cup all-purpose flour, plus more as needed

1 teaspoon baking powder

3 tablespoons corn oil

1/4 cup water

1 Cut the tofu into 4 equal slabs and wrap each one in plastic wrap. Place in the freezer until frozen, at least several hours, or overnight.

2 Remove the tofu from the freezer and let thaw.

3 Once it is thawed, squeeze or press as much water as you can out of the tofu, then crumble it into a bowl. Sprinkle the soy sauce over the tofu and season with salt and pepper to taste. Mix well.

4 In a small bowl, combine the flour and baking powder. Add I tablespoon of the oil and the water and stir until the mixture forms a paste. Add the paste to the tofu, mixing well. Divide the mixture into 8 portions, then wet your hands and shape each one into a disk.

5 Cut sixteen 4-inch squares of waxed paper, lay out on a work surface, and sprinkle each one with flour. Place the tofu disks on 8 of the squares, cover each one with another square, and press until flat. Freeze the patties, with the waxed paper still in place, for at least 30 minutes.

6 Remove the waxed paper from the patties. Heat the remaining 2 tablespoons oil in a large skillet over medium heat. Add the patties, in batches, and brown on both sides. Keep the first batch of cooked patties warm in a low oven while you cook the rest. Serve hot.

Serves 4 to 6

Savory Soy Scrapple

While growing up in Pennsylvania, I was raised on scrapple. It wasn't until I became an adult that I found out that it was made from leftover "scraps" of pork combined with cornmeal and spices. Needless to say, it's been many years since I've had the traditional kind. I now enjoy a delicious vegetarian version that I've adapted from a recipe in *Instead of Chicken, Instead of Turkey* by Karen Davis (Book Publishing Company, 1999). It is important to chill the scrapple before slicing and frying it so it holds together. Freezing tofu changes its texture dramatically, making it firmer and chewier. Once it has thawed, be sure to squeeze all the excess water from the tofu before using it. Serve with home fries and top with ketchup, or a drizzle of maple syrup, for a hearty breakfast or brunch entrée.

---

1 pound extra-firm tofu

3 tablespoons olive oil

1 small yellow onion, grated

2 garlic cloves, finely minced

1 1/4 cups coarse yellow cornmeal

1/2 teaspoon dried thyme

1/2 teaspoon dried sage

1/2 teaspoon salt

1/4 teaspoon freshly ground black pepper

3 cups vegetable stock (page 36)

All-purpose flour for dredging

1 Cut the tofu into 4 equal slabs and wrap each one in plastic wrap. Place in the freezer until frozen, at least several hours, or overnight.

2 Remove the tofu from the freezer and let thaw.

3 Heat 1 tablespoon of the oil in a large saucepan over medium heat. Add the onion and garlic, cover, and cook, stirring a few times, until softened, about 5 minutes. Stir in the cornmeal, thyme, sage, salt, and pepper, then slowly add the stock, whisking until smooth. Bring to a boil, whisking constantly. Reduce the heat to low and continue to cook, stirring frequently, until thick, about 15 minutes. Remove from the heat.

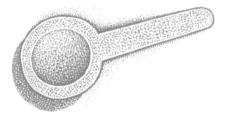

4 Squeeze the excess water from the thawed tofu and crumble it into very small pieces. Stir the tofu into the cornmeal mixture until well combined. Press the mixture into a well-oiled 9 x 5-inch loaf pan and refrigerate for at least 4 hours, or overnight.

5 Remove the scrapple from the loaf pan and cut it into $1/2$-inch-thick slices. Dredge the slices in flour, tapping off any excess. Heat the remaining 2 tablespoons oil in a large skillet over medium heat. Add the scrapple, in batches, and cook, turning once, until browned on both sides, 2 to 3 minutes per side. Keep the first batch warm in a low oven while you cook the remaining scrapple. Serve hot.

Serves 6

Grilled Portobello Mushrooms with Garlic and Herb-Infused Olive Oil

Meaty portobello mushrooms readily absorb the flavor of the garlic and fresh herbs in this flavorful marinade, and they look and smell as good as they taste. While the mushrooms are marinating, you can get the rest of dinner ready.

3 garlic cloves, minced

1 teaspoon chopped fresh rosemary
  leaves

1 teaspoon chopped fresh thyme leaves

1 teaspoon chopped fresh marjoram
  leaves

1/3 cup extra virgin olive oil

Salt and freshly ground black pepper

4 large portobello mushroom caps

1 teaspoon snipped fresh chives for
  garnish

1 In a small saucepan, combine the garlic, rosemary, thyme, marjoram, oil, and salt and pepper to taste. Heat over medium heat until fragrant. Keep warm over low heat.

2 With a sharp knife or spoon, carefully scrape the dark brown gills from the underside of the mushroom caps. Place the mushrooms in a shallow bowl. Pour the hot oil mixture over them, turning to coat. Set aside to marinate for 30 minutes.

3 Preheat the grill. Remove the mushrooms from the marinade (reserve the marinade) and grill, turning once, until tender, about 5 minutes. Serve garnished with a drizzle of the reserved marinade and a sprinkle of the chives.

Serves 4

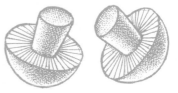

Ginger-Sesame-Glazed Portobello Steaks over Sesame-Wasabi Mashers

An aromatic marinade adds complexity to these mushrooms, which resemble flank steak when sliced on an angle. The wasabi-infused mashed potatoes are an ideal accompaniment.

2 garlic cloves, mashed

1 tablespoon peeled and minced fresh ginger

1 tablespoon tahini (sesame paste)

$^1/_2$ cup tamari or other soy sauce

$^1/_3$ cup toasted sesame oil

1 tablespoon firmly packed light brown sugar

3 tablespoons sake or dry white wine

4 portobello mushroom caps

1 tablespoon peanut oil

Sesame-Wasabi Mashers (page 207)

1 In a small bowl, combine the garlic, ginger, and tahini. Stir in the tamari, sesame oil, brown sugar, and sake, blending well.

2 Place the mushroom caps in a shallow bowl. Add the marinade, turning to coat the mushrooms, and let stand for 15 to 30 minutes, turning once.

3 Heat the peanut oil in a large skillet over medium-high heat. Add the mushrooms (reserve the marinade) and sear, turning once, until well browned and slightly softened, about 5 minutes.

4 Cut each mushroom on a slight angle into $^1/_4$-inch-thick slices. Place a serving of hot mashed potatoes on each of four dinner plates. Fan out the mushroom slices over the potatoes.

5 Meanwhile, heat the reserved marinade in a small saucepan.

6 Drizzle a little of the marinade around the edges of each plate and serve hot.

Serves 4

Chipotle-Glazed Portobello Fajitas

The meaty texture of portobello mushrooms wrapped in soft flour tortillas is complemented by the smoky heat of the chipotle chiles in adobo sauce, available in many supermarkets and specialty food shops. For extra richness, serve with guacamole for each person to add as desired.

One 6-ounce can chipotle chiles in
   adobo sauce

Juice of 1 lime

4 portobello mushroom caps

1 tablespoon olive oil

1 large red onion, cut into strips

Salt and freshly ground black pepper

8 flour tortillas, warmed

1 In a blender or food processor, combine the chiles, with their sauce, and the lime juice and puree. Set aside.

2 With a sharp knife or a spoon, carefully scrape the dark brown gills from the underside of the mushroom caps. Cut the caps into $1/4$-inch-thick slices.

3 Heat the oil in a large skillet over medium-high heat. Add the onion, cover, and cook, stirring a few times, until softened, about 5 minutes. Add the mushroom slices, season with salt and pepper, and cook, stirring, until softened slightly. Pour in the pureed chiles and cook, stirring gently to coat with the sauce, until the mushrooms and onion are glazed with sauce.

4 To serve, spoon the mushrooms and onions into the centers of the tortillas and roll up.

Serves 4

Great Stuffed Mushrooms

~~~

In this recipe, the "great" refers not only to the taste, but also to the size—large portobellos are used to make entrée-sized stuffed mushrooms. Topped with Good Gravy, or another sauce such as Marvelous Mushroom Sauce (page 303), they can be served with mashed potatoes, green beans, and cranberry sauce for a quick and easy holiday meal.

4 large portobello mushroom caps

2 tablespoons olive oil

1 tablespoon tamari or other soy sauce

2 shallots, minced

1/2 cup chopped cooked spinach, squeezed dry

2 1/2 cups finely diced bread

1/2 cup shredded mozzarella cheese or soy mozzarella

1 teaspoon minced fresh thyme leaves or 1/2 teaspoon dried

Salt and freshly ground black pepper

Vegetable stock (page 36) or water, if needed

Good Gravy (page 302), heated

1 Using a knife or a spoon, carefully scrape out the brown gills from the underside of the mushroom caps. Heat 1 tablespoon of the oil in a large skillet over medium-high heat, add the mushrooms, gill side up, and sear until browned. Add the tamari, turn the caps over, and cook for 30 seconds. Remove the mushrooms from the skillet and set aside.

2 Preheat the oven to 375 degrees F. Heat the remaining 1 tablespoon oil in a small skillet. Add the shallots, cover, and cook, stirring a few times, until softened, about 5 minutes. Transfer to a bowl and add the spinach, bread, cheese, thyme, and salt and pepper to taste. Mix well, adding a little stock or water if the mixture is too dry.

3 Divide the stuffing mixture into 4 equal portions and shape into balls. Flatten the balls into patties and gently press into the mushroom caps.

4 Place the stuffed mushrooms in a lightly oiled baking dish and bake until hot, about 10 minutes. Serve topped with the gravy.

Serves 4

Eggplant Teriyaki

Eggplant tends to absorb the flavors of the ingredients around it, so why not surround it with a scrumptious teriyaki sauce? Small Japanese eggplants are used here, but a regular eggplant can be substituted if necessary. Whether you peel the eggplant or not is up to you. Serve over freshly cooked rice. Brown rice syrup is available at natural food stores.

---

3 or 4 small Japanese eggplants, ends trimmed and cut into ¼-inch-thick rounds

Salt and freshly ground black pepper

3 tablespoons tamari or other soy sauce

3 tablespoons fresh orange juice

1 garlic clove, minced

1 tablespoon brown rice syrup or maple syrup

3 tablespoons toasted sesame oil

2 tablespoons peanut oil

1 Place the eggplant slices in a large shallow dish and season with salt and pepper. In a small bowl, combine the tamari, orange juice, garlic, syrup, and sesame oil, blending well. Pour the marinade over the eggplant, turning to coat well. Let the eggplant marinate in the refrigerator, turning it occasionally, for at least I hour, and up to 4 hours.

2 Transfer the eggplant to a platter, reserving the marinade.

3 Heat the peanut oil in a large skillet over medium heat. Add the eggplant, in batches if necessary, and cook, turning once, until browned on both sides, 3 to 5 minutes total. Add the reserved marinade (return all the eggplant to the pan if necessary) and simmer, turning once, until the eggplant is soft, about I0 minutes. Serve hot.

Serves 4

Eggplant Braciole with Tomato Concassé

The eggplant slices should be as thin as possible—no more than $1/4$ inch thick—to make them more pliable. A mandoline or other vegetable slicer works best to get thin, uniform slices. Otherwise, use a sharp knife.

1 large eggplant, ends trimmed, peeled,
    and cut lengthwise into thin slices
3 tablespoons olive oil
Salt and freshly ground black pepper
$1/4$ cup minced onion
$1/2$ cup dry bread crumbs
$1/2$ cup freshly grated Parmesan cheese
    or soy Parmesan
$1/4$ cup ground walnuts
$1/4$ cup raisins
Tomato Concassé (page 315)

1 Preheat the oven to 375 degrees F. Place the 8 largest eggplant slices (from the center) on a lightly oiled baking sheet and brush with I tablespoon of the oil. (Reserve the remaining eggplant for another use.) Season the eggplant slices with salt and pepper, cover with a sheet of aluminum foil, and bake until softened, about 10 minutes. Remove from the oven and set aside to cool slightly. Leave the oven on.

2 Heat the remaining 2 tablespoons oil in a small skillet over medium heat. Add the onion, cover, and cook, stirring a few times, until softened, about 5 minutes. Transfer to a bowl and add the bread crumbs, $1/4$ cup of the Parmesan, the walnuts, raisins, and salt and pepper to taste. Blend well.

3 Arrange the eggplant slices on a work surface. Divide the filling among them, gently spreading it over each slice. Beginning with the short end nearest you, roll up each slice, then arrange seam side down in a large oiled baking dish. Top each roll with about 2 tablespoons of the tomato concassé and sprinkle with the remaining $1/4$ cup Parmesan.

4 Bake to heat through and lightly brown the cheese on top, about 15 minutes. Serve with the remaining tomato concassé.

Serves 4

Spinach-and-Tofu-Stuffed Eggplant Roulades

With the eggplant, chickpeas, and tahini, this dish has a decidedly Middle Eastern flavor. I like to assemble the roulades ahead of time for a no-fuss meal. When preparing the eggplant slices, be sure to bake them until just soft enough to roll up. If you bake them too long, they will get crisp and become difficult to roll.

1 large eggplant, ends trimmed, peeled, and cut lengthwise into 1/4-inch-thick slices

3 tablespoons olive oil

Salt and freshly ground black pepper

8 ounces spinach, thick stems trimmed and washed well

1 cup cooked or canned chickpeas, drained and rinsed if canned

1 large garlic clove, chopped

1/4 cup tahini (sesame paste)

1/2 cup vegetable stock (page 36)

1 tablespoon fresh lemon juice

1 shallot, minced

8 ounces extra-firm tofu, crumbled

1 tablespoon minced fresh parsley leaves

1 Preheat the oven to 375 degrees F. Place the eggplant slices on a lightly oiled baking sheet, brush with 2 tablespoons of the oil, and season with salt and pepper. Bake, turning once, until just soft, about 10 minutes. Remove from the oven and set aside.

2 Meanwhile, steam the spinach until just wilted, about 3 minutes. Let cool, then squeeze the excess liquid from the spinach and coarsely chop. Set aside.

3 In a food processor, combine the chickpeas and garlic and process until finely minced. Add the tahini, stock, lemon juice, and salt and pepper to taste and process until smooth. Transfer to a small saucepan and set aside.

4 Heat the remaining 1 tablespoon oil in a medium-size skillet over medium heat. Add the shallot, cover, and cook, stirring a few times, until softened, about 5 minutes. Add the tofu, spinach, parsley, and salt and pepper to taste and mix well. Remove from the heat.

5 Put 2 tablespoons of the tofu mixture on one short end of each slice of eggplant and roll up. Arrange the eggplant roulades seam side down in a lightly oiled baking dish. Bake until lightly browned and heated through, 15 to 20 minutes.

6 Meanwhile, reheat the sauce over low heat. Top the hot roulades with the sauce and serve.

Serves 4

note: The roulades can be assembled up to 8 hours ahead, covered, and refrigerated. Return to room temperature before baking.

Vegetable Towers with Red Wine Sauce

⁓⁓⁓

This impressive-looking entrée is much simpler to make than it appears. Much of the prep work can be done in advance, and the delicious results are more than worth the time it takes to assemble the ingredients. I like to serve them with sautéed green beans and pine nuts, arranged in three spoke-like groups around each tower.

---

2 large Yukon Gold potatoes, each cut into four large ¼-inch-thick slices (reserve the remaining potatoes for another use, if desired)

Olive oil

4 large ¼-inch-thick slices red onion

4 large ¼-inch-thick rings yellow bell pepper, seeds removed

4 large portobello mushroom caps

1 large ripe tomato, seeded and cut into four ½-inch-thick slices

Salt and freshly ground black pepper

1 cup Red Wine Sauce (page 301), warmed

1 Preheat the oven to 400 degrees F. Lightly oil a baking sheet. Spray or brush the potato slices with oil and place on the baking sheet. Bake until soft and golden brown, about 20 minutes, turning once about halfway through.

2 Meanwhile, on a separate baking sheet, follow the same procedure with the onion slices. After turning the onion slices, place the bell pepper rings on the same baking sheet and bake until the onions and peppers have softened, 20 to 25 minutes total for the onion, 10 to 15 minutes for the peppers.

3 With a sharp knife or a spoon, carefully remove the dark brown gills from the underside of the mushroom caps. Lightly oil the mushrooms, place on a small baking sheet, and bake until softened, about 10 minutes.

4 When all the vegetables are cooked, allow them to cool slightly. Reduce the oven temperature to 350 degrees F.

5 Assemble the towers, seasoning each layer with salt and pepper: First, arrange 4 potato slices in a lightly oiled shallow baking dish. Top each with an onion slice, followed by a pepper ring. Top with another potato slice, followed by a tomato slice, and then a mushroom cap.

6 Tightly cover the baking dish with aluminum foil and place in the oven. Bake until hot, 15 to 20 minutes.

7 Using a metal spatula, carefully remove the towers and place one in the center of each dinner plate. Surround each with $^{1}/_{4}$ cup of the sauce and serve at once.

Serves 4

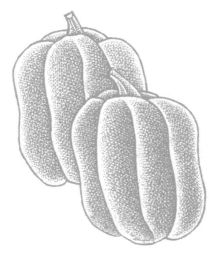

Vegetable Lover's Mixed Grill

—*mn*—

This collection of grilled vegetables can be served on a bed of rice, pasta, or even salad greens, with crusty garlic bread on the side. Other vegetables, such as sliced potatoes, fennel, or bell peppers, can be used in addition to or instead of any of the vegetables in this recipe.

---

3 tablespoons olive oil

2 tablespoons tamari or other soy sauce

1 tablespoon Dijon mustard

1 teaspoon minced fresh basil leaves

1 teaspoon minced fresh thyme leaves

1 large red onion, cut crosswise into
    4 thick slices

2 baby eggplants, ends trimmed and
    halved lengthwise

2 small zucchini, ends trimmed and
    halved lengthwise

4 portobello mushroom caps

2 large ripe tomatoes, halved crosswise

Salt and freshly ground black pepper

1 Preheat the grill. In a small bowl, combine the oil, tamari, mustard, basil, and thyme, blending well. Place the onion, eggplant, zucchini, mushrooms, and tomatoes in a shallow bowl and coat well with the oil mixture. Season with salt and pepper to taste.

2 Arrange the vegetables cut side down on the grill, starting with the onion and finishing with the tomatoes. Grill the vegetables, turning once, until tender on the inside and slightly charred on the outside. As the individual vegetables finish cooking, place them on a baking sheet and keep warm in a low oven until all of them are cooked.

3 To serve, divide the vegetables among four plates, arranging them attractively.

Serves 4

Marinated Vegetables en Brochette

Serve these skewered morsels of perfectly grilled vegetables on a bed of rice pilaf. Whether you grill them outside or in, or bake in a hot oven, these brochettes make an elegant and easy entrée and turn ordinary ingredients into something special. If using bamboo skewers, soak them in water for 20 to 30 minutes before using to prevent them from burning.

1/2 cup dry red wine

1/4 cup olive oil

2 tablespoons tamari or other soy sauce

2 garlic cloves, minced

1/4 teaspoon freshly ground black pepper

1 large red onion, quartered

1 large red bell pepper, seeded and cut
   into 2-inch squares

8 white button mushroom caps

2 small zucchini, ends trimmed and cut
   into 3/4-inch-thick rounds

8 large cherry tomatoes

1 In a shallow bowl, combine the wine, oil, tamari, garlic, and black pepper. Add the onion, bell pepper, mushrooms, and zucchini, toss to coat well, cover, and refrigerate for at least 1 hour, turning once or twice.

2 Preheat the grill or broiler, or preheat the oven to 450 degrees F. With a slotted spoon, remove the vegetables from the marinade; set the marinade aside. Skewer the marinated vegetables and the cherry tomatoes onto 8 skewers, alternating the ingredients and ending with the tomatoes.

3 Grill or broil the brochettes, or bake on a lightly oiled rimmed baking sheet, turning once and basting with the marinade, until the vegetables are tender.

4 When the vegetables are cooked, place the remaining marinade in a small saucepan and reduce by half over high heat.

5 Arrange the brochettes on serving plates, spoon the reduced marinade over them, and serve.

Serves 4

CHAPTER SIX

Hot
from the Oven

What's cozier on a cold winter night than a blazing fire and a warming aroma from the oven wafting through the house? Some of the consummate "meat and potatoes" dishes come from the oven, such as meat loaf and roasted potatoes. Casseroles and other oven-baked meals are cold-weather fixtures at my house. The warmth and fragrance of dinner baking in the oven evokes nostalgic childhood memories.

Since many old-fashioned classics, such as shepherd's pie, are high in fat and cholesterol, you may have forsaken your favorite baked dishes in favor of lighter fare. Thanks to healthful ingredients such as tofu, seitan, and tempeh, everyone can enjoy those familiar tastes and aromas that only oven baking can provide.

In this chapter, you will find recipes for vegetarian versions of timeless traditions such as meat loaf, potpies, and cassoulet. These familiar dishes are lightened up to provide a complete, well-balanced meal in one delicious no-fuss dish that goes directly from oven to table. It's just one more way to put the "comfort" back in comfort food.

Pizza lovers will be happy to find a selection of recipes for home-baked pizzas with a variety of flavorful toppings, from vegetarian pepperoni to pesto and potatoes.

Vegetarian Pot Roast

This dish can be made either entirely in the oven or entirely on top of the stove, but I prefer to use both methods. I begin by browning the ingredients on top of the stove and then finish cooking in the oven. Although using one large piece of seitan will produce more of a "pot roast" look, cutting it into slices allows the flavors of the seasonings to permeate it better. An alternative preparation is to "pot roast" the vegetables and, near the end of cooking time, add slices of seitan that have been browned in a skillet.

1/4 cup olive oil

2 garlic cloves, crushed

1 teaspoon dried thyme

Salt and freshly ground black pepper

1 pound seitan (page 127), cut into
 1/4-inch-thick slices

1 cup dry red wine

6 cipolline or other small white onions,
 unpeeled

8 ounces baby carrots

1 pound small new red or white potatoes,
 halved

2 1/2 cups vegetable stock (page 36)

1 teaspoon tomato paste

1 tablespoon tamari or other soy sauce

1 1/2 tablespoons cornstarch, dissolved in
 2 tablespoons water

1 Rub 2 tablespoons of the oil, the garlic, thyme, and salt and pepper to taste into the seitan. Place the seitan in a shallow bowl and add the wine. Cover and refrigerate for at least I hour, and up to 8 hours.

2 Parboil the onions in boiling water for 5 minutes (this makes them easier to peel). Drain, let cool enough to handle, and then peel; set aside.

3 Preheat the oven to 375 degrees F. Remove the seitan from the marinade; reserve the marinade. Heat I tablespoon of the oil in an ovenproof pot over medium-high heat. Add the seitan slices and brown on both sides, cooking in batches if necessary. Remove the seitan from the pot and set aside. (Note: If you don't have an ovenproof pot, brown the seitan and then the vegetables in a skillet; transfer the vegetables to a lightly oiled baking dish, and set the seitan aside until ready to use.)

4 Add the remaining I tablespoon oil to the pot and heat over medium heat. Add the onions, carrots, and potatoes and brown quickly all over, stirring frequently. Season the vegetables with salt and pepper to taste and add 1/2 cup of the stock.

continued

5 Cover the pot tightly and bake until the vegetables are tender, about 1 hour. About 15 minutes before the end of cooking time, add the seitan.

6 Meanwhile, in a small saucepan, combine the remaining 2 cups stock, the tomato paste, tamari, and the reserved marinade and bring to a boil. Reduce the heat to low and simmer for 10 minutes to reduce slightly. Whisk in the cornstarch mixture and boil, stirring, for 1 minute, or until the sauce is thickened. Adjust the seasonings if necessary and keep warm over very low heat.

7 When the vegetables are cooked, arrange them on a serving platter with the seitan. Spoon the sauce over the seitan and serve.

Serves 4

"Meat" Made from Wheat

Seitan, as it is known in Japan, is also called "wheat-meat" because it is made from whole wheat flour. It has a chewy meat-like texture and appearance and is perhaps the most versatile of the meat alternatives. Seitan is made by kneading and rinsing a whole wheat dough until the starch and bran are removed, leaving only the gluten. Seitan is high in protein, calcium, niacin, and other nutrients. It keeps well under refrigeration for several days and freezes well for several months.

Roasted Wheat-Meat with Oyster Mushroom and "Sausage" Stuffing

This recipe uses raw seitan, or wheat-meat. It can be made using the recipe on page 127 or with a product called Seitan Quick Mix from Harvest Direct, available in natural food stores, which will cut preparation time significantly.

1 pound raw seitan (see headnote)

1/2 cup tamari or other soy sauce

3 tablespoons olive oil

1 small yellow onion, minced

8 ounces oyster mushrooms, coarsely
   chopped

8 ounces vegetarian sausage, cooked
   and crumbled

1 tablespoon minced fresh parsley leaves

1 teaspoon fresh minced thyme leaves or
   1/2 teaspoon dried

Salt and freshly ground black pepper

4 cups finely diced bread

1 1/2 cups Good Gravy (page 302)

1 Place the seitan in a shallow baking dish. Cover with the tamari and marinate for 30 minutes at room temperature.

2 While the seitan is marinating, preheat the oven to 375 degrees F. Heat the oil in a large skillet over medium heat. Add the onion, cover, and cook, stirring a few times, until softened, about 5 minutes. Add the mushrooms, vegetarian sausage, parsley, thyme, and salt and pepper to taste and cook, stirring often, for 5 minutes longer, then transfer to a large bowl.

3 Stir in the bread and mix well. If the mixture is too dry, add a small amount of water. Set aside.

4 Place the marinated seitan (reserve the marinade) between two sheets of plastic wrap and roll out with a rolling pin until it is approximately 1/4 inch thick. Using your hands, spread the stuffing over the seitan to within 1/2 inch of the edges, then roll it up. Place the rolled seitan seam side down in a lightly oiled shallow baking dish. Pierce it in several places with a fork.

5 Pour the reserved marinade over the roast and bake, uncovered, 40 to 45 minutes, basting it once after 20 minutes. When the surface of the roast is firm and

continued

golden brown, remove it from the oven and let it rest for 10 minutes.

6 Meanwhile, heat the gravy in a small saucepan.

7 Using a serrated knife, cut the roast into $1/2$-inch-thick slices. Arrange on a serving platter, and serve with the gravy.

Serves 8

Cranberry-Pecan-Stuffed Wheat-Meat Ballotine

The dried cranberries offer a sweet-tart accent to the stuffing and, along with the pecans, add texture and flavor. As in the preceding recipe, the seitan can be made from scratch or with a mix.

1 pound raw seitan (page 127)

$1/2$ cup tamari or other soy sauce

$3/4$ cup dried cranberries

2 tablespoons olive oil, plus extra for roasting

1 celery stalk, minced

2 shallots, minced

2 cups cooked brown rice

$1/2$ cup chopped pecans

1 cup fresh bread crumbs

$1/4$ cup minced fresh parsley leaves

1 Place the seitan in a shallow baking dish. Cover with the tamari and marinate for 30 minutes at room temperature.

2 While the seitan is marinating, soak the cranberries in a small bowl of hot water for 15 minutes. Drain and set aside.

3 Preheat the oven to 375 degrees F. Heat the oil in a large skillet over medium heat. Add the celery and shallots, cover, and cook, stirring a few times, until softened, about 5 minutes. Remove from the heat and stir in the rice, all but 2 tablespoons of the drained cranberries, the pecans, bread crumbs,

2 teaspoons minced fresh savory leaves
   or 1 teaspoon dried
Salt and freshly ground black pepper
1½ cups Good Gravy (page 302)

parsley, savory, and salt and pepper to taste. Mix well, adding a small amount of water if the mixture is too dry. Set aside.

4 Place the marinated seitan (reserve the marinade) between two sheets of plastic wrap and roll out with a rolling pin until it is approximately ¼ inch thick. Using your hands, spread the stuffing over the seitan to within ½ inch of the edges and roll it up like a jelly roll. Place the roast seam side down in an oiled shallow baking pan. Pierce it in several places with a fork and rub a small amount of oil over the surface.

5 Pour the reserved marinade over the ballotine and bake, uncovered, for about 45 minutes, basting once after 20 minutes. When the surface of the roast is firm and golden brown, remove it from the oven and let it rest for 10 minutes.

6 While the roast is resting, heat the gravy in a small saucepan and stir in the reserved 2 tablespoons dried cranberries.

7 Using a serrated knife, cut the roast into ½-inch-thick slices. Arrange on a serving platter, and serve with the gravy.

Serves 8

Meat-Free Meat Loaf with Good Gravy

Protein-rich lentils, walnuts, tofu, and tahini combine with crumbled vegetarian burgers to produce the proper consistency in this meat-less loaf. Serve it with oven-roasted potatoes and carrots and a green vegetable. Top with the Good Gravy, or serve with ketchup, salsa, or chutney.

1 tablespoon olive oil

1 small onion, minced

1 small carrot, grated

4 vegetarian burgers, thawed

$1/2$ cup ground walnuts

1 cup fresh bread crumbs

1 cup cooked brown lentils, drained well

$1/4$ cup soft tofu

2 tablespoons tahini (sesame paste)

1 tablespoon tamari or other soy sauce

1 tablespoon minced fresh parsley leaves

Salt and freshly ground black pepper

Good Gravy (page 302)

1 Preheat the oven to 350 degrees F. Lightly oil a 9 x 5-inch loaf pan.

2 Heat the oil in a small skillet over medium heat. Add the onion and carrot, cover, and cook, stirring a few times, until softened, 5 to 7 minutes. Set aside.

3 Chop or crumble the vegetarian burgers and place in a large bowl. Add the walnuts, bread crumbs, and the onion mixture. Pulse the lentils in a food processor until coarsely chopped, and add to the mixture.

4 In the food processor, process the tofu, tahini, tamari, and parsley until well blended. Stir into the walnut mixture, season to taste with salt and pepper, and transfer to the prepared pan. Smooth the top of the loaf.

5 Bake the loaf until firm and golden brown, 40 to 50 minutes. Let rest for 10 to 15 minutes.

6 Meanwhile, heat the gravy in a small saucepan.

7 Slice the loaf and serve with the gravy.

Serves 4 to 6

Curried Lentil Loaf

This fragrantly spiced lentil loaf has the potatoes and veggies baked right inside. I like to serve it with a sweet-hot chutney, basmati rice, and a green vegetable.

2 tablespoons corn oil

1 large carrot, grated

1 medium-size yellow onion, grated

1 large all-purpose potato, peeled and grated

1 small red bell pepper, seeded and minced

1 garlic clove, minced

2 ripe plum tomatoes, seeded and finely chopped

1 tablespoon tomato paste

1 tablespoon curry powder

1/8 teaspoon cayenne

Salt

2 cups cooked brown lentils, drained and mashed

2 tablespoons creamy natural peanut butter

1/4 cup dry bread crumbs

1 Preheat the oven to 375 degrees F. Lightly oil a 9 x 5-inch loaf pan.

2 Heat the oil in a large skillet over medium heat. Add the carrot, onion, potato, bell pepper, and garlic, cover, and cook, stirring a few times, until the vegetables begin to soften, about 5 minutes. Stir in the tomatoes, tomato paste, curry powder, cayenne, and salt to taste and cook for 1 minute, stirring, to mix well. Cover and simmer until the vegetables are soft, about 10 minutes. Remove from the heat and stir in the lentils.

3 In a food processor or blender, combine the peanut butter and 1 cup of the lentil mixture and process until smooth. Stir into the remaining lentil mixture, add the bread crumbs, and mix well. Taste to adjust the seasoning, then transfer to the prepared loaf pan, spreading the mixture evenly and smoothing the top.

4 Bake the loaf until firm, 30 to 40 minutes. Let sit for at least 15 minutes before slicing.

Serves 4 to 6

Shepherd's Vegetable Pie

This rich and flavorful vegetarian shepherd's pie can also be made with 3 chopped veggie burgers or about 12 ounces of tempeh or tofu, if you prefer. If you use tempeh, poach it in water for 10 minutes first. If using tofu, sauté it lightly in a little tamari first to give it some color. The crowning glory of this home-style favorite is the rich, buttery top layer of mashed Yukon Gold potatoes.

---

2 pounds Yukon Gold potatoes, peeled and diced

1/4 cup regular or soy milk

2 tablespoons olive oil

1 medium-size yellow onion, chopped

1 medium-size carrot, chopped

11/2 cups vegetarian burger crumbles

1/2 cup frozen peas

1/2 cup frozen corn kernels

1 tablespoon tamari or other soy sauce

1 teaspoon minced fresh thyme leaves or 1/2 teaspoon dried

1 to 11/2 cups Good Gravy (page 302)

Salt and freshly ground black pepper

1 Place the potatoes in a medium-size saucepan, cover with salted water, and bring to a boil. Reduce the heat to medium-low, cover, and simmer until tender, 20 to 30 minutes.

2 Drain the potatoes and return to the pan. Add the milk and mash until smooth, then season with salt to taste.

3 Meanwhile, preheat the oven to 350 degrees F. Lightly oil a shallow 11/2-quart baking dish.

4 Heat 1 tablespoon of the oil in a large skillet over medium heat. Add the onion and carrot, cover, and cook, stirring a few times, until softened, 5 to 7 minutes. Stir in the burger crumbles, peas, corn, tamari, thyme, and 1 cup of the gravy, adding up to 1/2 cup more if necessary to moisten. Season with salt and pepper to taste.

5 Spoon the filling mixture into the prepared baking dish. Spread the mashed potatoes on top and drizzle with the remaining 1 tablespoon oil.

6 Bake until heated through and the top is golden, 20 to 30 minutes. Serve hot.

Serves 4

Indian-Spiced Sweet Potato Potpie

~~~

The rich flavor of the sweet potatoes in both the filling and the crust blends harmoniously with the aromatic curry spices. A green salad with raisins, peanuts, and bits of apple makes a delightful accompaniment.

Filling:

3 tablespoons corn oil

1 small yellow onion, chopped

1 medium-size carrot, chopped

12 ounces extra-firm tofu, cut into

$^1/_4$-inch dice

1 tablespoon tamari or other soy sauce

2 teaspoons curry powder or paste

1 cup peeled and diced sweet potato,

boiled in water to cover until tender

and drained

$^1/_2$ cup frozen peas

1 tablespoon minced fresh parsley leaves

Salt

2 tablespoons all-purpose flour

1 cup regular or soy milk

$^1/_2$ cup vegetable stock (page 36) or

water

Crust:

1 cup all-purpose flour, or more if needed

$^3/_4$ teaspoon baking powder

$^1/_4$ teaspoon salt

$^1/_4$ cup corn oil, chilled

$^1/_2$ cup cold mashed sweet potatoes

1 Preheat the oven to 350 degrees F. Lightly oil a 1$^1/_2$-quart casserole dish.

2 Make the filling: Heat 1 tablespoon of the oil in a medium-size skillet over medium heat. Add the onion and carrot, cover, and cook, stirring a few times, until softened, 5 to 7 minutes. Remove from the skillet with a slotted spoon and set aside.

3 Add the tofu and tamari to the skillet and cook, stirring gently to coat the tofu with the tamari, for about 3 minutes. Return the onion and carrot to the skillet and stir in 1 teaspoon of the curry powder, the diced sweet potato, peas, parsley, and salt to taste. Stir gently to combine, then transfer the mixture to the prepared casserole.

4 Heat the remaining 2 tablespoons oil in a small saucepan over medium heat. Stir in the flour and cook, stirring constantly, for 1 minute. Gradually add the milk, stock, and the remaining 1 teaspoon curry powder, stirring until smooth. Bring the sauce almost to a boil and remove from the heat. Season with salt to taste. Pour the sauce over the tofu and vegetables in the casserole dish and set aside.

5 Make the crust: In a food processor, combine the flour, baking powder, and salt, pulsing to blend. Add the oil, processing until the mixture is crumbly. Add

continued

the mashed sweet potatoes, processing to blend. If the mixture is too wet, add more flour.

6 On a lightly floured work surface, roll out the dough to a $1/4$-inch-thick round a little larger than the casserole dish. Carefully place the crust on top of the casserole, crimping the edges to seal.

7 Bake until heated through and the crust is lightly browned on top, about 45 minutes. Let rest for 10 minutes before serving.

Serves 4

Flaky Vegetable Potpie

Blustery Sunday afternoons are my favorite time to make this comfort food classic enriched with soy protein. Tender vegetables and creamy sauce topped with a flaky golden crust provide a taste of down-home goodness.

Filling:

1 all-purpose potato, diced

2 teaspoons olive oil

1/2 cup chopped onions

1/2 cup chopped carrots

2 cups extra-firm tofu, cut into 1/4-inch
   dice

1/2 cup frozen peas, thawed

1 tablespoon minced fresh parsley leaves

1 1/4 cups Good Gravy (page 302)

Crust:

1 cup all-purpose flour

1/4 teaspoon salt

1/4 cup corn oil, chilled

1 to 2 tablespoons ice water

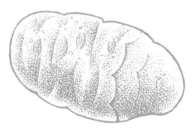

1 Preheat the oven to 350 degrees F. Lightly oil a 1 1/2-quart casserole dish.

2 Make the filling: Cook the potato in boiling salted water until tender. Drain, rinse, and set aside.

3 Heat the oil in a medium-size skillet over medium heat. Add the onions and carrots, cover, and cook, stirring occasionally, until tender. Transfer the onions and carrots to the prepared casserole dish, add the tofu, peas, parsley, and potato, and stir to mix. Add the gravy, stirring to combine, and set aside.

4 Make the crust: In a food processor, combine the flour and salt, pulsing to blend. Add the oil and process until the mixture is crumbly. With the machine running, slowly add the water and process until the mixture forms a ball.

5 On a lightly floured work surface, roll out the dough to a 1/4-inch-thick round a little larger than the casserole dish. Place the crust over the filled casserole and crimp the edges to seal.

6 Bake until heated through and the crust is browned, 40 to 45 minutes. Let rest for 10 minutes before serving.

Serves 6

Quiche and Tell

⟨ornament⟩

Real men *do* eat quiche, and if it's this quiche they're eating, they also eat tofu and spinach. You might call this dish a spinach tart or gratin.

Crust:

1 cup all-purpose flour

1/8 teaspoon salt

1/4 cup corn oil, chilled

1 to 2 tablespoons cold water

Filling:

1 tablespoon olive oil

1/2 cup minced onion

One 10-ounce package frozen spinach,
    cooked according to package
    directions, drained, squeezed dry, and
    chopped

2 cups firm tofu, drained and crumbled

1 cup regular or soy milk

1 tablespoon Dijon mustard

1/2 teaspoon salt

1/8 teaspoon cayenne

Pinch of ground nutmeg

1 cup grated mozzarella cheese or soy
    mozzarella

1 Make the crust: In a food processor, combine the flour and salt, pulsing to blend. Add the oil and process until the mixture is crumbly. With the machine running, slowly add the water and process until the mixture forms a ball. Turn the dough out, flatten it into a disk, and wrap it in plastic. Refrigerate for at least 30 minutes.

2 Meanwhile, make the filling: Preheat the oven to 375 degrees F. Heat the oil in a small skillet over medium heat. Add the onion, cover, and cook, stirring a few times, until softened, about 5 minutes. Remove from the heat and add the spinach, stirring to combine. Set aside.

3 On a lightly floured work surface, roll the dough out into a 12-inch round. Fit it into a 9-inch fluted quiche pan or pie plate. Set aside.

4 In the food processor, process the tofu, milk, mustard, salt, cayenne, and nutmeg until well blended. Spoon the spinach mixture into the crust and sprinkle with the mozzarella. Pour the tofu mixture over the spinach and mozzarella, making sure it is evenly distributed.

5 Bake until the filling is firm and lightly browned on top, 45 to 50 minutes. Let the quiche cool slightly to firm up before cutting.

Serves 4 to 6

Country Vegetable Cassoulet

While sausage and other meats are traditional in the classic French cassoulet, one of the key ingredients is white beans slowly baked with vegetables and herbs. In this tasty meat-free version, the beans and vegetables are cooked ahead of time, to significantly cut down on the oven time. Using canned beans makes it quicker still. Serve with crusty French bread and a green salad.

1 cup pearl onions, unpeeled

2 medium-size carrots, sliced diagonally

3 tablespoons olive oil

2 garlic cloves, minced

1 tablespoon tomato paste

1/2 cup dry white wine

One 28-ounce can diced tomatoes, with
  their juices

3 cups cooked Great Northern or other
  white beans or two 15-ounce cans,
  drained and rinsed

1 tablespoon chopped fresh parsley
  leaves

1 teaspoon minced fresh thyme leaves or
  1/2 teaspoon dried

1/2 teaspoon minced fresh marjoram
  leaves or 1/4 teaspoon dried

2 bay leaves

Salt and freshly ground black pepper

3/4 cup dry bread crumbs

1 Preheat the oven to 350 degrees F. Lightly oil a 2-quart casserole dish.

2 Place the onions in a small saucepan with water to cover, bring to a boil, and let simmer until just tender, about 15 minutes (this makes it easier to peel the onions). Rinse under cold running water until cool enough to handle, then peel and set aside.

3 Lightly steam the carrots until softened, about 5 minutes. Set aside.

4 Heat 2 tablespoons of the oil in a large skillet over medium heat. Add the garlic and cook until fragrant, about 30 seconds. Remove from the heat and stir in the onions and carrots, coating with the oil and garlic. Transfer the vegetable mixture to the prepared casserole dish.

5 Add the tomato paste to the skillet and cook over medium heat for 1 minute, then blend in the wine. Add to the mixture in the casserole dish, along with the tomatoes, beans, parsley, thyme, marjoram, bay leaves, and salt and pepper to taste, stirring to mix well. Cover tightly and bake until hot and bubbly, about 30 minutes.

continued

6 While the cassoulet is baking, lightly toss the bread crumbs in a small bowl with the remaining 1 tablespoon oil.

7 When the cassoulet is done, remove the cover and remove and discard the bay leaves. Top with the crumbs, and return to the oven for 5 to 10 minutes to brown the crumbs. Serve hot.

Serves 4 to 6

Biryani Vegetables

This recipe was inspired by the traditional Indian biryani, a layered casserole that includes a variety of vegetables, dried fruits, and nuts. To save time, I combine everything and begin cooking the ingredients on top of the stove. It then finishes baking in the oven, and is served directly from the casserole dish. (If you prefer to cook it entirely on top of the stove, I give alternate instructions for that method.) The preparation for this dish is somewhat similar to that for stir-frying, in that the ingredients need to be assembled before cooking begins so they can be added quickly in succession. A prepared Indian spice blend such as garam masala can be used instead of the individual spices.

3 garlic cloves, peeled

2 teaspoons peeled and chopped fresh ginger

2 1/2 cups plus 2 tablespoons water

1 teaspoon ground coriander

1 teaspoon ground cumin

1/2 teaspoon cayenne

1/2 teaspoon turmeric

1/4 teaspoon ground cinnamon

1 Combine the garlic, ginger, and 2 tablespoons of the water in a blender and grind to a paste. Set aside.

2 In a small bowl, combine the coriander, cumin, cayenne, turmeric, cinnamon, black pepper, and cloves and set aside.

3 Soak and rinse the rice in several changes of water until the water remains clear; set aside.

4 Preheat the oven to 375 degrees F. Lightly oil a 2 1/2-quart casserole dish.

1/4 teaspoon freshly ground black pepper

1/8 teaspoon ground cloves

1 1/2 cups basmati rice

2 tablespoons peanut oil

1 large yellow onion, diced

1 small red bell pepper, seeded and diced

1 cup bite-size cauliflower florets

1 large carrot, thinly sliced

3/4 teaspoon salt

1 1/2 cups cooked chickpeas or one
   15-ounce can, drained and rinsed
   (see Note)

1/2 cup golden raisins

1/2 cup unsweetened coconut milk

Toasted slivered almonds for garnish

5 Heat the oil in a large saucepan over medium heat. Add the onion, cover, and cook, stirring a few times, until softened, about 5 minutes. Add the bell pepper, cauliflower, and carrot and cook, stirring a few times, until slightly softened, about 2 minutes. Add the spice mixture and cook for 2 minutes longer, stirring to coat the vegetables well with the spices. Stir in the garlic/ginger paste, 1 cup water, and 1/4 teaspoon of the salt and cook, covered, until the vegetables soften, 5 to 7 minutes. Stir in the rice, chickpeas, raisins, coconut milk, 1 1/2 cups water, and the remaining 1/2 teaspoon salt.

6 Transfer the mixture to the prepared casserole dish, cover tightly, and bake until the vegetables are tender and the rice is cooked, about 45 minutes. (Or, to finish cooking on top of the stove, cover tightly and cook over low heat until the rice absorbs the liquid and the rice and vegetables are tender, about 30 minutes.) Sprinkle with almonds and serve.

Serves 4

note: Canned chickpeas are convenient, but if you prefer using dried chickpeas, consider cooking them in a pressure cooker to save time: Soak 1 cup chickpeas in water to cover for 8 to 12 hours. Rinse and drain, then place in a pressure cooker with 3 to 4 cups water, or enough to cover, and pressure-cook for about 20 minutes after the cooker comes to full pressure.

Molasses-Baked Beans and "Franks"

This quick and easy baked bean recipe can be made without the vegetarian hot dogs, if you prefer, but I like the way they absorb the zesty flavors of the sauce. Not all veggie dogs are created equal, so experiment with different brands to find one you like best. Homemade coleslaw (pages 92–94) is a great accompaniment to this dish.

1 tablespoon olive oil

1 small yellow onion, chopped

One 14.5-ounce can crushed tomatoes

1/4 cup molasses

2 tablespoons cider vinegar

1/4 cup prepared barbecue sauce of your
choice

1 tablespoon prepared mustard of your
choice

1 tablespoon tamari or other soy sauce

3 cups cooked navy or other white beans
or two 15-ounce cans, drained and
rinsed

One 16-ounce package vegetarian hot
dogs (8 hot dogs)

1 Preheat the oven to 350 degrees F. Heat the oil in a large skillet over medium heat. Add the onion, cover, and cook, stirring a few times, until softened, about 5 minutes. Add the tomatoes, molasses, vinegar, barbecue sauce, mustard, and tamari and stir to combine. Add the beans and heat through.

2 Transfer half the bean mixture to a shallow 2-quart baking dish and top with the hot dogs, followed by the remaining bean mixture. Cover the dish tightly and bake until hot and bubbly, 20 to 30 minutes. Serve hot.

Serves 4

Savory Vegetable Bread Pudding

This bread pudding is great for a company brunch, a party buffet, or even a weeknight supper. It can be assembled in advance and refrigerated until ready to bake. Return it to room temperature before baking.

1 pound fresh spinach, tough stems
   removed and washed well, or one
   10-ounce package frozen chopped
   spinach
1 tablespoon olive oil
1 large yellow onion, chopped
2 garlic cloves, minced
8 ounces white button mushrooms, sliced
1 pound soft tofu, crumbled
2 cups regular or soy milk
1¹/₂ teaspoons Dijon mustard
1 teaspoon minced fresh marjoram
   leaves or ¹/₂ teaspoon dried
¹/₈ teaspoon ground nutmeg
Salt and freshly ground black pepper
4 ounces mozzarella cheese or soy
   mozzarella, shredded
1 loaf Italian bread, cut into thick slices

1. Lightly steam the fresh spinach, or cook the frozen spinach according to the package directions. Drain well and squeeze dry. Set aside.

2. Heat the oil in a large skillet over medium heat. Add the onion, cover, and cook, stirring a few times, until softened, about 5 minutes. Stir in the garlic and mushrooms and cook, uncovered, until the mushrooms release their liquid and it begins to evaporate, 2 to 3 minutes. Stir in the spinach and set aside.

3. In a food processor or blender, combine the tofu, milk, mustard, marjoram, nutmeg, and salt and pepper to taste and process until smooth. Stir this into the vegetable mixture, along with the cheese.

4. Preheat the oven to 350 degrees F. Lightly oil a 9 x 13-inch baking dish.

5. Arrange the bread slices in the prepared baking dish. Pour the vegetable mixture over the bread, using a fork to distribute the vegetables evenly. Let soak until the liquid is absorbed, about 20 minutes.

6. Bake the bread pudding for 30 minutes, then increase the oven temperature to 400 degrees F and continue to bake until golden brown on top, about 10 minutes. Let stand for 10 minutes before serving.

Serves 6 to 8

Mexican Tortilla Bake

Soft tortillas layered with pinto beans, salsa, and other Mexican ingredients make a hearty casserole, which can be assembled ahead of time for a quick weeknight supper.

1 tablespoon olive oil

1 large garlic clove, minced

1¹/₂ cups cooked pinto beans or one
   15-ounce can, drained and rinsed

One 14.5-ounce can diced tomatoes,
   drained

1¹/₂ tablespoons chili powder

Salt and freshly ground black pepper

1¹/₂ cups prepared salsa of your choice

4 ounces soft or silken tofu

2 tablespoons fresh lime juice

Twelve 6-inch flour tortillas

1 cup shredded Monterey Jack or soy
   cheese

1. Preheat the oven to 350 degrees F. Lightly oil a 9 x 13-inch baking dish.

2. Heat the oil in a large skillet over medium heat. Add the garlic and cook until fragrant, about 30 seconds. Add the pinto beans, tomatoes, chili powder, and salt and pepper to taste and simmer for 5 minutes. Remove from the heat.

3. In a food processor or blender, combine the salsa, tofu, lime juice, and ¹/₂ cup of the bean mixture. Process until well blended.

4. Spread a thin layer of the tofu-and-salsa mixture over the bottom of the prepared baking dish. Arrange 6 of the tortillas on top, overlapping as necessary. Spread the remaining bean mixture over the tortillas and cover with another layer of tortillas. Top with the remaining tofu-and-salsa mixture and sprinkle with the shredded cheese.

5. Bake until hot and bubbly and lightly browned on top, about 30 minutes. Let rest for 10 minutes before serving.

Serves 6

Classy Casseroles

The casserole, a savory blend of ingredients baked in a dish of the same name, has its roots in many ethnic traditions. While some casseroles are vegetarian, most others can easily be adapted to meatless and dairy-free dining. Many of us regard the humble casserole as a casual family meal, but its upscale distant cousins, the gratin and tart, can be elegant fare for guests. In a broad sense, casseroles can also include such oven-going delights as lasagna, quiche, and spanakopita, as well as potpies, vegetable cobblers, and bread puddings.

Casseroles have long been a part of mealtime traditions, yet the many virtues of these bubbly baked wonders are often overlooked. Infinitely versatile, casseroles are usually made with precooked ingredients, making them the perfect strategy for using up leftover grains, pasta, and vegetables. Since they can be made ahead and reheated, casseroles are great for an easy dinner as well as parties and potlucks. They are an economical way of feeding a crowd.

Easy to assemble, most casseroles are simply popped into a moderate oven to bake until heated through and bubbly, freeing the cook to do other things while dinner cooks itself. Therein lies yet another virtue of the casserole: It is baked and served in the same dish. For an attractive presentation, a casserole can be topped with crumbs or cheese that turn golden brown during baking. Other flavorful, often crunchy casserole toppings include cracker crumbs, crumbled potato chips or tortilla chips, and ground nuts.

Double Eggplant Moussaka

T raditional moussaka contains layers of ground lamb and sliced eggplant, but this version uses the eggplant in both roles for a flavorful vegetarian casserole redolent of Greek spices.

3 tablespoons olive oil

1 large yellow onion, chopped

2 large eggplants, ends trimmed, 1 peeled and finely chopped, 1 cut into 1/4-inch-thick slices

2 garlic cloves, chopped

1 tablespoon minced fresh oregano leaves or 1 1/2 teaspoons dried

1/2 teaspoon ground cinnamon

One 14.5-ounce can diced tomatoes, drained

2 tablespoons tomato paste

1/2 cup dry white wine

1/4 cup chopped fresh parsley leaves

Salt and freshly ground black pepper

1 cup cooked brown rice

3/4 cup soft or silken tofu

2 cups regular or soy milk

Pinch of ground nutmeg

1/2 cup freshly grated Parmesan cheese or soy Parmesan

1 Heat I tablespoon of the oil in a large skillet over medium heat. Add the onion, cover, and cook, stirring a few times, until softened, about 5 minutes. Add the finely chopped eggplant, garlic, oregano, cinnamon, and tomatoes. Stir the tomato paste into the wine, then add to the skillet, along with the parsley and salt and pepper to taste. Cook over low heat for 10 minutes to blend the flavors. Stir in the rice and set aside.

2 Preheat the oven to 350 degrees F. Lightly oil a 9 x 13-inch baking dish. In a blender or food processor, combine the tofu, milk, nutmeg, and salt and pepper to taste and process until smooth. Set aside.

3 Heat the remaining 2 tablespoons oil in a large skillet over medium heat. Add the eggplant slices (you may need to do this in batches) and cook, turning once, until lightly browned on both sides, about 2 minutes per side. Arrange a layer of one-third of the sliced eggplant in the prepared baking dish. Spread half the chopped eggplant mixture over the top. Arrange another layer of eggplant slices on top, followed by the remaining eggplant mixture and a final layer of eggplant slices. Pour the tofu sauce over all and sprinkle with the cheese.

4 Bake until bubbly and lightly browned on top, about 45 minutes. Let stand for 20 minutes before cutting into squares to serve.

Serves 6 to 8

Eggplant Parmesan

This Italian classic is one of the most popular ways to serve eggplant. When the eggplant slices are breaded and fried, the fat and calorie content soars. Cooking the eggplant slices in the oven takes care of that problem and makes for a lighter dish.

1 large eggplant, ends trimmed, peeled, and cut into ¼-inch-thick slices

2 tablespoons olive oil

1 small onion, minced

2 garlic cloves, minced

One 28-ounce can crushed tomatoes

2 tablespoons minced fresh parsley leaves

1 tablespoon minced fresh basil leaves

1 teaspoon minced fresh oregano leaves or ½ teaspoon dried

Salt and freshly ground black pepper

½ cup freshly grated Parmesan cheese or soy Parmesan

1 cup shredded mozzarella cheese or soy mozzarella

1 Preheat the oven to 375 degrees F. Arrange the eggplant slices on a lightly oiled baking sheet and bake, turning once, until soft, about 15 minutes. Remove from the oven and set aside. Leave the oven on.

2 Heat the oil in a large skillet over medium heat. Add the onion and garlic, cover, and cook, stirring a few times, until softened, about 5 minutes. Stir in the tomatoes, parsley, basil, oregano, and salt and pepper to taste and simmer for 10 minutes to blend the flavors. Remove from the heat.

3 Spread a layer of the tomato sauce over the bottom of a 2½-quart casserole dish. Top with a layer of eggplant slices and sprinkle with a small amount of the Parmesan and mozzarella. Continue layering until the ingredients are used up, ending with a layer of sauce sprinkled with the remaining cheeses.

4 Bake until hot and bubbly, about 40 minutes. Let sit for 10 minutes before serving.

Serves 4

Provençal Vegetable Gratin

⌇⌇⌇

This lovely gratin is a celebration of summer's harvest, using a variety of fresh vegetables and herbs. A mandoline or other vegetable slicer makes short work of slicing the vegetables, but a good sharp knife gets the job done as well. Peel or don't peel the potatoes, as you prefer.

2$^1/_2$ tablespoons olive oil

6 small new red potatoes, thinly sliced

1 medium-size yellow onion, thinly sliced

1 medium-size zucchini, ends trimmed
   and thinly sliced

4 ripe plum tomatoes, cut into $^1/_4$-inch-
   thick rounds

1 small yellow bell pepper, seeded and
   minced

2 garlic cloves, minced

1 tablespoon minced fresh rosemary
   leaves or 1$^1/_2$ teaspoons dried

1 teaspoon minced fresh basil leaves or
   $^1/_2$ teaspoon dried

$^1/_2$ teaspoon minced fresh thyme leaves
   or $^1/_4$ teaspoon dried

Salt and freshly ground black pepper

$^1/_4$ cup vegetable stock (page 36)

$^3/_4$ cup dry bread crumbs

$^1/_2$ cup freshly grated Parmesan cheese
   or soy Parmesan

1 Preheat the oven to 375 degrees F. Generously oil a large gratin dish with 1$^1/_2$ teaspoons of the oil.

2 Arrange alternating and overlapping slices of the potato, onion, zucchini, and tomato in the prepared dish, layering as you go. Sprinkle with the bell pepper, garlic, rosemary, basil, and thyme and season with salt and pepper to taste. Drizzle with 1 tablespoon of the oil, and pour the stock over all.

3 Cover and bake until the vegetables begin to soften, about 30 minutes. Uncover and continue to bake until the vegetables are soft, the top layer is lightly browned, and the liquid is absorbed, about 30 minutes longer.

4 Meanwhile, in a small bowl, combine the bread crumbs, cheese, and the remaining 1 tablespoon oil.

5 Remove the gratin from the oven and top with the crumb mixture. Return to the oven for 5 to 10 minutes to brown the topping. Let sit for 10 minutes before serving.

Serves 6

Asian-Inspired Stuffed Kabocha Squash

~mm~

Japanese kabocha squash, also called Hokkaido pumpkin, has a deep green skin and blushing orange flesh that is sweeter than that of any other squash I've tasted. It can be found at Asian markets and some well-stocked supermarkets. If it is unavailable, substitute Buttercup or butternut squash. The mirin, tamari, sesame oil, and other Asian ingredients in the stuffing complement the Japanese origins of the squash. A rich mushroom sauce made with miso would be especially good with this dish.

1 medium-size kabocha squash, halved
    and seeded

Salt

1 tablespoon peanut oil

1 small yellow onion, minced

2 garlic cloves, minced

1 tablespoon peeled and minced fresh
    ginger

3 scallions, minced

2 tablespoons tamari or other soy sauce

1 tablespoon mirin (rice wine)

2$^1/_2$ cups finely diced bread

1$^1/_2$ cups cooked brown rice

$^1/_4$ cup minced fresh parsley leaves

1 teaspoon toasted sesame oil

1   Preheat the oven to 350 degrees F. Season the squash halves with salt and place them cut side down in a lightly oiled shallow baking pan. Add $^1/_4$ inch of water to the pan and cover tightly. Bake for 20 minutes, or until slightly softened.

2   While the squash is baking, heat the peanut oil in a large skillet over medium heat. Add the onion, cover, and cook, stirring a few times, until softened, about 5 minutes. Stir in the garlic, ginger, and scallions and cook until fragrant, about 30 seconds. Stir in the tamari and mirin, then transfer to a large bowl. Add the bread, rice, parsley, and sesame oil, mixing thoroughly. Taste to adjust the seasonings. If additional moisture is needed, add a little water or vegetable stock.

3   Turn the squash halves over and fill the cavities with the stuffing. Cover with a sheet of aluminum foil and bake until the stuffing is hot and the squash is tender, about 40 minutes. Uncover for the last 10 minutes of cooking time to brown the stuffing on top. Slice the squash in half to serve.

Serves 4

Savory Stuffed Beefsteak Tomatoes

~uu~

If you're like me, when red ripe beefsteak tomatoes are in season, you can't get enough of them. For a nice change from eating them "as is," I like to stuff them and serve them as a hot entrée. Garlic and fresh herbs complement the flavor of the tomatoes, and pine nuts add texture.

---

4 large ripe tomatoes

2 tablespoons olive oil

1 small yellow onion, minced

1 garlic clove, minced

2 cups cooked brown basmati or other
    long-grain rice

1/4 cup pine nuts

2 tablespoons minced fresh parsley
    leaves

1 tablespoon minced fresh basil leaves
    or 1 1/2 teaspoons dried

1 teaspoon minced fresh marjoram or
    1/2 teaspoon dried

1/8 teaspoon red pepper flakes

1/2 teaspoon salt

1/4 teaspoon freshly ground black pepper

1/2 cup dry bread crumbs

1/2 cup freshly grated Parmesan cheese
    or soy Parmesan

1 Preheat the oven to 375 degrees F. Lightly oil a small baking dish.

2 Slice the tops off the tomatoes and carefully remove the pulp and seeds. Chop the pulp, and set the tomatoes aside.

3 Heat I tablespoon of the oil in a large skillet over medium heat. Add the onion, cover, and cook, stirring a few times, until softened, about 5 minutes. Add the garlic, tomato pulp, rice, pine nuts, parsley, basil, marjoram, red pepper flakes, salt, and pepper and cook over low heat for 5 minutes. Remove from the heat and allow to cool slightly.

4 Stuff the rice mixture into the tomatoes and place in the prepared baking dish. In a small bowl, combine the remaining I tablespoon oil with the bread crumbs and Parmesan, tossing with a fork to mix. Sprinkle over the tomatoes.

5 Cover with a sheet of aluminum foil and bake until the tomatoes are soft and the filling is hot, about 20 minutes. Remove the foil and bake for 5 to 10 minutes longer to brown the topping. Serve hot.

Serves 6

Pepper-Stuffed Peppers

~~~

Zesty Italian cherry peppers and tiny peppercorn-shaped pasta (*acini di pepe*) combine with a variety of ingredients to make a flavorful stuffing for bell peppers. Use any color bell peppers you prefer, or mix and match for a colorful entrée. If vegetarian sausage is unavailable, use thawed and chopped veggie burgers or TVP.

4 large bell peppers

2 tablespoons olive oil

1 small yellow onion, minced

1 small zucchini, ends trimmed and
   chopped

1 garlic clove, minced

3 or 4 hot Italian cherry peppers, to your
   taste, seeded and minced

Salt and freshly ground black pepper

2 1/2 cups tomato sauce, homemade
   (page 241) or store-bought

1 cup cooked *acini di pepe* or other tiny
   pasta shape (1/4 cup uncooked)

8 ounces vegetarian sausage, cooked
   and crumbled

1 tablespoon minced fresh parsley leaves

1 teaspoon minced fresh basil leaves or
   1/2 teaspoon dried

1/4 cup dry bread crumbs

1/2 cup freshly grated Parmesan cheese
   or soy Parmesan

1   Cut the bell peppers lengthwise in half and remove the seeds and membranes. Place the peppers in a pot of boiling water, reduce the heat to medium, and simmer just long enough to soften slightly, 3 to 4 minutes. Drain and set aside.

2   Preheat the oven to 375 degrees F. Heat the oil in a large skillet over medium heat. Add the onion, cover, and cook, stirring a few times, until softened, about 5 minutes. Add the zucchini, garlic, cherry peppers, and salt and pepper to taste and cook, stirring a few times, until the vegetables are tender, about 5 minutes longer. Stir in 1/2 cup of the tomato sauce, cover, and simmer for 10 minutes. Remove from the heat and add the cooked pasta, vegetarian sausage, parsley, and basil, mixing well.

3   Stuff the pepper halves with the sausage mixture and arrange in a lightly oiled shallow baking dish just large enough to hold them. Sprinkle with the bread crumbs and Parmesan.

4   Bake until the stuffing is heated through and the tops are lightly browned, about 30 minutes.

continued

5 Meanwhile, heat the remaining 2 cups tomato sauce in a small saucepan.

6 To serve, arrange 2 pepper halves on each plate and spoon a little sauce onto each pepper. Pass the rest of the sauce on the side.

Serves 4

Simply Stuffed!

Certain vegetables, in addition to being delicious in their own right, make fabulous edible containers for other foods.

When you stuff vegetables, you get a delicious meal of moist stuffing that is made more flavorful by the permeating essence of the vegetable holding it all together. As an added bonus, you get an artfully presented and aesthetically pleasing dish—and you can eat the container.

Whether you stuff a tiny cherry tomato with pesto or hummus or fill a large beefsteak tomato to overflowing with rice and vegetables, using fresh produce to hold your food is a delicious and practical way to showcase nature's bounty. Bell peppers make great holders for dips and salsas and, like tomatoes, can be served as a main course when stuffed with a grain-and-vegetable mixture and baked.

Other terrific "stuffing" vegetables include eggplants, sweet yellow or red onions, potatoes, and zucchini and other squashes—which are often stuffed with themselves, the inner pulp scooped out, chopped, and sautéed with herbs and other ingredients, then spooned back in. Stuffed mushrooms make elegant appetizers, as do stuffed artichokes. Many baked stuffed vegetables can be served as a main dish, depending on the heartiness of the stuffing.

Stuffed Peppers on Sliced Potatoes

The first time I had stuffed peppers made this way was back in the late 1960s, when my then newly married sister prepared them for dinner one evening. The flavor combination has stuck with me since then, especially the way the potato slices soak up the flavor of the peppers and tomatoes. As an alternative to the lentils, substitute another cooked bean variety, or use chopped vegetarian burgers or TVP.

4 large red bell peppers, tops cut off and
    seeds and membranes removed

2 tablespoons olive oil

1 small yellow onion, minced

1 garlic clove, minced

One 14.5-ounce can diced tomatoes,
    drained

1 tablespoon firmly packed light brown
    sugar

2 tablespoons minced fresh parsley
    leaves

1 teaspoon minced fresh basil leaves or
    $1/2$ teaspoon dried

$1/2$ teaspoon salt

$1/4$ teaspoon freshly ground black pepper

$1 1/2$ cups cooked brown lentils, drained

$1 1/2$ cups cooked long-grain white rice or
    brown rice

2 medium-size all-purpose potatoes

1 Place the peppers in a pot of boiling water, reduce the heat to medium, and simmer just long enough to soften slightly, 3 to 4 minutes. Drain and set aside.

2 Preheat the oven to 375 degrees F. Heat I tablespoon of the oil in a large skillet over medium heat. Add the onion, cover, and cook, stirring a few times, until softened, about 5 minutes. Add the garlic, tomatoes, brown sugar, parsley, basil, salt, and pepper and simmer over low heat for 10 minutes to blend the flavors. Remove from the heat.

3 In a large bowl, combine the lentils, rice, and half of the tomato mixture. Stir to combine and set aside.

4 Cut the potatoes into $1/4$-inch-thick slices and arrange in the bottom of a lightly oiled baking dish just large enough to hold the peppers. Stuff the peppers with the filling and place on the potato slices. Pour the remaining tomato mixture over all and cover tightly with a sheet of aluminum foil.

5 Bake until the peppers and potatoes are tender, about 30 minutes. Serve hot.

Serves 6

Basic Pizza Dough

This makes enough dough for one 12-inch pizza or two 8-inch pizzas, but the recipe is easily doubled if you are cooking for a crowd. The dough can be mixed by hand, if you like, but I prefer using a food processor.

1½ teaspoons active dry yeast

²/₃ cup plus 2 tablespoons warm water

2 cups all-purpose flour

1 teaspoon salt

1 tablespoon olive oil

1 In a small bowl, dissolve the yeast in 2 tablespoons of the warm water and let stand for 5 minutes.

2 Combine the flour and salt in a food processor, pulsing to blend. With the machine running, pour in the yeast mixture, oil, and the remaining ²/₃ cup water and process to form a ball.

3 Turn the dough out onto a lightly floured work surface and knead until smooth and elastic, about 3 minutes. Transfer the dough to a large oiled bowl. Spread a small amount of oil on top of the dough, cover with plastic wrap, and set aside in a warm place to allow the dough to rise until doubled, about 1 hour. The dough is now ready to be used.

**Makes enough for
1 large or 2 small pizzas**

Pile-It-On Pepperoni Pizza

Quick and easy toppings are yours with the help of your favorite pantry ingredients. Choose from among sliced olives, roasted red peppers, marinated artichoke hearts, and even pine nuts. Can't decide? Pile them all on and enjoy. Vegetarian pepperoni, available in natural food stores and well-stocked supermarket, adds a spicy accent.

Basic Pizza Dough (page 194)

4 ounces vegetarian pepperoni, sliced

1 tablespoon olive oil

1 cup seasoned tomato sauce or pizza sauce, homemade or store-bought

1 1/2 cup shredded mozzarella cheese or soy mozzarella

Optional toppings: sliced olives, roasted red peppers, artichoke hearts, pine nuts, etc.

1 While the dough is rising, preheat the oven to 450 degrees F. Place the pepperoni slices in a small bowl and drizzle with the oil, tossing to coat. Set aside.

2 Punch down the dough and divide it in half if desired. On a lightly floured work surface, roll out the dough into a circle or circles about $1/4$ inch thick. Place on a lightly oiled pizza pan or baking sheet. Bake on the lower rack of the oven for 5 minutes.

3 Remove from the oven and top with the tomato sauce, spreading it thinly to $1/2$ inch from the edges of the dough. Sprinkle the cheese over the sauce, along with the vegetarian pepperoni slices and any other toppings, as desired. Bake until the crust is golden brown, 12 to 15 minutes.

Serves 4

Grilled Vegetable Pizza

About the only thing I like more than grilled vegetables is pizza, so a pizza topped with grilled veggies is my idea of heaven. Whether you cook them outdoors or indoors, your vegetables will take on a depth of flavor that only grilling can provide. Vary the vegetables according to personal preference and seasonal availability.

Basic Pizza Dough (page 194)

1 small red onion, sliced

1/2 small yellow bell pepper, seeded

1 large portobello mushroom cap, brown gills removed with a sharp knife or a spoon

2 tablespoons olive oil

Salt and freshly ground black pepper

1/4 cup freshly grated Parmesan cheese or soy Parmesan

1 teaspoon minced fresh basil leaves or 1/2 teaspoon dried

1 teaspoon minced fresh oregano leaves or 1/2 teaspoon dried

1 large ripe tomato, seeded and sliced

1 cup shredded mozzarella cheese or soy mozzarella

1 While the dough is rising, preheat the grill or broiler and cook the vegetables: Brush the onion, bell pepper, and mushroom with the oil. Season with salt and pepper to taste and grill or broil, turning once or twice, until soft and lightly charred. Let cool slightly, then cut the vegetables into bite-size pieces and set aside. Preheat the oven to 450 degrees F.

2 Punch down the dough and divide it in half if desired. On a lightly floured work surface, roll out the dough into a circle or circles about 1/4 inch thick. Place on a lightly oiled pizza pan or baking sheet. Bake on the lower rack of the oven for 5 minutes.

3 Remove from the oven and sprinkle with the Parmesan, basil, oregano, and salt and pepper to taste. Arrange the grilled vegetables and tomato slices on top, to within 1/2 inch from the edges of the dough. Sprinkle the mozzarella over the top and bake until the crust is golden brown, 12 to 15 minutes.

Serves 4

Artichoke, Fennel, and Mushroom Pizza

Aromatic fennel combines with flavorful artichoke hearts and cremini mushrooms for a special topping that signals this is no ordinary pizza. I've served this for company by doubling the recipe and shaping the dough into individual-sized pizzas. Serve with a salad and crisp white wine.

Basic Pizza Dough (page 194)

2 tablespoons olive oil

1 small fennel bulb, stalks removed and discarded, bottom trimmed, and bulb cut into thin strips

3 ounces cremini or other mushrooms, sliced

One 9-ounce box frozen artichoke hearts, cooked according to package directions, drained, and sliced

1 teaspoon minced fresh marjoram leaves or 1/2 teaspoon dried

Salt and freshly ground black pepper

1/2 cup freshly grated Parmesan cheese or soy Parmesan

1 While the dough is rising, preheat the oven to 450 degrees F. Heat the oil in a large skillet over medium heat. Add the fennel and cook, stirring, until softened, about 5 minutes. Add the mushrooms and artichokes and cook until the mushrooms have released their liquid and most of it evaporates, 3 to 5 minutes. Season with the marjoram and salt and pepper to taste and set aside.

2 Punch down the dough and divide in in half if desired. On a lightly floured work surface, roll out the dough into a circle or circles about 1/4 inch thick. Place on a lightly oiled pizza pan or baking sheet and bake on the bottom rack of the oven for 5 minutes.

3 Remove from the oven and spread the vegetable mixture over the dough to within 1/2 inch from the edges of the dough. Sprinkle with the Parmesan and bake until the crust is golden brown, 12 to 15 minutes.

Serves 4

White on White Pizza with Baby Spinach

When we lived in my hometown of Hazleton, Pennsylvania, my husband and I would frequent a local restaurant where we enjoyed an incredible white pizza and fresh spinach salad. Inspired by that memory, I've combined the two, and the result is a tasty and attractive pizza.

Basic Pizza Dough (page 194)

1 tablespoon olive oil

1 small yellow onion, thinly sliced

2 garlic cloves, minced

8 ounces baby spinach, washed well

1/4 teaspoon red pepper flakes

Salt and freshly ground black pepper

1/3 cup freshly grated Parmesan cheese
   or soy Parmesan

1 1/2 cups grated mozzarella cheese or
   soy mozzarella

1 While the dough is rising, preheat the oven to 450 degrees F. Heat the oil in a large skillet over medium heat. Add the onion and garlic, cover, and cook, stirring a few times, until softened, about 5 minutes. Add the spinach, red pepper flakes, and salt and pepper to taste. Cook until the spinach is wilted, 1 to 2 minutes. Set aside.

2 Punch down the dough and divide it in half if desired. On a lightly floured work surface, roll out the dough into a circle or circles about 1/4 inch thick. Place on a lightly oiled pizza pan or baking sheet. Bake on the lower rack of the oven for 5 minutes.

3 Remove from the oven and sprinkle with the Parmesan. Spread the spinach topping mixture to within 1/2 inch of the edges of the dough. Sprinkle on the mozzarella and bake until the crust is golden brown, 12 to 15 minutes.

Serves 4

Pesto-Potato Pizza

Potatoes on pizza may seem like a carb-lover's fantasy meal, but, like pasta with potatoes and pesto, it is a delicious combination enjoyed in Italy.

Basic Pizza Dough (page 194)

4 small new white potatoes

2 tablespoons olive oil

Salt and freshly ground black pepper

$^1/_2$ cup basil pesto, homemade
   (page 313) or store-bought

1 cup shredded mozzarella cheese or soy
   mozzarella

1 While the dough rises, preheat the oven to 450 degrees F. Peel the potatoes, cut into slices about $^1/_4$ inch thick, and place on a lightly oiled baking sheet. Drizzle with I tablespoon of the oil, tossing to coat, and season with salt and pepper to taste. Bake, turning once, until just tender, about 15 minutes. Remove from the oven and set aside. Leave the oven on.

2 In a shallow bowl, combine the pesto with the remaining I tablespoon oil. Add the potato slices, tossing gently to coat with the pesto. Set aside.

3 Punch down the dough and divide it in half if desired. On a lightly floured work surface, roll out the dough into a circle or circles about $^1/_4$ inch thick. Place on a lightly oiled pizza pan or baking sheet. Bake on the lower rack of the oven for 5 minutes.

4 Remove from the oven and top with the pesto-coated potato slices, arranging them to within $^1/_2$ inch of the edges of the dough. Sprinkle the mozzarella on top and bake until the crust is golden brown, 12 to 15 minutes.

Serves 4

Calzone Crazy

~~~

Acalzone can be described as a kind of pizza turnover, made with pizza dough that is rolled out and folded over a savory filling. Calzones can vary in size from bite-sized appetizers to large family-size creations; this recipe makes two 8-inch calzones. Virtually anything that can top a pizza can fill a calzone, so experiment with different fillings.

Basic Pizza Dough (page 194)

1 tablespoon olive oil

2 garlic cloves, minced

1 cup drained canned diced tomatoes

1 pound extra-firm tofu, drained and
   crumbled

1 tablespoon minced fresh basil leaves
   or 1 1/2 teaspoons dried

1 teaspoon minced fresh oregano leaves
   or 1/2 teaspoon dried

1 cup shredded mozzarella cheese or soy
   mozzarella

1/4 cup freshly grated Parmesan or soy
   Parmesan

Salt and freshly ground black pepper

1 While the dough is rising, preheat the oven to 375 degrees F. Heat the oil in a large skillet over medium heat. Add the garlic and cook until fragrant, about 30 seconds. Add the tomatoes and tofu and stir until all the liquid evaporates. Add the basil and oregano, stirring to combine. Remove from the heat and stir in the mozzarella and Parmesan until they melt. Season with salt and pepper to taste and set aside to cool.

2 Punch down the dough and divide it in half. On a lightly floured work surface, roll out each piece into a 1/4-inch-thick circle. Spread an equal amount of the filling over half of each of the dough circles, leaving a 1-inch border along the edge. Fold the other half of each dough circle over the filling and press the edges together with your fingers, then press the edges with a fork to seal.

3 Transfer the calzones to a lightly oiled pizza pan or baking sheet. Bake until golden brown, about 30 minutes. Allow to sit for 10 minutes before serving.

Serves 4

Spicy Eggplant Calzones

Red pepper flakes add a bit of heat to the flavorful eggplant filling—use more or less according to personal preference. Be sure to cook the filling until all the moisture is evaporated, to prevent the crust from becoming soggy.

Basic Pizza Dough (page 194)

1 tablespoon olive oil

2 garlic cloves, minced

1 large eggplant, ends trimmed, peeled, and chopped

One 14.5-ounce can diced tomatoes, drained

$1/2$ teaspoon red pepper flakes

1 teaspoon minced fresh oregano leaves or $1/2$ teaspoon dried

Salt and freshly ground black pepper

1 cup shredded mozzarella cheese or soy mozzarella

$1/4$ cup freshly grated Parmesan or soy Parmesan

1 While the dough is rising, preheat the oven to 375 degrees F. Heat the oil in a large skillet over medium heat. Add the garlic and eggplant, cover, and cook, stirring occasionally, until softened, about 5 minutes. Stir in the tomatoes, red pepper flakes, oregano, and salt and pepper to taste. Cook until the eggplant is soft and all the liquid has evaporated, about 10 minutes. Remove from the heat and stir in the mozzarella and Parmesan until melted. Set aside to cool.

2 Punch down the dough and divide it in half. On a lightly floured work surface, roll out each piece into a $1/4$-inch-thick circle. Spread an equal amount of the filling over half of each of the dough circles, leaving a 1-inch border along the edge. Fold the other half of each dough circle over the filling and press the edges together with your fingers, then press the edges with a fork to seal.

3 Transfer the calzones to a lightly oiled pizza pan or baking sheet. Bake until golden brown, about 30 minutes. Allow to sit for 10 minutes before serving.

Serves 4

CHAPTER SEVEN

More Potatoes, Please

Meet the potato—the better half of the "meat and potatoes" pairing that both vegetarians and carnivores can agree on. Everyone loves potatoes. Who didn't grow up virtually addicted to French fries and potato chips? We eat mountains of fluffy mashers and make meals out of delectable stuffed baked potatoes.

From basic baked, boiled, mashed, or fried spuds to homey kugel, potato cakes, and gnocchi, potatoes are at the top of everyone's list of favorite comfort foods—a pure and fundamental food that warms and soothes like few others do. Real potato lovers sneak a few extra potatoes into the oven or pot whenever they prepare potatoes. They know the extras will inspire yet another delicious potato concoction the next day.

Not long ago, potato varieties were limited to "baking" or "boiling" potatoes, and sweet potatoes were reserved for Thanksgiving dinner. These days, however, most supermarkets carry a wide range, from tiny creamers, b-reds, and fingerlings to purple potatoes and buttery Yukon Golds. Sweet potatoes have begun to make the scene year round. No longer hiding under their holiday marshmallow shroud, they are now prepared in many of the same ways regular potatoes are.

Originating in ancient South America, potatoes are enjoyed the world over today, from Africa to Europe to parts of Asia. Whether exploring the exotic tastes of Indian-style potatoes redolent of heady spices or settling into a plateful of comforting Polish pierogi, you can eat your way around the world enjoying global potato dishes.

Many of the recipes in this chapter hold up their end of the "meat and potatoes" partnership by including vegetarian "meats" as well. In addition, there are several recipes for potato dishes where the glorious spud is the main event. And do check out the potato salads on pages 66–76.

Garlic Smashers

Here buttery Yukon Gold potatoes are "smashed" with lots of flavorful garlic and a drizzle of olive oil. Use a hand potato masher to achieve potatoes that are more "smashed" than "mashed." Leave the skins on the potatoes for more flavor, nutrition, and texture.

---

2 pounds Yukon Gold potatoes

Salt

3 to 4 garlic cloves, to your taste, crushed

2 tablespoons extra virgin olive oil

$1/3$ to $1/2$ cup regular or soy milk, as
   needed, warmed

Cayenne

1 Cut the potatoes into quarters and place in a large saucepan with cold water to cover. Salt the water, add the garlic, and bring to a boil. Boil until the potatoes and garlic are fork-tender, about 30 minutes.

2 Drain the potatoes and return them to the saucepan. Add the oil and milk. Coarsely mash with a potato masher, allowing some of the potato pieces to remain intact rather than smooth. Season with salt and cayenne to taste and serve hot.

Serves 4

Creamy Mashed Potatoes with Fresh Chives

—mm—

Vegans and cholesterol-watchers, take note: these creamy chive-flecked mashed potatoes can be made with virtuous soy milk and olive oil instead of the usual cream and butter.

---

2 pounds russet or Yukon Gold potatoes

Salt

2 tablespoons butter or extra virgin olive oil

1/3 to 1/2 cup regular or soy milk, as needed, warmed

1 tablespoon minced fresh chives

Freshly ground black pepper

1 Peel the potatoes and cut into quarters. Place them in a large saucepan with cold water to cover. Salt the water and bring to a boil. Let continue to boil until the potatoes are fork tender, about 30 minutes.

2 Drain the potatoes and mash with a potato masher, ricer, food mill, or rotary mixer. Add the butter and milk, mixing until smooth. Stir in the chives, season with salt and pepper to taste, and serve hot.

Serves 4

Potato Pointers

- The flesh of peeled or cut potatoes darkens when it comes in contact with air, so if you prepare them in advance, place them in a bowl of cold water to cover until ready to use.

- Buy firm potatoes with no cracks, green areas, eyes, or other signs of sprouting. Avoid bruised potatoes. If you find that any of your potatoes have some green parts, cut them out, as they will be bitter. (If a potato is mostly green, discard it.)

- Scrub potatoes well to remove dirt and trim of any imperfections before cooking them.

- Before baking potatoes, pierce them with a fork to allow steam to escape, or you may find exploded potato all over the inside of your oven.

- When boiling potatoes for mashing, for best results, start them in cold water.

- Starchy potatoes with low moisture content, such as Idahos or russets, make the best mashed or baked potatoes and French fries.

- Thin-skinned waxy potatoes, such as red or white "new" (see page 220) potatoes, are best for boiling, steaming, or roasting.

Sesame-Wasabi Mashers

〜〜〜

The subtle heat of wasabi, also known as Japanese horseradish, complemented by a drizzle of toasted sesame oil lends an element of surprise to these creamy East-West mashers. Wasabi powder can be found in Asian markets and well-stocked supermarkets.

---

2 pounds russet or Yukon Gold potatoes, peeled

Salt

1 tablespoon wasabi powder

2 tablespoons water

$1/3$ to $1/2$ cup regular or soy milk, as needed, warmed

$1^1/_2$ tablespoons toasted sesame oil

1 Quarter the potatoes and place in a large saucepan with cold water to cover. Salt the water, bring to a boil, and boil until the potatoes are fork-tender, about 30 minutes.

2 Meanwhile, in a small bowl, combine the wasabi powder and water to make a paste. Set aside.

3 Drain the potatoes and mash with a potato masher, ricer, food mill, or rotary mixer. Stir in the wasabi paste, milk, sesame oil, and salt to taste, mixing until smooth. Serve hot.

Serves 4

Maple-Mashed Sweet Potatoes

The rich flavor of fresh maple syrup complements the natural sweetness of the potatoes without being cloying. You don't have to wait for Thanksgiving to serve them—they taste great anytime.

1¹/₂ pounds sweet potatoes, peeled and cut into chunks

Salt

¹/₂ cup apple juice

¹/₄ cup pure maple syrup

¹/₄ teaspoon ground cinnamon

1 Place the sweet potatoes in a large saucepan with cold water to cover. Salt the water and bring to a boil. Boil until the potatoes are fork-tender, 20 to 30 minutes.

2 Drain the potatoes and place in a large bowl. Add the apple juice, maple syrup, and cinnamon and mash with an electric mixer or a potato masher until smooth. Season to taste with salt and serve hot.

Serves 4

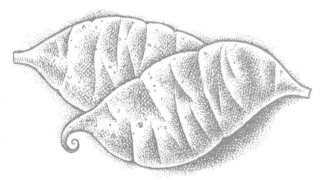

Mushroom-Stuffed Dinner Jacket Potatoes

W hat does a well-scrubbed potato wear for dinner? Why, his dinner jacket, of course. At least, that's what I thought of the first time I heard the phrase "in the jacket" as a reference to baked potatoes.

4 medium-size russet or other baking
   potatoes, well scrubbed

1 tablespoon olive oil

1 cup sliced white mushrooms

1 tablespoon tamari or other soy sauce

Dash of cayenne

3 ounces soft tofu, mashed

Salt

2 tablespoons freshly grated Parmesan
   cheese or soy Parmesan

1 Preheat the oven to 375 degrees F. Prick the potatoes with a fork and bake until soft, about 1 hour. Set aside to cool briefly. Leave the oven on.

2 Meanwhile, heat the oil in a medium-size skillet over medium heat. Add the mushrooms and cook, stirring, until softened, about 2 minutes. Add the tamari, stirring to coat the mushrooms. Set aside.

3 Slice off about $1/2$ inch from the top of each potato, essentially cutting out a lid. Scoop the pulp from the lids into a large bowl, and discard the lids. Carefully scoop out the potato centers, leaving a shell about $1/4$ inch thick, and add to the bowl. Add the tofu and mushrooms, including the pan juices, and season with salt to taste. Mash the potato pulp, mixing well.

4 Spoon one-fourth of the stuffing into each of the hollowed-out potatoes and arrange the stuffed potatoes on a baking sheet. Sprinkle with the Parmesan and return to the oven until the potatoes are heated through and the cheese is melted.

Serves 4

Twice-Baked Spinach-Stuffed Potatoes

These potatoes can be made ahead up through Step 2 and refrigerated; bring them back to room temperature before baking. Each potato makes 2 substantial portions, so the serving amount will depend on what else is on the menu—if the potatoes are the featured dish, this recipe serves 4; if served as a side dish, the recipe accommodates 8.

4 large russet or other baking potatoes, well scrubbed

8 ounces spinach

$1/2$ cup sour cream or tofu sour cream

$1/4$ cup shredded mozzarella cheese or soy mozzarella

Salt and freshly ground black pepper

2 tablespoons freshly grated Parmesan cheese or soy Parmesan

1 Preheat the oven to 375 degrees F. Prick the potatoes with a fork and bake until soft, about 1 hour. Let cool for 10 minutes. Leave the oven on.

2 While the potatoes are baking, steam the spinach over boiling water until tender. Drain well, squeeze the excess liquid from the spinach, and finely chop. Set aside.

3 Halve the potatoes lengthwise. Scoop out the center of each half, leaving a $1/4$-inch shell, and place in a large bowl. Add the spinach, sour cream, mozzarella, and salt and pepper to taste and mix well. Spoon the stuffing into the potato skins and arrange the stuffed potato halves in a large shallow baking dish.

4 Sprinkle the potatoes with the Parmesan and return them to the oven until they are heated through and the cheese is melted.

Serves 4 to 8

Chili-Topped Baked Potatoes

This is an easy variation on the stuffed potato theme. Instead of scooping out the potato flesh, mixing it with other ingredients, and spooning it back inside the potato shells, the baked potatoes are simply split open and topped with a savory vegetarian chili. Other topping ideas could include Roasted Ratatouille (page 272), Garlicky Escarole and Borlotti Beans (page 268), or simply a spoonful of pesto.

4 large russet or other baking potatoes, well scrubbed

2 cups Chili con Frijoles (page 121)

1 Preheat the oven to 375 degrees F. Prick the potatoes with a fork and bake until soft, about I hour.

2 Meanwhile, heat the chili in a saucepan and keep warm.

3 When the potatoes are tender, cut an X in the top of each and press gently against the sides of the potato to open it. Spoon one-fourth of the chili onto each potato and serve hot.

Serves 4

Twice-Spiced Purple Potatoes

The purple color of these potatoes won't be the only cause of a double take. Twice the spice will make your guests sit up and take notice too. Spice them once before baking and again when they come out, for a bold flavor sensation. Small red or white new potatoes may be used if purple potatoes are unavailable. Larger potatoes can be halved or quartered as necessary.

1 1/2 to 2 pounds small purple potatoes

2 tablespoons olive oil

1 teaspoon garlic powder

1 teaspoon sweet paprika

1 teaspoon ground coriander

1/4 teaspoon ground allspice

1 teaspoon salt

1/2 teaspoon ground fennel

1/4 teaspoon cayenne

1 tablespoon chopped fresh parsley
   leaves

1 tablespoon minced fresh chives

1 Preheat the oven to 400 degrees F. Place the potatoes in a large bowl and add the oil, tossing to coat. Sprinkle with the garlic powder, paprika, coriander, allspice, $1/2$ teaspoon of the salt, $1/4$ teaspoon of the fennel, and $1/8$ teaspoon of the cayenne, tossing to coat well.

2 Arrange the potatoes in a single layer on a baking sheet and roast, turning occasionally, until tender, 45 to 50 minutes, depending on their size.

3 Transfer to a serving dish, sprinkle with the remaining $1/2$ teaspoon salt, $1/4$ teaspoon fennel, and $1/8$ teaspoon cayenne, the parsley, and chives, and serve immediately.

Serves 4 to 6

Oven-Browned Steak Fries

These crispy "steak-cut" potatoes are baked in the oven for a healthful alternative to traditional French fries. If you cut the potatoes in advance, be sure to submerge them in a bowl of water so they don't turn brown. Dry them well before using.

4 medium-size russet or other baking
   potatoes, well scrubbed

2 tablespoons olive oil

1/2 teaspoon salt

1/4 teaspoon sweet paprika

1/8 teaspoon freshly ground black pepper

1 Preheat the oven to 425 degrees F. Lightly oil a large baking sheet.

2 Halve the (unpeeled) potatoes lengthwise, then cut each half into 1/4-inch-wide wedges. Place in a large bowl and add the oil, salt, paprika, and pepper. Toss gently to coat the potatoes well.

3 Spread the potatoes in a single layer on the prepared baking sheet. Bake until golden brown and crisp on the outside and soft on the inside, about 25 minutes. Serve hot.

Serves 4 to 6

Sweet Potato Fries

Sweet potatoes, rich in beta carotene and other nutrients, make a colorful and tasty alternative to regular French fries. I find that this is a great way to make sweet potato converts of those who don't like the typical overly sweet glazed or marshmallow-topped preparations. Oven-roasting them this way brings out the natural flavor.

4 large sweet potatoes

2 tablespoons olive oil

$1/2$ teaspoon salt

$1/8$ teaspoon freshly ground black pepper

1 Preheat the oven to 425 degrees F. Lightly oil a large baking sheet and set aside.

2 Peel the sweet potatoes, then cut them lengthwise in half and cut each half into $1/4$-inch-wide wedges. Place the potatoes in a large bowl and add the oil, salt, and pepper. Toss gently to coat the potatoes well.

3 Spread the potatoes in a single layer on the prepared baking sheet. Bake until lightly browned and crisp on the outside and soft on the inside, about 25 minutes. Serve immediately.

Serves 4 to 6

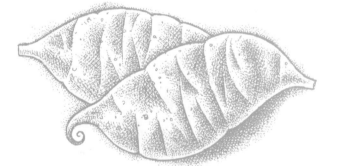

Steamed Purple Potatoes with Fresh Herbs

Tiny Peruvian potatoes in shades of purple or blue are increasingly available in well-stocked supermarkets and specialty greengrocers. These small heirloom potatoes are distinctive for their unusual color, but they also have a sweet, rich flavor. If unavailable, substitute any small new potato. Vary the fresh herbs according to availability and your personal taste.

1½ pounds small purple potatoes

2 tablespoons extra virgin olive oil

1 tablespoon minced fresh parsley leaves

1 tablespoon minced fresh tarragon leaves

1 teaspoon minced fresh chives

Salt and freshly ground black pepper

1 Steam the potatoes over boiling water until tender, about 30 minutes.

2 Transfer the potatoes to a medium-size serving bowl and drizzle with the oil. Sprinkle on the parsley, tarragon, chives, and salt and pepper to taste. Toss gently, and serve at once.

Serves 4

Spanish-Style "Hot Potatoes"

Both temperature hot and spicy hot, these flavorful potatoes are a typical Spanish preparation.

2 tablespoons olive oil

1½ pounds small red potatoes, cut into ¼-inch-thick slices

Salt and freshly ground black pepper

1 teaspoon sweet paprika

¼ to ½ teaspoon cayenne, to taste

1½ tablespoons white wine vinegar

1½ teaspoons tomato paste

1 Heat the oil in a large skillet over medium heat. Add the potato slices and cook until lightly browned on both sides, about 5 minutes. Reduce the heat to low and season to taste with salt and pepper. Cover the skillet and cook until the potatoes are soft, 15 to 20 minutes. Sprinkle the potatoes with the paprika and cayenne, turning gently to coat.

2 In a small bowl, combine the vinegar and tomato paste and blend well. Stir the mixture into the skillet and cook for 2 to 3 minutes, turning the potatoes to coat. Serve hot.

Serves 4

Indian Potatoes and Cauliflower

When I crave a taste of India, I sometimes make this dish, which I serve over basmati rice with a lentil dal. Its lovely golden color is as captivating as its delicious taste and aroma.

1½ pounds all-purpose potatoes, peeled and cut into 1-inch dice

1 small head cauliflower, cut into bite-size florets

½ teaspoon salt

½ teaspoon turmeric

½ teaspoon ground cumin

¼ teaspoon ground coriander

2 tablespoons olive oil

1 small yellow onion, chopped

3 garlic cloves, chopped and mashed to a paste

½ cup unsweetened coconut milk

1 Place the potatoes in a large saucepan with cold water to cover. Salt the water, bring to a boil, and boil until the potatoes are just fork-tender, 15 to 20 minutes. Drain and set aside.

2 Meanwhile, steam the cauliflower until just tender, 5 to 7 minutes. Set aside.

3 In a small bowl, combine the salt, turmeric, cumin, and coriander; set aside.

4 Heat the oil in a large skillet over medium-high heat. Add the onion, cover, and cook, stirring a few times, until softened, about 5 minutes. Stir in the garlic paste and the spice mixture and cook, stirring, until fragrant, about 30 seconds. Add the potatoes and cauliflower and cook, stirring gently to coat with the spice mixture, until lightly browned, about 5 minutes. Gently stir in the coconut milk and heat through before serving.

Serves 4 to 6

New Potato and Walnut Sauté

mm

The crunch of walnuts adds a flavorful surprise to this sophisticated potato dish. Serve it as an accompaniment for a special dinner, or add some sliced seitan or cooked chickpeas and serve it as an entrée. The walnut oil intensifies the flavor of the walnuts, but even made without it, the dish tastes great.

2 pounds small red new potatoes

1 tablespoon olive oil

2 shallots, minced

1/2 teaspoon salt

1/8 teaspoon cayenne

1/2 cup walnut pieces

1 tablespoon walnut oil (optional)

1 tablespoon fresh lemon juice

1 tablespoons minced fresh parsley
  leaves

1 Place the potatoes in a large saucepan with cold water to cover. Salt the water, bring to a boil, and boil until the potatoes are fork-tender, about 30 minutes. Drain well and let cool slightly.

2 Halve or quarter the potatoes, depending on their size. Set aside.

3 Heat the olive oil in a large skillet over medium heat. Add the shallots, cover, and cook, stirring a few times, until softened, 3 to 5 minutes. Add the potatoes and cook, turning occasionally, until browned on all sides, 7 to 10 minutes. Sprinkle with the salt and cayenne. Add the walnuts and cook, stirring occasionally, until they are lightly toasted, about 5 minutes.

4 Transfer the potatoes to a large serving bowl. Add the walnut oil, if using, lemon juice, and parsley and toss gently to coat. Serve at once.

Serves 4 to 6

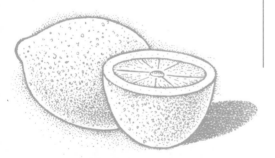

Rum-Kissed Sweet Potato Sauté with Pecans and Cranberries

Even people who don't like sweet potatoes will give this dish a second look. The color, texture, and flavor of the sweet-tart cranberries and crunchy pecans combine beautifully with the sliced sweet potatoes. A splash of rum adds an extra flavor dimension.

2 tablespoons olive oil

1 pound sweet potatoes, peeled and cut into 1/4-inch-thick slices

Salt and freshly ground black pepper

2 tablespoons dark rum

1/2 cup dried cranberries

1/2 cup pecan halves, toasted (page 9)

1/2 teaspoon light brown sugar

1/4 teaspoon ground allspice

1 Heat the oil in a large skillet over medium heat. Add the sweet potato slices and season lightly with salt and pepper. Cover, reduce the heat to low, and cook, turning occasionally, until tender, 15 to 20 minutes.

2 Add the rum, cranberries, pecans, brown sugar, and allspice and cook for another 2 minutes, turning gently to combine. Taste to adjust the seasonings. Serve hot.

Serves 4

Sunday Morning Hash Brown Potatoes

Cooking up a skillet of hash browns is a Sunday morning treat in our house. If you have difficulty flipping the entire "cake" of potatoes, cut it into wedges and flip a portion at a time. Although you can start with raw potatoes, I think they taste better if cooked ahead of time.

1 1/2 pounds russet or other baking
   potatoes, cooked, peeled, and finely
   diced or grated (about 3 cups)
3 tablespoons grated onion
3/4 teaspoon salt
1/8 teaspoon freshly ground black pepper
2 tablespoons olive oil

1 In a large bowl, combine the potatoes, onion, salt, and pepper and mix well.
2 Heat the oil in a large skillet over medium heat. Add the potato mixture and press down with a metal spatula to form a cake. Cook until the potatoes turn golden brown on the bottom, 5 to 7 minutes.
3 Loosen the potatoes from the pan with the spatula and flip them over onto a large plate. Slide back into the pan and cook to brown the other side, about 5 minutes longer. Serve hot.

Serves 4

Tater Trivia

Potatoes are the most popular vegetable in the United States and among the most versatile as well. They are enjoyed on their own in a variety of ways and combine well with root vegetables, squash, and dark leafy greens in soups, stews, and braised or roasted dishes.

Potatoes are rich in potassium and vitamin C, and they also contain vitamin B6, niacin, and iron. Varieties include starchy russets or baking potatoes, semi-waxy "all-purpose" potatoes, and waxy new potatoes, which are actually not a variety at all, but simply freshly dug young potatoes of any type. The buttery Yukon Gold potatoes can be considered an all-purpose potato, and their great taste adds to its popularity. In addition, there are a number of specialty potatoes, such as tiny purple potatoes and the finger-shaped fingerling potatoes, which are best prepared steamed to appreciate their delicate flavor. Sweet potatoes are tubers that are not related to potatoes, although they can be cooked in similar ways.

Lemon-Oregano Home Fries

Greek-inspired flavors turn leftover potatoes into something special.

3 tablespoons olive oil

1 small yellow onion, finely minced

1 small red bell pepper, seeded and
chopped

3 to 4 leftover baked potatoes, peeled
and cut into $1/2$-inch dice

1 teaspoon minced fresh oregano leaves
or $1/2$ teaspoon dried

1 teaspoon sweet paprika

Salt and freshly ground black pepper

2 tablespoons fresh lemon juice

1 Heat the oil in a large skillet over medium heat. Add the onion, cover, and cook, stirring a few times, until softened, about 5 minutes. Add the bell pepper and cook for 2 minutes to soften slightly. Add the potatoes and cook, turning occasionally, until golden brown, 10 to 15 minutes.

2 Add the oregano, paprika, and salt and pepper to taste and cook for 2 to 3 minutes to blend the flavors. Just before serving, drizzle on the lemon juice and toss gently to combine.

Serves 4

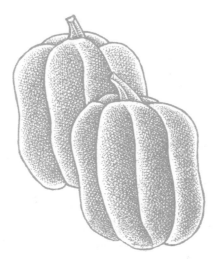

Sam's Truck-Stop Hash with Red Onion–Green Apple Marmalade

My friend Samantha Ragan likes to experiment with new dishes. She came up with this stick-to-your-ribs meatless hash that reminded us of the hearty hash often served at truck-stop diners—but without the indigestion. The red onion marmalade elevates it to a special brunch dish, or, if you prefer, serve it truck stop–style with ketchup. This is an ideal destination for leftover baked potatoes and can be made with chopped tempeh or seitan instead of the veggie burgers, if you like.

1 tablespoon olive oil

1 large yellow onion, chopped

1 small red bell pepper, seeded and chopped

3 large cooked potatoes, diced

2 or 3 frozen vegetarian burgers, thawed and chopped

1 tablespoon tamari or other soy sauce

1/2 teaspoon salt, or more to taste

1/8 teaspoon freshly ground black pepper

Red Onion–Green Apple Marmalade (page 323)

1 Heat the oil in a large skillet over medium heat. Add the onion and bell pepper, cover, and cook, stirring a few times, until softened, about 5 minutes.

2 Add the potatoes and cook, stirring frequently, until lightly browned, 3 to 5 minutes. Stir in the veggie burgers and cook until lightly browned, about 3 minutes. Add the tamari, salt, and pepper and cook until the flavors are blended, about 5 minutes. Serve with the onion marmalade or ketchup.

Serves 4 to 6

Red Flannel Hash

Like the original, this hash gets its vibrant red color from beets. Unlike the original, it's made with tempeh rather than beef. For a more intense flavor, use roasted beets and potatoes (it's a great way to use leftovers).

4 small red beets

3 medium-size all-purpose potatoes

8 ounces tempeh

2 tablespoons olive oil

1 large red onion, chopped

1 tablespoon tamari or other soy sauce

1/2 teaspoon salt or more to taste

1/8 teaspoon cayenne

1 Cook the beets in boiling salted water to cover until tender, about 30 minutes. Drain and cool under cold water. Peel and chop; set aside.

2 Peel and dice the potatoes. Steam over boiling water until tender, about 20 minutes. Drain and set aside.

3 Place the tempeh in a small saucepan with water to cover and bring to a simmer over medium heat. Let simmer for 10 minutes, then drain and allow to cool.

4 Finely chop or grate the tempeh and set aside.

5 Heat the oil in a large skillet over medium heat. Add the onion, cover, and cook, stirring a few times, until softened, about 5 minutes. Add the potatoes, beets, and tempeh, increase the heat to medium-high, and cook, stirring frequently, until the potatoes and tempeh are lightly browned, about 5 minutes. Add the tamari, salt, and cayenne and cook until the flavors are blended, about 5 minutes. Serve hot, with ketchup.

Serves 4 to 6

Fettuccine with Potatoes and Pesto

C an't decide on pasta or potatoes for dinner tonight? Surprise everyone and serve them both. Although strong on carbohydrates, this intriguing combination is a favorite in many areas of Italy.

3/4 pound small new potatoes, peeled
and cut into 1/4-inch-thick slices

2 tablespoons olive oil

2 garlic cloves, minced

3/4 cup basil pesto, homemade
(page 313) or store-bought

1 pound fettuccine

Salt and freshly ground black pepper

1 Steam the potatoes over boiling water until just tender, 8 to 10 minutes. Set aside.

2 Heat the oil in a large skillet over medium heat. Add the garlic and cook until fragrant, about 30 seconds. Add the potatoes and pesto, stirring to coat the potatoes. Keep warm over low heat.

3 Cook the fettuccine in a large pot of boiling salted water, stirring occasionally, until *al dente*, about 8 minutes. Drain the pasta, reserving 1/3 cup of the pasta cooking water, and place in a large shallow serving bowl.

4 Add the potato mixture and the reserved pasta water to the pasta. Season to taste with salt and pepper and toss gently to combine. Serve immediately.

Serves 4 to 6

Potato-Tofu "Frittata"

This adaptation of a hearty Italian omelet is made with tofu instead of eggs. As with a traditional frittata, the cooking begins on top of the stove and finishes in the oven. This is another good use for leftover baked potatoes.

1 pound firm tofu, crumbled

1/4 cup regular or soy milk

1/4 cup chopped fresh parsley leaves

1/8 teaspoon turmeric

1/2 cup shredded mozzarella cheese or soy mozzarella

Salt and freshly ground black pepper

1 tablespoon olive oil

2 garlic cloves, minced

2 large Yukon Gold or russet potatoes, baked or roasted and cut into 1/2-inch dice

1 Preheat the oven to 400 degrees F. Place half the tofu in a food processor, along with the milk, parsley, turmeric, 1/4 cup of the cheese, and salt and pepper to taste. Process until smooth. Set aside.

2 Heat the oil in a large ovenproof skillet over medium heat. Add the garlic and potatoes and cook, turning occasionally, until the potatoes are lightly browned on all sides, about 5 minutes. Add the remaining crumbled tofu and the pureed tofu mixture, stirring to combine well. Cook for 5 minutes, or until the mixture is beginning to set.

3 Transfer the frittata to the oven and bake until firm and hot, about 20 minutes.

4 Sprinkle with the remaining 1/4 cup cheese and return to the oven to melt the cheese, about 5 minutes. Let stand for 10 minutes before cutting into wedges to serve.

Serves 4

Potato-Tomato Gratin

～～～

Gratins are often made with a small amount of liquid, either broth or cream. Because of the high water content of the tomatoes in this gratin, however, no additional liquid is necessary.

1½ pounds Yukon Gold or other all-
purpose potatoes, peeled and cut into
¼-inch-thick slices

¼ cup olive oil

1 large yellow onion, minced

2 garlic cloves, minced

½ teaspoon dried basil

Salt and freshly ground white pepper

3 large ripe tomatoes, peeled and cut
into thin slices

2 tablespoons chopped capers

½ cup fresh bread crumbs

½ cup freshly grated Parmesan cheese
or soy Parmesan

¼ teaspoon sweet paprika

1 Preheat the oven to 375 degrees F. Lightly oil a 2-quart gratin dish. Cook the potato slices in a pot of boiling salted water until slightly softened, 3 to 5 minutes. Drain, rinse, and set aside.

2 Heat 2 tablespoons of the oil in a large skillet over medium heat. Add the onion, garlic, basil, and salt and pepper to taste, cover, and cook, stirring a few times, until the onion is softened, about 5 minutes. Set aside.

3 Arrange half of the potatoes in the bottom of the prepared gratin dish, overlapping them. Top with half of the onion mixture and half of the tomatoes. Season with salt and pepper and sprinkle on half of the chopped capers. Top with a layer of the remaining potatoes, then the remaining onion mixture and remaining tomatoes, the remaining capers, and salt and pepper to taste.

4 In a small bowl, combine the bread crumbs with the remaining 2 tablespoons oil, the Parmesan, and paprika. Blend gently with a fork to combine, and sprinkle on top of the gratin.

5 Cover the gratin with a sheet of aluminum foil and bake for 30 minutes, then remove the foil and bake until the potatoes are soft and the top is golden brown, about 30 minutes longer. Serve hot.

Serves 4 to 6

Provençal Potato and Vegetable Tian

A classic tian is a slow-cooked casserole of vegetables, olive oil, and aromatic herbs that hails from the South of France. In this version, potatoes take center stage but get lots of support—and flavor—from the surrounding vegetables. A shallow casserole dish may be used in place of the earthenware baking dish for which the tian is named. Herbes de Provence is a mixture of dried herbs that usually includes thyme, savory, basil, rosemary, and, sometimes, lavender. It is available at specialty food shops and gourmet markets.

1½ pounds small waxy potatoes, peeled and thinly sliced

1 small yellow onion, chopped

1 small red bell pepper, seeded and diced

1 small carrot, thinly sliced

3 garlic cloves, minced

3 ripe plum tomatoes, peeled, seeded, and chopped

¼ cup vegetable stock (page 36) or water

¼ cup olive oil

1 teaspoon dried herbes de Provence

Salt and freshly ground black pepper

1 cup fresh bread crumbs

1 Preheat the oven to 400 degrees F. In a large bowl, combine the potatoes, onion, bell pepper, carrot, garlic, and tomatoes. Add the vegetable stock and 3 tablespoons of the oil. Season with the herbes de Provence and salt and pepper to taste. Toss well to coat the vegetables with the oil and seasonings.

2 Transfer the mixture to a large shallow baking dish and spread out evenly. Cover tightly with a sheet of aluminum foil and bake until the potatoes and carrots are tender, about 45 minutes.

3 Meanwhile, in a small bowl, combine the bread crumbs with the remaining 1 tablespoon oil.

4 Remove the tian from the oven, uncover, and sprinkle the bread crumb mixture on top. Return to the oven and bake for about 15 minutes longer to brown the crumbs. Serve hot.

Serves 4 to 6

Golden Potato Kugel

The flavor of this potato kugel is similar to that of potato pancakes, but it's considerably less time-consuming to prepare and healthier, since it isn't fried. Enriched with soy protein, the dish makes a worthy brunch entrée or hearty side dish. Made with Yukon Gold potatoes and a pinch of turmeric, it has a lovely golden color; ground almonds add texture and flavor.

1½ pounds Yukon Gold or other
   all-purpose potatoes

1 large yellow onion

8 ounces soft or silken tofu

3/4 cup regular or soy milk

1 large garlic clove, pressed

1 teaspoon salt

1/4 teaspoon turmeric

1/8 teaspoon cayenne

1/8 teaspoon freshly ground black pepper

1/4 cup finely minced fresh parsley leaves

1/2 cup finely ground almonds

1 Preheat the oven to 400 degrees F. Lightly oil a shallow 9 x 14-inch baking dish.

2 Peel the potatoes. Grate the potatoes and onion, using a box grater or food processor, and place in a colander. Press out the excess moisture and transfer to a large bowl.

3 In a food processor or blender, combine the tofu, milk, garlic, salt, turmeric, cayenne, and black pepper and blend until smooth. Stir the tofu mixture into the potato mixture, blending well. Stir in the parsley.

4 Transfer the mixture to the prepared baking dish. Cover with a sheet of aluminum foil and bake for 45 minutes.

5 Remove the foil, sprinkle with the ground almonds, and bake until they are lightly browned, 10 to 15 minutes longer. Let stand for 10 minutes before cutting into squares.

Serves 4

Potato-Onion Pierogi

B e sure to cool the filling before assembling these, or they will self-destruct. Pierogi are delicious served with dairy or nondairy sour cream or applesauce on the side. Uncooked pierogi freeze well. To freeze, arrange them in a single layer on a baking sheet and place in the freezer until frozen hard, then remove from the sheet and store in a freezer bag. Defrost before cooking. Flaxseeds are available in natural food stores.

Filling:

1 1/2 pounds russet potatoes, peeled and
   cut into chunks

1 teaspoon salt

1/4 teaspoon freshly ground black pepper

2 tablespoons olive oil

1 large yellow onion, finely minced

Dough:

1 tablespoon ground flaxseeds

1 cup water

3 cups all-purpose flour

1 teaspoon salt

Butter or olive oil for cooking

1 *Make the filling:* Place the potatoes in a large saucepan with cold water to cover. Salt the water, bring to a boil, and boil until tender, about 20 minutes. Drain the potatoes and mash with a potato masher or ricer. Season with the salt and pepper and set aside.

2 Heat the oil in a medium-size skillet over medium heat. Add the onion, cover, and cook, stirring a few times, until softened, about 5 minutes. Stir the onion into the mashed potatoes and taste to adjust the seasonings. Set aside to cool completely.

3 *Make the dough:* Combine the ground flaxseeds and 1/4 cup of the water in a blender and blend until thick and frothy. Set aside.

4 Combine the flour and salt in a large bowl and make a well in the center. Add the flax mixture and the remaining 3/4 cup water and stir to form a stiff dough. Turn out onto a lightly floured work surface and knead until smooth. Divide the dough into 2 equal portions.

5 One at a time, roll out the dough portions on the floured work surface to a rectangle about 1/8 inch thick. Cut into 3- to 4-inch-wide strips and then cut

continued

across the strips to create 3- to 4-inch squares. Put a heaping tablespoon of filling onto one half of each dough square. Moisten the edges of each square and fold in half to form a triangle. Using your fingers, press the edges together to seal well. For a decorative edge, press the tines of a fork into $1/4$ inch of the edges of each pierogi.

6 To cook, bring a large pot of salted water to a boil. Carefully add the pierogi, in batches, and cook until they float to the top, 2 to 3 minutes. Drain well and place on a platter.

7 To serve, lightly brown the pierogi, in batches, in a large skillet using a tablespoon or so of butter or oil. Transfer to a platter and cover to keep warm while you cook the remaining pierogi. Serve hot.

Serves 6

Potato Pancakes with Apples and Cinnamon

These potato cakes are imbued with the tart-sweet taste of Granny Smith apples. I like to serve them as part of a brunch buffet, but the temptation is to eat them for dessert. Serve them with regular or soy yogurt or sour cream. Flaxseeds are available at natural food stores.

1 tablespoon ground flaxseeds

3 tablespoons water

1 pound russet or other baking potatoes

1 small yellow onion

1 large Granny Smith apple, peeled and cored

1/4 cup all-purpose flour

1 teaspoon ground cinnamon

1 teaspoon light brown sugar

3/4 teaspoon salt

Peanut oil for frying

1 Combine the flaxseeds and water in a blender and blend until thick and frothy, about 1 minute. Set aside.

2 Peel the potatoes. Using a hand grater or a food processor, grate the potatoes, onion, and apple. Place them in a colander and press out the excess liquid. Transfer the mixture to a large bowl and stir in the flax mixture, flour, cinnamon, brown sugar, and salt, blending well.

3 Preheat the oven to 250 degrees F. Pour a thin layer of oil into a large nonstick skillet and heat over medium-high heat. Using a large spoon, scoop out a spoonful of the potato mixture and shape into a pancake. Place in the hot skillet and flatten with a metal spatula. Repeat to make more pancakes, without crowding the pan. Cook until crisp and golden brown on the bottom, about 5 minutes. Turn and cook until browned on the other side, about 3 to 5 minutes longer. Drain the pancakes on paper towels, then transfer them to an ovenproof platter and keep warm in the oven. Repeat with the remaining potato mixture, adding more oil to the pan as necessary. Serve hot.

Serves 4 to 6

Plan-Ahead Potato Cakes

I learned this version of potato pancakes, made with leftover mashed potatoes, from my mother. But when I make mashed potatoes, there are rarely leftovers, so if I want to serve these delicious potato cakes, I have to plan ahead to make extra mashers and put them aside so they don't disappear.

1³/₄ cups cold mashed potatoes

2 scallions, minced

1 tablespoon minced fresh parsley leaves

Salt and freshly ground black pepper

All-purpose flour for dredging

2 tablespoons olive oil

1 Place the mashed potatoes in a large bowl, add the scallions, parsley, and salt and pepper to taste, and mix well.

2 Scoop out a spoonful of the potato mixture and, using your hands, shape it into a patty about ¹/₄ inch thick. Repeat until all the mixture is used up. You should end up with 8 to 10 potato cakes. Dredge the cakes in flour, tapping off any excess, and set aside.

3 Preheat the oven to 250 degrees F. Heat the oil in a large skillet over medium-high heat. Add the potato cakes, in batches, and cook, turning once, until crisp and golden brown on both sides, about 10 minutes total. Drain on paper towels, then transfer to an ovenproof platter and keep warm in the oven. Serve hot.

Serves 4

Chive-Flecked Potato Latkes

Some versions of latkes, or potato pancakes, call for eggs and flour in the mixture, but I prefer to make them without. The chives add extra flavor and a bit of color. If they are unavailable, finely mince the green part of 1 or 2 scallions. Be sure to wait until the pancakes are crisp and well browned on the first side before turning them. Serve with applesauce or regular or soy sour cream.

1¹/₂ pounds russet or other baking
　　potatoes

1 small yellow onion

2 tablespoons minced fresh chives

1 teaspoon salt

Freshly ground black pepper

Olive oil for frying

1　Peel the potatoes. Using a hand grater or a food processor, grate the potatoes and onion. Place them in a colander and press out the excess liquid. Transfer to a large bowl, add the chives and salt and pepper to taste, and mix well.

2　Preheat the oven to 250 degrees F. Heat a thin layer of oil in a large nonstick skillet over medium-high heat. In batches, place large spoonfuls of the potato mixture in the hot skillet and flatten with a metal spatula. Cook, turning once, until golden brown on both sides, about 5 minutes per side. Transfer to paper towels to drain and keep warm on a heatproof platter in the oven. Repeat with remaining potato mixture, adding more oil to the pan as necessary. Serve hot.

Serves 4 to 6

Four-Vegetable Latkes

Carrots and zucchini share the spotlight with the traditional potatoes and onions in this yummy latke adaptation. It's a good way to get finicky family members to eat their veggies. Like traditional latkes, these are delicious with applesauce or dairy or nondairy sour cream.

1 large russet or other baking potato

1 small carrot

1 small yellow onion

1 small zucchini, ends trimmed

1 large egg or egg replacer for 1 egg (see page 342)

1/4 cup all-purpose flour

1 teaspoon salt

1/2 teaspoon dried basil

1/8 teaspoon cayenne

Peanut oil for frying

1 Peel the potato and carrot. Using a hand grater or a food processor, grate the potato, carrot, onion, and zucchini. Place them in a colander and press out the excess liquid. Transfer the mixture to a large bowl. Add the egg, flour, salt, basil, and cayenne and mix well.

2 Preheat the oven to 250 degrees F. Heat a thin layer of oil in a large nonstick skillet over medium-high heat. In batches, place large spoonfuls of the potato mixture in the hot skillet and flatten with a metal spatula. Cook, turning once, until golden brown on both sides, about 5 minutes per side. Transfer to paper towels to drain and keep warm on a heatproof platter in the oven. Repeat with the remaining potato mixture. Serve hot.

Serves 4 to 6

Potato Gnocchi

Gnocchi are at once simple to make and yet a bit fussy. It is important to make sure the potatoes are still warm when you make the dough. Although gnocchi don't keep well under refrigeration, they do freeze well. To freeze, place the raw gnocchi on baking sheets in the freezer for several hours, or overnight; once they are frozen hard, transfer them to plastic bags and store in the freezer for up to a month. Gnocchi are delicious served with tomato sauce, pesto sauce, or simply a bit of melted butter and grated cheese.

2 large russet or other baking potatoes

1 cup all-purpose flour, or more as needed

3/4 teaspoon salt

1/4 teaspoon freshly ground black pepper

2 tablespoons minced fresh parsley leaves

1/4 cup freshly grated Parmesan cheese or soy Parmesan (optional)

1 Preheat the oven to 400 degrees F. Pierce the potatoes in several places with a fork and bake until soft, about 1 hour. Meanwhile, put the flour in a large bowl and sprinkle with the salt and pepper. Set aside.

2 While the potatoes are still hot, peel and run them through a potato ricer, or mash with a potato masher until they are fluffy.

3 Make a well in the center of the flour and place the mashed potatoes in the well, along with the parsley and cheese, if using. With a spoon, gradually draw the flour into the potatoes to form a slightly sticky dough, adding more flour as necessary. Knead the dough for about 3 minutes, just long enough to make a smooth dough; do not overwork. Divide the dough into 6 pieces.

4 On a floured board, roll each piece of dough under the palms of your hands into a 1/2-inch-thick rope. Using a knife, cut each dough rope into 3/4-inch lengths. Roll each piece of dough between your fingers briefly to round off the edges, pressing the tines of a fork against one side to achieve the classic gnocchi shape, if desired.

continued

5 To cook the gnocchi, bring a large pot of salted water to boil. Add the gnocchi and cook, uncovered, until they float to the top, 1 to 2 minutes. Drain carefully and serve at once with your favorite sauce.

Serves 4

Sweet Potato Gnocchi with Caramelized Shallot Rings

Sweet potatoes can be used to make delicious and colorful gnocchi that are equally at home as an entrée or side dish.

2 large sweet potatoes, well scrubbed

1¼ cups all-purpose flour

¾ teaspoon salt

⅛ teaspoon freshly ground black pepper

2 tablespoons extra virgin olive oil

3 or 4 shallots, to your taste, thinly sliced
    and pulled apart into rings

1 teaspoon minced fresh marjoram
    leaves

1 Preheat the oven to 400 degrees F. Pierce the potatoes in several places with a fork. Bake until soft, about 1 hour. Remove from the oven and let cool slightly. Reduce the oven temperature to 300 degrees F.

2 While the potatoes are baking, place the flour in a large bowl and sprinkle with the salt and pepper.

3 As soon as the potatoes are cool enough to touch, peel and run them through a potato ricer, or mash with a potato masher until they are fluffy.

4 Make a well in the center of the flour and place the potatoes in the well. Using a spoon, gradually draw

the flour into the potatoes until a dough is formed. Knead for 5 minutes, then divide into 6 pieces.

5 On a floured board, roll each piece of dough under the palms of your hands into a rope about $1/2$ inch in diameter. With a knife, cut each rope into $3/4$-inch lengths. Roll each piece between your fingers briefly to shape into a ball. Or, if desired, roll each piece briefly to round off the edges, pressing the tines of a fork to achieve the classic gnocchi shape.

6 To cook the gnocchi, bring a large pot of salted water to a boil. Add the gnocchi and cook until they float to the top, 1 to 2 minutes. Remove with a slotted spoon and place in a colander to drain well, then transfer the gnocchi to a baking sheet or large shallow baking dish, arranging them in a single layer. Place in the oven to keep warm while you prepare the shallots.

7 Heat the oil in a large skillet over medium-high heat. Add the shallots and cook, stirring occasionally, until crisp and golden brown, about 10 minutes.

8 Remove the gnocchi from the oven, sprinkle with the marjoram and shallots, drizzle with the oil in which the shallots cooked, and serve hot.

Serves 4

Pasta and Other Comforts

I n some areas of the world, favorite "meat and potatoes" comfort foods don't center around meat or potatoes at all, but rather around pasta, grains, and vegetable dishes. Consider the satisfying *Vegetable Donburi* of Japan or the *Jasmine Fried Rice* and *Pad Thai* of Thailand. Among other global vegetarian comfort foods are Italy's polenta and creamy risotto dishes, Russia's *Kasha Varnishkas*, and Mexican favorites such as *Bean and Chile Burritos*.

In addition to pasta and grain dishes, this chapter includes a selection of versatile vegetable side dishes that are so delicious and full of flavor I think of them as being in the same class of comfort foods, because when you eat them, you want more—the tastes you can't get enough of. *Coconut Creamed Spinach* and *Roasted Asparagus* are among the vegetable accompaniments that can be served alongside your favorite vegetarian meat and potatoes meal.

Spaghetti and "Meatballs"

Ziti with Mushroom and Green Peppercorn
  Sauce

Baked Ziti and Eggplant

Layered Vegetable Lasagna

Baked Macaroni with a Twist

Creamy Tahini Broccoli and Pasta Bake

Caraway Cabbage and Noodles

Chinese Noodle Pancake

Pad Thai

Couscous with Pistachios and
  Dried Cranberries

Cilantro Polenta Wedges with Black Beans
  and Roasted Yellow Peppers

Baked Polenta with Porcini Mushrooms

Butternut Squash Risotto

Jasmine Fried Rice

Vegetable Donburi

Kasha Varnishkas

Millet-Cauliflower "Mashed Potatoes"

Fruity Bulgur Pilaf

Rasta Red Beans and Rice

Bean and Chile Burritos

Garlicky Escarole and Borlotti Beans

Sesame Green Beans and Shallots

Coconut Creamed Spinach

Roasted Asparagus with Orange-Thyme Aïoli

Roasted Ratatouille

Niçoise Vegetable Sauté

Underground Vegetable Sauté

Spaghetti and "Meatballs"

⌁⌁⌁

As in many Italian-American families, spaghetti and meatballs was the equivalent of "meat and potatoes" in my house while growing up. I find the consistency of most brands of veggie burgers to be ideal to shape into "meatballs," because they hold together well. For a great-tasting tomato sauce without "meatballs," simply omit the first three ingredients (and reduce the oil to I tablespoon), and proceed with the recipe. Serve over pasta, as in the recipe, or use in other recipes such as the lasagna on page 246.

---

4 frozen vegetarian burgers, thawed

2 tablespoons minced fresh parsley leaves

1 tablespoon freshly grated Parmesan cheese or soy Parmesan, plus more for serving

2 tablespoons olive oil

1 small yellow onion, chopped

2 garlic cloves, minced

2 tablespoons tomato paste

One 28-ounce can crushed tomatoes

$^1/_2$ cup dry red wine

$^1/_2$ teaspoon dried oregano

$^1/_2$ teaspoon dried basil

Salt and freshly ground black pepper

1 pound spaghetti

1 Place the veggie burgers in a large bowl, add I table-spoon of the parsley and the Parmesan, and, using your hands, mix until well combined. Divide the mixture evenly into 12 portions and shape into "meatballs."

2 Heat I tablespoon of the oil in a large skillet over medium-high heat, add the "meatballs," and cook, turning occasionally, until browned on all sides, 5 to 7 minutes. Keep warm over very low heat or in a low oven.

3 Heat the remaining I tablespoon oil in a large sauce-pan over medium heat. Add the onion and garlic, cover, and cook, stirring a few times, until softened, about 5 minutes. Stir in the tomato paste. Add the tomatoes, wine, oregano, basil, and salt and pepper to taste, reduce the heat to low, and simmer, uncovered, for I5 to 20 minutes to blend the flavors.

continued

4 While the sauce is simmering, cook the spaghetti in a large pot of boiling salted water, stirring occasionally, until it is *al dente*, about 10 minutes. Drain well.

5 Divide the pasta among four plates or shallow bowls. Top each plate of pasta with 3 of the "meatballs" and ladle the sauce over all. Serve at once, with additional cheese to pass at the table.

Serves 4

Ziti with Mushroom and Green Peppercorn Sauce

B ottled green peppercorns add a surprising bite to this satisfying pasta sauce made with tomatoes, garlic, and an abundance of chopped mushrooms. Although regular white mushrooms are used here, a more woodsy variety may be used instead if you prefer. The credit for this dish goes to my husband, Jon, who created it one day after foraging in the refrigerator.

1 tablespoon olive oil

1 small yellow onion, minced

8 ounces white button mushrooms, chopped

3 large garlic cloves, minced

One 28-ounce can diced tomatoes, drained

1 teaspoon bottled green peppercorns, drained

Salt and freshly ground black pepper

1 pound ziti or other tubular pasta

1 Heat the oil in a large skillet over medium heat. Add the onion, cover, and cook, stirring a few times, until softened, about 5 minutes. Add the mushrooms and garlic and cook, stirring a few times, until the mushrooms release their liquid and are tender, about 5 minutes. Stir in the tomatoes, peppercorns, and salt and pepper to taste. Simmer for 5 to 10 minutes to allow the flavors to develop. Keep warm over low heat.

2 Meanwhile, cook the ziti in a large pot of boiling salted water, stirring occasionally, until *al dente*, 8 to 10 minutes. Drain well.

3 Transfer the ziti to a large bowl, add the sauce, and toss gently to combine. Serve hot.

Serves 4

Baked Ziti and Eggplant

To add protein and increase the yield, a pound of crumbled tofu can be incorporated to this tasty casserole, which can be assembled ahead of time and popped in the oven when ready to eat.

2 tablespoons olive oil

1 medium-size yellow onion, minced

1 medium-size eggplant, ends trimmed, peeled, and chopped

1 garlic clove, minced

One 28-ounce can crushed tomatoes

$1/2$ cup dry red wine

$1/4$ cup chopped fresh parsley leaves

1 tablespoon chopped fresh basil leaves or $1^1/_2$ teaspoons dried

Salt and freshly ground black pepper

1 pound ziti

$1/2$ cup freshly grated Parmesan cheese or soy Parmesan

8 ounces mozzarella cheese or soy mozzarella, shredded

1 Preheat the oven to 375 degrees F. Heat the oil in a large skillet over medium heat. Add the onion, cover, and cook, stirring a few times, until softened, about 5 minutes. Add the eggplant and garlic, cover, and cook, stirring a few times, for 5 minutes. Stir in the tomatoes, wine, parsley, basil, and salt and pepper to taste and simmer, uncovered, for 15 minutes to blend the flavors.

2 Meanwhile, cook the ziti in a large pot of boiling salted water, stirring occasionally, until just *al dente*, 8 to 10 minutes. Drain and set aside.

3 In a large bowl, combine the cooked ziti with the sauce, Parmesan, and half of the mozzarella. Spoon the mixture into a large baking dish and sprinkle with the remaining mozzarella. Bake until hot and lightly browned on top, 30 to 40 minutes. Serve hot.

Serves 6

Extraordinary Eggplant

Eggplant is popular in the cuisines of much of the world, including Asia, India, and the Mediterranean regions. Its meatiness makes it an ideal vegetarian ingredient in recipes that benefit from its texture. Extremely versatile, eggplant can prepared in a number of ways—halved and stuffed, sliced and fried, chopped and sautéed, roasted and pureed.

The large dark purple pear-shaped eggplant is the most well known variety in the United States. Other varieties include the smaller globe-shaped Italian, long thin Chinese and Japanese, and small white egg-shaped eggplants, which all tend to be less bitter than the large American eggplant.

While it is often recommended that eggplant be sliced, salted, and weighted to remove the bitterness, I haven't found the difference in flavor to be worth the trouble. My feeling is that you either love the taste of eggplant or you don't. Still, if you're on the fence about eggplant because you think it might be bitter, the simplest solution is to buy the smaller varieties.

Any way you slice it, eggplant is one of the great vegetarian "meats."

Layered Vegetable Lasagna

O ffering a delicious surprise in every bite, this sumptuous lasagna is endowed with layers of sliced artichoke hearts, portobello mushrooms, and zucchini. Use your favorite bottled pasta sauce or make your own, following the recipe on page 241.

3 large portobello mushroom caps

2 tablespoons olive oil

1 large zucchini, ends trimmed and thinly
   sliced on a diagonal

Salt and freshly ground black pepper

12 ounces lasagna noodles

2 pounds firm tofu

1/4 cup minced fresh parsley leaves

1/4 cup freshly grated Parmesan cheese
   or soy Parmesan

3 cups tomato sauce, homemade or
   store-bought

1 1/2 cups shredded mozzarella cheese or
   soy mozzarella

One 9-ounce package frozen artichoke
   hearts, cooked according to package
   instructions, drained, and thinly sliced

1 With a sharp knife or a spoon, carefully remove the dark brown gills from the underside of the mushrooms. Cut the mushrooms horizontally to make 6 slices total. Set aside.

2 Heat the oil in a large skillet over medium heat. Add the zucchini slices, season with salt and pepper to taste, and cook, stirring several times, until softened, about 5 minutes. Remove from the skillet and set aside.

3 Add the portobellos to the skillet and cook until they release their liquid, 2 to 3 minutes. Transfer to paper towels to drain.

4 Preheat the oven to 350 degrees F. Cook the lasagna noodles in a large pot of salted boiling water until *al dente*, about 10 minutes. Drain and lay out on a work surface so they don't stick together.

5 In a large bowl, combine the tofu, parsley, Parmesan, and salt and pepper to taste, blending well. Spread a thin layer of tomato sauce in the bottom of a 9 x 13-inch baking dish. Top with a layer of noodles. Top the noodles with half of the tofu mixture, then a layer of half the zucchini slices and

another layer of noodles. Spread some sauce over the noodles and sprinkle with one-quarter of the mozzarella. Top with the remaining tofu mixture, then the mushroom and artichoke slices and another layer of noodles. Top with the remaining tomato sauce and mozzarella.

6 Bake until bubbly, about 45 minutes. Let stand for 10 to 15 minutes before cutting.

Serves 6 to 8

Baked Macaroni with a Twist

There's actually more than one twist to this updated interpretation of classic macaroni and cheese. Made with rotini pasta "twists" instead of the traditional elbow macaroni, it also contains a twist of lemon, and tofu and miso paste for flavor and substance. Miso paste is available in natural food stores and Asian markets.

1 tablespoon olive oil

1 medium-size yellow onion, minced

2 cups regular or soy milk

12 ounces soft or silken tofu

1 tablespoon fresh lemon juice

1 teaspoon white miso paste

Dash of Tabasco sauce

Pinch of turmeric

Salt and freshly ground black pepper

12 ounces rotini pasta

1 cup grated Monterey Jack or soy cheese

$^1/_2$ cup dry bread crumbs

1 Preheat the oven to 375 degrees F. Lightly oil a $2^1/2$-quart casserole dish.

2 Heat the oil in a small skillet over medium heat. Add the onion, cover, and cook, stirring a few times, until softened, about 5 minutes. Transfer to a food processor or blender and add the milk, tofu, lemon juice, miso, Tabasco, turmeric, and salt and pepper to taste. Process until well blended. Set aside.

3 Cook the pasta in a large pot of salted boiling water until *al dente*, about 8 minutes. Drain the pasta and place it in a large bowl.

4 Add the sauce and half of the cheese to the pasta and stir to combine, then transfer to the prepared casserole dish and top with the bread crumbs and the remaining cheese.

5 Cover and bake for 30 minutes. Uncover and bake until the top is lightly browned, 5 to 10 minutes longer. Let sit for 5 to 10 minutes before serving.

Serves 4 to 6

Creamy Tahini Broccoli and Pasta Bake

This "melting pot" casserole combines Italian pasta and cheese, Middle Eastern sesame paste, and Japanese tofu and soy sauce for an all-American one-dish meal, which can be assembled ahead of time. If radiatore are unavailable, elbow macaroni or another bite-size pasta shape can be substituted.

12 ounces radiatore pasta

3 cups chopped broccoli florets

2 tablespoons olive oil

1 small onion, minced

2 garlic cloves, chopped

12 ounces soft or silken tofu, crumbled

1/2 cup tahini (sesame paste)

2 tablespoons tamari or other soy sauce

2 tablespoons fresh lemon juice

1/4 cup chopped fresh parsley leaves

Salt and freshly ground black pepper

1/3 cup dry bread crumbs

1 cup shredded mozzarella cheese or soy mozzarella

1 Preheat the oven to 375 degrees F. Lightly oil a 2-quart casserole dish.

2 Cook the pasta in a large pot of boiling salted water, stirring occasionally, until *al dente*, 8 to 10 minutes. About 5 minutes before the pasta is cooked, add the broccoli. Drain well and set aside.

3 Meanwhile, heat 1 tablespoon of the oil in a large skillet over medium-high heat. Add the onion and garlic, cover, and cook, stirring a few times, until softened, about 5 minutes. Set aside.

4 In a food processor or blender, combine the tofu, tahini, tamari, lemon juice, parsley, the onion mixture, and salt and pepper to taste and process until smooth. Taste to adjust the seasonings.

5 In a large bowl, combine the pasta and broccoli with the tofu-tahini mixture, mixing well. Spoon the mixture into the prepared casserole dish. In a small bowl, combine the bread crumbs and cheese with the remaining 1 tablespoon oil. Sprinkle over the top of the pasta.

6 Bake until the pasta is hot and lightly browned on top, about 30 minutes. Let sit for 10 minutes before serving.

Serves 6

Caraway Cabbage and Noodles

~~~

Noodles and cabbage is a soul-satisfying comfort food combination throughout Eastern Europe, with slight variations. In Austria, for example, egg noodles are combined with butter, cabbage, onion, and a bit of sugar. In countries such as Poland and Hungary, the sugar is omitted and sour cream is added. Some variations add caraway seeds. In this recipe, the ingredients can be prepared ahead of time, then combined in a casserole dish to be heated when ready to eat. Alternatively, the cooked noodles and cabbage can be quickly heated together on top of the stove and served, omitting the sour cream and bread crumbs as well as the finishing in the oven.

2 tablespoons olive oil

1 large yellow onion, finely chopped

4 cups shredded Savoy cabbage (1 small
    head)

Salt and freshly ground black pepper

$1/_3$ cup water

12 ounces egg noodles or fettucine,
    broken into thirds

2 teaspoons caraway seeds

1 cup sour cream or tofu sour cream
    (optional)

$1/_4$ cup dry bread crumbs (optional)

1 If finishing the dish in the oven, preheat the oven to 350 degrees F. Lightly oil a $2^1/_2$-quart casserole dish.

2 Heat the oil in a large skillet over medium heat. Add the onion, cover, and cook, stirring occasionally, until soft and golden brown, about 10 minutes. Add the cabbage and salt and pepper to taste and cook until the cabbage begins to brown slightly. Add the water, cover, reduce the heat to low, and continue to cook until the cabbage is soft, about 10 minutes.

3 While the cabbage is cooking, cook the noodles in a large pot of boiling water, stirring occasionally, until *al dente*, 8 to 10 minutes. Drain and place in a large shallow bowl.

4 Add the cabbage to the pasta and toss gently to combine. Add the caraway seeds and the sour cream, if using, and stir gently to combine. Serve, or proceed with the recipe.

5 Spread the cabbage mixture in the prepared casserole dish and sprinkle the top with the bread crumbs. Bake until hot and the crumbs are lightly browned, about 15 minutes. Serve hot.

Serves 4

Chinese Noodle Pancake

Wholesome, satisfying, and simple to make, this noodle pancake looks great on the plate and makes a terrific accompaniment to a spicy stir-fry. While Chinese egg noodles are traditional, I've had good luck preparing this dish with regular spaghetti.

8 ounces thin fresh or dried Chinese
   noodles or spaghetti

3 scallions, finely minced

1 tablespoon tamari or other soy sauce

1 tablespoon toasted sesame oil

2 tablespoons peanut oil

1 Cook the noodles or spaghetti according to the package directions until tender but not soft. Drain and rinse under cold running water to stop the cooking process.

2 Place the noodles in a medium-size bowl and add the scallions, tamari, and sesame oil. Toss to combine.

3 Heat the peanut oil in a large nonstick skillet over medium-high heat. Add the noodle mixture and spread it evenly in the skillet, pressing down with a metal spatula. Cook for about 2 minutes, then reduce the heat to low and cook until the pancake is browned and crisp on the bottom, about 5 minutes longer. Slide the pancake onto a large plate, cover it with another plate, invert, and slide the pancake back into the skillet to brown the other side. Cook until the second side is browned and crisp.

4 To serve, transfer the pancake to a large plate and cut into wedges. Serve hot.

Serves 4

Pad Thai

⌇⌇⌇

I think of pad thai as a basic "meat and potatoes" dish of Thai cuisine. It is certainly the most popular Thai dish in America, probably because it's mild but still quite flavorful. For best results, assemble all of the ingredients ahead of time before beginning to stir-fry. If dried rice stick noodles are unavailable, substitute fettuccine.

---

8 ounces rice sticks

1/4 cup tamari or other soy sauce

2 tablespoons fresh lime juice

1 tablespoon tomato paste

2 teaspoons light brown sugar

1/8 teaspoon cayenne

1 tablespoon peanut oil

4 ounces extra-firm tofu, cut into
   1/2-inch-wide strips

1 small red bell pepper, seeded and cut
   into 1/4-inch-wide strips

3 scallions, chopped

2 garlic cloves, minced

2 tablespoons chopped fresh cilantro
   leaves

1 cup fresh bean sprouts

1/4 cup chopped unsalted roasted
   peanuts

Lime wedges for garnish

1 Bring a large pot of water to a boil. Add the rice sticks and turn off the heat. Allow the rice sticks to soak until soft, about 15 minutes. Drain and set aside.

2 In a small bowl, combine the tamari, lime juice, tomato paste, brown sugar, and cayenne, stirring to blend. Set aside.

3 In a large wok or skillet, heat the oil over medium-high heat. Add the tofu and cook, stirring, until golden brown on all sides, about 3 minutes. Remove from the wok with a slotted spoon and set aside.

4 Add the bell pepper, scallions, and garlic to the wok and stir-fry until softened, 2 to 3 minutes. Add the tamari mixture and bring to a simmer. Stir in the drained noodles, cilantro, and tofu and stir-fry until heated through, about 2 minutes.

5 Transfer to dinner plates and sprinkle with the bean sprouts and peanuts. Garnish with lime wedges and serve hot.

Serves 4

Couscous with Pistachios and Dried Cranberries

The red cranberries and green pistachios make this dish a natural at Christmastime, but the great taste says serve it anytime.

2 tablespoons olive oil

2 large shallots, minced

2 cups quick-cooking couscous

$1/2$ cup dried cranberries

3 cups vegetable stock (page 36), brought to a boil

$1/2$ teaspoon ground cardamom

$1/8$ teaspoon cayenne

Salt

$1/3$ cup pistachio nuts

2 tablespoons minced fresh parsley leaves

1 Heat the oil in a large skillet over medium heat. Add the shallots, cover, and cook, stirring a few times, until softened, about 5 minutes. Add the couscous and stir to coat with the oil. Stir in the cranberries and hot stock and bring to a boil. Reduce the heat to low, stir in the cardamom and cayenne, and season to taste with salt. Cover and cook until the water is absorbed, 5 to 7 minutes.

2 Remove from the heat, stir in the pistachios and parsley, and serve.

Serves 6

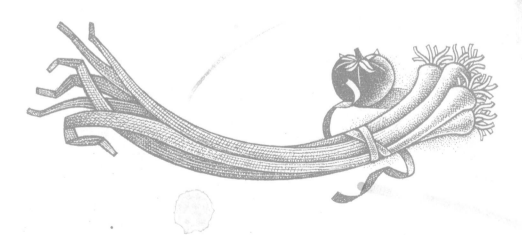

Cilantro Polenta Wedges with Black Beans and Roasted Yellow Peppers

~mm~

Cilantro, green chile, and black beans give a Southwestern flavor to these rich polenta triangles. I like to make this recipe using a springform pan so it's easy to remove the polenta. If you don't have a springform pan, use a cake pan.

1 large yellow bell pepper

3¹/₂ cups vegetable stock (page 36)

1 cup coarse yellow cornmeal

2 tablespoons minced fresh cilantro leaves

3 tablespoons olive oil

Salt and freshly ground black pepper

1 hot green chile, seeded and minced

2 garlic cloves, minced

1¹/₂ cups cooked black beans or one 15-ounce can, drained and rinsed

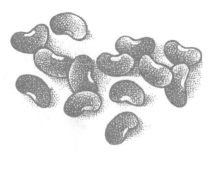

1 Roast the pepper over an open flame or under the broiler, turning often, until the skin is blackened on all sides. Place in a paper bag, seal the bag, and let steam for 5 minutes. Remove the pepper from the bag and cut it lengthwise in half. Scrape off the charred skin, remove the stem and seeds, and cut into thin strips. Set aside.

2 Bring the stock to a boil in a large saucepan. Reduce the heat to medium and slowly add the cornmeal, whisking constantly. Reduce the heat to low and cook, whisking frequently, until thick, 20 to 25 minutes.

3 Stir in 1 tablespoon of the cilantro, 1 tablespoon of the oil, and salt and pepper to taste. Spoon the polenta into a well-oiled 10-inch springform pan and refrigerate for 1 hour to firm up.

4 Heat 1 tablespoon of the oil in a medium-size skillet over medium heat. Add the chile and garlic and cook, stirring, until fragrant, about 30 seconds. Stir in the beans and the remaining 1 tablespoon cilantro and season with salt and pepper to taste. Simmer until the flavors are blended, about 10 minutes. Keep warm over very low heat.

5 When the polenta is firm, remove the sides from the springform pan and cut the polenta into 6 wedges.

6 Heat the remaining I tablespoon oil in a large skillet or griddle over medium heat. Add the polenta wedges and cook, turning once, until hot and lightly browned on both sides. (Alternatively, the polenta wedges can be brushed with oil and heated in a preheated 375 degree F oven.)

7 To serve, place each polenta wedge on a plate, spoon a portion of the warm black bean mixture over each one, and top with a few strips of roasted bell pepper. Serve at once.

Serves 6

Baked Polenta with Porcini Mushrooms

In the 1970s, we were fortunate enough to live near a friend who was a wild mushroom expert. I have fond memories of picking mushrooms with Walter Throne, one time bringing home a massive ram's head mushroom the size of a basketball. We sliced it and sautéed it in garlic and olive oil and served it with baked polenta, much the same as this recipe. Fresh porcini are quite expensive and can be difficult to find. Fresh cremini mushrooms may be used instead or about $^1/_2$ cup dried porcini, also called cepes, may be substituted. Soak dried porcini in warm water for 30 minutes and drain before using.

3 cups vegetable stock (page 36)

1 cup coarse yellow cornmeal

$^1/_2$ cup regular or soy milk

$^1/_4$ cup olive oil

8 ounces mozzarella cheese or soy
  mozzarella, shredded

Salt and freshly ground black pepper

$^1/_2$ cup freshly grated Parmesan cheese
  or soy Parmesan

3 garlic cloves, chopped

8 ounces porcini mushrooms, sliced

2 tablespoons dry white wine

1 tablespoon minced fresh parsley leaves

1 Preheat the oven to 400 degrees F. Generously oil a 9 x 13-inch baking dish.

2 Bring the stock to a boil in a large saucepan. Slowly add the cornmeal, whisking constantly. Reduce the heat to low and cook, whisking frequently, until the polenta is thick, 20 to 25 minutes. Stir in the milk, 2 tablespoons of the oil, and half the mozzarella, season with salt and pepper to taste, and stir until the cheese is melted.

3 Transfer the polenta to the prepared baking dish and sprinkle on the remaining mozzarella and the Parmesan. Bake until the top is golden brown, 20 to 30 minutes.

4 While the polenta is baking, prepare the mushrooms: Heat the remaining 2 tablespoons oil in a large skillet over medium-high heat. Add the garlic and cook until fragrant, about 30 seconds. Add the porcini and cook, stirring a few times, until softened, about 5 minutes longer. Add the wine, parsley,

and salt and pepper to taste and cook for 5 minutes longer to blend the flavors. Keep warm over very low heat.

5 When the polenta is done, let it stand for 10 minutes before cutting into squares. Serve topped with the mushrooms.

Serves 4 to 6

Butternut Squash Risotto

The diced squash continues to cook in the creamy risotto, adding its color and flavor. I use butternut squash because it's readily available, easy to prepare, and consistently flavorful.

1 small butternut squash, peeled, halved, seeded, and cut into 1/2-inch dice
1 tablespoon olive oil
1/2 cup seeded and finely chopped red bell pepper
2 garlic cloves, minced
1 1/2 cups Arborio rice
1/4 cup dry white wine
4 1/2 cups vegetable stock (page 36), heated to a simmer
Salt and freshly ground black pepper

1 Steam the squash over boiling water until tender, about 15 to 18 minutes. Measure out 2 cups of the squash and set aside; reserve any remaining squash for another use.

2 Heat the oil in a large saucepan over medium heat. Add the bell pepper and garlic, cover, and cook, stirring a few times, until softened, about 5 minutes. Add the rice and stir to coat with the oil. Add the squash and wine and stir gently until the liquid is absorbed. Add 1/2 cup of the stock and cook, stirring, until it is absorbed. Continue to add the stock 1/2 cup at a time, stirring each time until the liquid is absorbed before the next addition, until the risotto is creamy and the rice is just *al dente*. It should take about 25 minutes total.

3 Season with salt and pepper to taste and serve hot.

Serves 4 to 6

Jasmine Fried Rice

Although many Thai dishes are notoriously hot, there are several that have no trace of heat, such as this one, in which the full flavors of the fragrant Jasmine rice and Thai basil dominate. Nothing tastes quite like Thai basil, but if you can't find it, you can use regular basil or even mint, which will give the dish a slightly different character.

1 tablespoon peanut oil

1 small red onion, finely chopped

1/2 medium-size red bell pepper, seeded and finely chopped

1 small carrot, grated

1 teaspoon peeled and minced fresh ginger

3 1/2 cups cold cooked jasmine rice

1/4 cup frozen peas, thawed

2 tablespoons tamari or other soy sauce

2 tablespoons minced fresh Thai basil leaves

2 tablespoons chopped unsalted roasted peanuts

1 Heat the oil in a large skillet over medium-high heat. Add the onion and stir-fry until softened, 3 to 4 minutes. Add the bell pepper, carrot, and ginger and stir-fry until softened and fragrant, about 2 minutes. Add the rice, peas, and tamari and stir-fry until the rice is heated through, about 3 minutes. Stir in the basil.

2 Sprinkle with the peanuts and serve hot.

Serves 4

Vegetable Donburi

mm

Donburi was one of the first Japanese dishes I ever tasted, when, in the early 1970s, a friend took us to a tiny Japanese restaurant in New York City, where we were the only Caucasians. I remember that the warming feeling from my first taste of donburi made me feel comfortable in unfamiliar surroundings. Now I make donburi at home, using tofu instead of the customary eggs. Traditionally donburi is served in individual rice bowls.

---

1 tablespoon peanut oil

1 medium-size yellow onion, finely
   chopped

4 shiitake mushrooms, stems removed
   and caps thinly sliced

8 ounces firm tofu

2 tablespoons tamari or other soy sauce

3 cups hot cooked medium- or long-grain
   white rice

2 teaspoons toasted sesame oil

1 tablespoon sesame seeds, toasted

1 Heat the peanut oil in a large skillet over medium heat. Add the onion, cover, and cook, stirring a few times, until softened about 5 minutes. Add the mushrooms and cook for 1 minute longer.

2 Squeeze the excess water from the tofu and crumble it into the skillet. Add the tamari and cook, stirring to combine well, until heated through.

3 Divide the hot rice among individual bowls, top with the tofu mixture, and drizzle with the sesame oil. Top each with a sprinkling of the sesame seeds and serve hot.

Serves 4

Toasting Sesame Seeds

Toast sesame seeds in a dry skillet over medium heat, stirring occasionally, until they turn golden brown and smell fragrant, about 3 minutes. Do not leave them unattended, as they can brown and burn quickly. Once toasted, remove from the pan, or they will continue to brown and possibly burn.

Kasha Varnishkas

Kasha, or buckwheat groats, and bow-tie pasta is a hearty Eastern European dish and a great cold-weather comfort food meal. Kasha is available in well-stocked supermarkets and natural food stores. The coarse grain is the best texture to use for this dish.

2 tablespoons olive oil

1 large yellow onion, chopped

1 cup coarse kasha (buckwheat groats)

2 to 2 1/4 cups vegetable stock (page 36) or water

12 ounces bow-tie pasta

2 tablespoons minced fresh parsley leaves

Salt and freshly ground black pepper

1 Heat 1 tablespoon of the oil in a large skillet over medium heat. Add the onion and cook, stirring occasionally, until browned, about 10 minutes.

2 Stir in the kasha, add 2 cups of the stock, and bring to a boil. Reduce the heat to low. Cover and simmer until the kasha is tender, about 20 minutes. Set aside.

3 Meanwhile, cook the bow-ties in a large pot of boiling salted water, stirring occasionally, until *al dente*, about 10 minutes. Drain well and return to the pot.

4 Add the kasha mixture, parsley, the remaining 1 tablespoon oil, and salt and pepper to taste to the bow-ties. Place the pot over medium heat and stir gently to heat through, 3 to 4 minutes. If the mixture seems too dry, add up to 1/4 cup more stock while it heats. Serve hot.

Serves 4

Millet-Cauliflower "Mashed Potatoes"

This recipe provides a delicious way to enjoy millet—a very nourishing grain that is seldom used in the United States. It's also a great way to disguise cauliflower for family members who don't like it. The seemingly unlikely combination of millet and cauliflower produces a mashed potato–like result in appearance and consistency that even tastes similar to potatoes. It is delicious as is, or serve it with brown gravy such as the one on page 302. Millet is available in natural food stores.

1½ cups millet

1 small head cauliflower, broken into small florets (about 3½ cups)

1 medium-size yellow onion, finely minced

3¾ cups water

Salt and freshly ground black pepper

1 teaspoon extra virgin olive oil

1 tablespoon minced fresh chives

1 Combine the millet, cauliflower, onion, and water in a large saucepan and bring to a boil. Reduce the heat to low, salt the water, cover, and simmer until the millet and vegetables are soft and the water has been absorbed, about 30 minutes.

2 Puree the mixture using a food mill or food processor and season to taste with salt and pepper. Transfer to a serving bowl, drizzle with the oil, sprinkle with the chives, and serve hot.

Serves 4 to 6

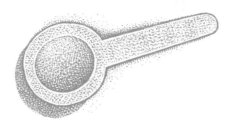

Fruity Bulgur Pilaf

Also called cracked wheat, bulgur is a quick-cooking grain with a hearty, nut-like flavor that is enhanced by the sweetness of the fruit in this colorful pilaf.

2 tablespoons olive oil

1 small yellow onion, finely chopped

1 small carrot, grated

1 cup medium-grade bulgur

2 cups vegetable stock (page 36) or
  water

1/4 cup chopped dried fruit, such as
  apricots, apples, and/or cranberries

1/4 cup golden raisins

Salt and freshly ground black pepper

1/4 cup slivered almonds

1 tablespoon chopped fresh mint leaves

1 Heat the oil in a large skillet over medium heat. Add the onion, cover, and cook, stirring a few times, until softened, about 5 minutes. Add the carrot and bulgur and stir to combine. Stir in the stock, dried fruit, and raisins and bring to a boil. Reduce the heat to low and season with salt and pepper to taste. Cover and simmer until the bulgur is tender and the liquid has been absorbed, about 15 minutes.

2 Remove the bulgur from the heat and stir in the almonds and mint. Cover and let stand for 15 minutes before serving.

Serves 4

Two Amazing Grains

Whole grains are important to any well-balanced diet and have long been a dietary staple in many cultures. They are a vital component of vegetarian cooking and an economical source of high-quality nutrition. Whole grains can be used in soups, stuffings, pilafs, salads, and desserts and as a bed for stews. Among the numerous varieties of grain, which include corn, oats, millet, barley, and quinoa, two stand out as the most widely used throughout the world: rice and wheat.

Rice, the world's most popular grain, is enjoyed throughout the Far East and India, the Middle East, much of Europe and Africa, and the United States. While refined white rice remains the most widely used, the more nutritious brown rice and exotic varieties such as basmati and jasmine are gaining in popularity.

In the United States, wheat is usually made into flour for breads, baked goods, and cereals, rather than eaten as a whole grain. In Eastern Europe, buckwheat groats, or kasha, as it is known after cooking, is a traditional ingredient with an intense, nutty flavor. In the Middle East, bulgur, partially cooked whole-grain wheat that has been dried and cracked, is used to make the traditional tabbouleh.

Grain Cooking 101

Most grains can be cooked in about two times as much water by volume as grain. More water may be required, depending on the cooking time of the particular grain. Combine the grain and water in a saucepan and bring the water to a boil. Cover, reduce the heat to low, and simmer until the grain is tender and the water has been absorbed. For 1 cup of uncooked grain, the average yield is 2 to 3 cups of cooked grain. To intensify the flavor of grains, lightly toast them in a dry skillet before cooking.

Rasta Red Beans and Rice

Rice and beans is a basic stick-to-your-ribs combination for many ethnic groups. It is especially popular on the Caribbean islands and in Louisiana and the American Southwest. This version takes its inspiration from island cooking, with typical seasonings including allspice, oregano, and chiles.

1 tablespoon olive oil

1 small yellow onion, minced

1 small hot chile, seeded and minced

3 garlic cloves, minced

One 14.5-ounce can crushed tomatoes

1 1/2 cups cooked dark red kidney beans or one 15-ounce can, drained and rinsed

3/4 teaspoon ground allspice

1/2 teaspoon dried oregano

1/2 teaspoon dried thyme

1/2 teaspoon light brown sugar

1/4 teaspoon ground nutmeg

Salt and freshly ground black pepper

1/3 cup water

2 tablespoons minced fresh parsley leaves

3 cups hot cooked long-grain white rice

1 Heat the oil in a large saucepan over medium heat. Add the onion, chile, and garlic, cover, and cook, stirring a few times, until softened, about 5 minutes. Add the tomatoes, kidney beans, allspice, oregano, thyme, brown sugar, nutmeg, and salt and pepper to taste. Stir in the water, cover, and simmer for 20 minutes to blend the flavors.

2 Stir in the parsley, and serve over the hot cooked rice. (Alternatively, the bean mixture and the rice can be combined before serving.)

Serves 4 to 6

A Brief Bean Bio

An ancient source of protein throughout the world, beans are a natural complement to whole grains and are traditionally paired with them in India, Mexico, and the Middle East. There are thousands of bean varieties, but only a few have made their way to the dinner tables of the United States. Black beans, navy beans, chickpeas, and Great Northern, kidney, lima, and pinto beans are among the most popular in the United States. They can be purchased raw, dried, canned, or, sometimes, frozen. When starting with dried beans, all of these varieties require overnight soaking and can take up to 2 or 3 hours to cook. For convenience, these longer-cooking beans can be cooked in large quantities, portioned, and frozen for later use. Some people use a pressure cooker when preparing dried beans to reduce the cooking time and improve digestibility.

The most useful and versatile bean of all is the soybean. For years, the soybean has been hailed as one of humanity's greatest nutritional treasures, because there are a number of high-protein foods derived from it, such as tofu, tempeh, and miso. Roasted soy "nuts" and edamame, boiled fresh soybeans in the pod, are other delicious ways to enjoy soy.

When cooked beans are eaten with brown rice or another whole grain, you are combining two wonderful sources of protein. Beans and grains are like the "meat and potatoes" of vegetarian cuisine. Add some steamed or stir-fried vegetables for a complete, well-balanced meal. It was once thought that beans and grains needed to be combined at the same meal to achieve the benefits of a complete protein, but it was later proven that they can be eaten at separate times during the day with the same positive nutritional results. Still, since so many ethnic dishes use beans and grains together, it's an easy choice to enjoy them that way.

Bean and Chile Burritos

Bean burritos rank high among Mexican-style comfort foods. If you prefer comfort without the kick, simply omit the chiles and use a mild salsa.

2 teaspoons olive oil

1 small yellow onion, minced

1 garlic clove, minced

2 jalapeños or other hot chiles, seeded
   and minced

1 teaspoon chili powder

Salt and freshly ground black pepper

1 1/2 cups cooked pinto beans or one
   15-ounce can, drained and rinsed

1 cup shredded cheddar cheese or soy
   cheddar

Eight 8-inch flour tortillas, warmed

Tomato–Red Onion Salsa (page 318)

1 Heat the oil in a large skillet over medium heat. Add the onion and garlic, cover, and cook, stirring a few times, until softened, about 5 minutes. Stir in the chiles, chili powder, and salt and pepper to taste.

2 Meanwhile, place the pinto beans in a food processor and pulse to a coarse puree.

3 Stir the beans into the onion mixture and heat through, about 3 minutes. Remove the skillet from the heat and stir in the cheese until it melts.

4 To serve, spoon an equal amount of the filling into the center of each tortilla (about $1/3$ cup each). Top with a spoonful of the salsa. Fold the bottom edge of each tortilla up over the filling, then fold the sides over, overlapping the edges. Or place all the ingredients on the table and allow everyone to assemble their own.

Serves 4

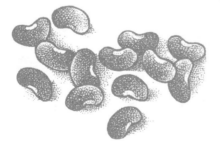

Garlicky Escarole and Borlotti Beans

Borlotti are meaty Italian beans that resemble large pinto beans. They are sometimes called Roman beans. I have only been able to find the canned variety at Italian grocery stores in my area, but they work fine. You can substitute cannellini beans or chickpeas if you prefer—the real stars here are the escarole and garlic.

1 large head escarole, trimmed and
   coarsely chopped

2 tablespoons olive oil

3 garlic cloves, finely minced

1½ cups cooked borlotti beans or one
   15-ounce can, drained and rinsed

Salt and freshly ground black pepper

1 Plunge the escarole into a pot of boiling salted water for 5 minutes. Drain well and set aside.

2 Heat the oil in a large skillet over medium heat. Add the garlic and cook until fragrant, about 30 seconds. Add the escarole and cook, stirring a few times, until tender, about 5 minutes. Add the beans and season with salt and pepper to taste. Cook for 5 minutes longer, stirring, to heat through and blend the flavors. Serve hot.

Serves 4

Sesame Green Beans and Shallots

Tender green beans luxuriate in a coating of creamy sesame tahini, which is rich in calcium and protein. Mirin is a Japanese cooking wine available in well-stocked supermarkets, Asian markets, and natural food stores.

1¹/₂ pounds green beans, ends trimmed

2 tablespoons tahini (sesame paste)

2 tablespoons tamari or other soy sauce

1 tablespoon mirin (rice wine)

¹/₂ teaspoon light brown sugar

1 tablespoon toasted sesame oil

2 tablespoons peanut oil

3 shallots, minced

2 garlic cloves, minced

2 teaspoons peeled and minced fresh
    ginger

1 Steam the green beans over boiling water until just tender, about 5 minutes. Set aside.

2 In a small bowl, combine the tahini, tamari, mirin, brown sugar, and sesame oil. Set aside.

3 Heat the peanut oil in a wok or large skillet over medium-high heat. Add the shallots, garlic, and ginger and stir-fry for 30 seconds. Add the green beans and stir-fry for 30 seconds. Stir in the tahini mixture and stir-fry until the beans are coated with the sauce and the ingredients are hot, about 1 minute. Serve immediately.

Serves 4

Coconut Creamed Spinach

Coconut milk and spices transform spinach into an exotic, almost decadent, delight. Fresh spinach is notoriously sandy, so be sure to wash it well.

---

1 pound spinach, tough stems removed and washed well

1 tablespoon olive oil

1 teaspoon peeled and grated fresh ginger

1/2 teaspoon ground cumin

1/8 teaspoon ground nutmeg

3/4 cup unsweetened coconut milk

Salt and freshly ground black pepper

1 Steam the spinach over boiling water until tender, 3 to 5 minutes. Press the excess liquid from the spinach, then chop it well. Set aside.

2 Heat the oil in a large skillet over medium heat. Add the ginger, cumin, and nutmeg and cook until fragrant, about 1 minute. Stir in the spinach, coconut milk, and salt and pepper to taste. Simmer, stirring frequently, until hot and creamy, 5 to 7 minutes. Serve hot.

Serves 4 to 6

Roasted Asparagus with Orange-Thyme Aïoli

Roasting asparagus gives it a sublime depth of flavor that is so delicious you'll find yourself craving more. While it is perfectly wonderful seasoned only with the olive oil and a little salt and pepper, a bit of Orange-Thyme Aïoli adds sophistication and enhances the flavor of the asparagus.

1¹/₂ pounds thin asparagus, tough
  bottoms snapped off

2 tablespoons olive oil

Salt and freshly ground black pepper

¹/₂ cup Orange-Thyme Aïoli (page 310), or
  more to taste

1 Preheat the oven to 425 degrees F. Toss the asparagus with the oil and arrange in a single layer on a lightly oiled baking sheet. Season with salt and pepper to taste.

2 Roast until just tender, about 10 minutes. (The timing will vary depending on the thickness of the asparagus.) Transfer to a shallow serving platter.

3 Top with a ribbon of aïoli and serve at once.

Serves 4 to 6

Roasted Ratatouille

~mm~

Roasting brings out the flavor of the vegetables in this interpretation of the classic vegetable stew from Provence. It is delicious served over rice or noodles, or with roasted potatoes or warm crusty bread. Diced canned tomatoes can be substituted for fresh if you prefer.

---

1 small eggplant, ends trimmed, peeled, and cut into ¹/₂-inch dice

1 small yellow onion, diced

1 small red bell pepper, seeded and cut into ¹/₂-inch dice

2 garlic cloves, minced

2 tablespoons olive oil

Salt and freshly ground black pepper

2 small zucchini, ends trimmed and cut into ¹/₂-inch-thick rounds

4 ripe plum tomatoes, chopped, or one 14.5-ounce can, drained and chopped

2 teaspoons minced fresh thyme leaves or 1 teaspoon dried

3 tablespoons basil pesto, homemade (page 313) or store-bought

1 tablespoon chopped fresh parsley leaves

1 Preheat the oven to 425 degrees F. Lightly oil a large roasting pan.

2 Add the eggplant, onion, bell pepper, and garlic to the pan, drizzle with the oil, and season with salt and pepper to taste. Toss gently to combine. Cover and roast until the vegetables are slightly softened, about 20 minutes.

3 Remove the pan from the oven, add the zucchini, tomatoes, and thyme, and toss gently. Roast, uncovered, until all the vegetables are tender, about 20 minutes longer.

4 Stir in the pesto, sprinkle with the parsley, and serve hot.

Serves 4 to 6

Niçoise Vegetable Sauté

This colorful vegetable medley takes its inspiration from the popular Niçoise salad. Like the salad, this sauté includes green beans, potatoes, tomatoes, and Niçoise olives. Unlike the salad, there is no tuna or lettuce, and the dish is served hot. I like to cook the potatoes and green beans in advance so that the sauté can be assembled quickly when ready to serve. Leave the tender peels on the potatoes for added nutrition.

2 tablespoons olive oil

1 small red onion, thinly sliced

3 garlic cloves, chopped

1 pound new red potatoes, boiled in salted water to cover until tender, drained, and quartered

12 ounces green beans, ends trimmed and steamed for 5 minutes

One 14.5-ounce can diced tomatoes, drained

2 tablespoon chopped fresh basil leaves

1 tablespoon chopped fresh parsley leaves

1 tablespoon capers, drained and chopped

1 teaspoon salt

$1/8$ teaspoon cayenne

$1/4$ cup Niçoise olives, halved and pitted

1 Heat the oil in a large saucepan over medium heat. Add the onion, cover, and cook, stirring a few times, until softened, about 5 minutes. Add the garlic, potatoes, and green beans and cook, stirring a few times, for 5 minutes longer. Add the tomatoes, basil, parsley, capers, salt, and cayenne and cook until all the vegetables are hot and the flavors have had time to mingle, about 10 minutes.

2 Stir in the olives and serve.

Serves 4 to 6

Underground Vegetable Sauté

~~~

This root vegetable celebration is enhanced by the sweet addition of orange marmalade. For a hearty one-dish meal, add diced potatoes and vegetarian sausage links.

2 tablespoons olive oil

2 shallots, chopped

3 medium-size carrots, cut into 1/4-inch-
thick slices

2 medium-size parsnips, peeled and cut
into 1/4-inch-thick slices

1 small rutabaga, peeled and cut into
1/2-inch dice

2 tablespoons orange marmalade

1/2 cup water

Salt and freshly ground black pepper

1 Heat the oil in a large skillet over medium heat. Add the shallots, carrots, parsnips, and rutabaga and cook, stirring a few times, until slightly softened, about 5 minutes. Stir in the marmalade, water, and salt and pepper to taste. Reduce the heat to low, cover, and simmer until the vegetables are soft but not mushy, about 10 minutes.

2 Remove the cover, increase the heat to medium-high, and stir gently to reduce the liquid and coat the vegetables with a marmalade glaze. Serve hot.

Serves 4 to 6

CHAPTER NINE

The Sandwich Board

Burger and fries. Sandwich and chips. Hot dog and potato salad. The typical American lunch often consists of one of these meat-and-potato pairs. For many health-conscious people, however, this typically high-fat fare is bypassed in favor of lighter choices. The good news is that you can enjoy hearty sandwiches and burgers and still eat nutritiously, thanks to the wide variety of vegetarian burgers, hot dogs, and cold cuts available in supermarkets and natural food stores.

Since these commercial products are used in the same way as their animal-based counterparts, there's no need to explain here how to make a vegetarian ham-and-cheese deli sandwich or prepare a tofu hot dog. Simply substitute the vegetable-based meat analogs in your favorite sandwich recipe and you're all set.

But sandwich options do not have to end with ham and cheese on white bread. Delicious sandwich fillings can be made using a variety of vegetables, beans, and ingredients such as tofu and tempeh. These fillings can be nestled in sprouted grain bread, tortillas, pita bread, boules, kaiser rolls, focaccia, baguettes, croissants, and many other international breads. By exploring ethnic cuisines that use different types of breads and fillings, you can experience a world of flavors through the satisfyingly simple meal of a sandwich.

The range of sandwiches in this chapter provides options for every taste and occasion, including a variety of burgers and healthful variations of a Philadelphia-style cheese steak (made with seitan and soy cheese) and a po' boy.

Spicy Tofu "Po' Boys"

Seitan "Cheese Steaks"

Grilled Portobello "Steak" Sandwiches

"Sausage" Subs with Peppers and Onions

Sloppy Giuseppes

Sizzling Soy Melts

The Shadrach

Tempeh "BLT"

Chicken-Out Salad

Tofu "Egg" Salad

Nothin's Fishy "Tuna" Salad

Marinated Tofu Wraps

Southwestern Refried Bean Wraps with
   Avocado and Salsa

Seared Wheat-Meat Tortilla Wraps

Hungry-for-Hummus Pita

Sunshine Burgers

Lentil-Walnut Burgers

Cajun Red Bean Burgers

Cardamom-Spiced Lentil-Potato Wraps

Spicy Tofu "Po' Boys"

Golden fried tofu nuggets stand in for the oysters in this filling sandwich inspired by the New Orleans tradition. Be sure to put the bottle of Tabasco on the table to spice things up.

Salt

8 ounces extra-firm tofu, cut into 1 x 3 x
   ¹/₂-inch pieces

¹/₂ cup dry bread crumbs

2 tablespoons olive oil

Old Bay seasoning

Two 6- to 7-inch sub rolls

2 tablespoons regular or soy mayonnaise
   (page 309)

4 romaine lettuce leaves, finely shredded

1 large ripe tomato, thinly sliced

Tabasco sauce

1 Salt the tofu pieces, then dredge them in the bread crumbs; set aside.

2 Heat the oil in a large skillet over medium-high heat. Add the tofu pieces and brown on all sides. Remove from the heat and sprinkle with Old Bay seasoning to taste.

3 Split the rolls lengthwise and spread on both sides with the mayonnaise. Line the bottom half of each roll with the lettuce and tomato slices. Top with the fried tofu and a splash of Tabasco. Serve with the bottle of Tabasco on the table.

Serves 2

Seitan "Cheese Steaks"

This substantial sandwich is best on sub rolls, or on lengths of split French or Italian bread. It can also be made with small boules or kaiser rolls. Thinly sliced seitan is an ideal substitute for beef in this recipe. You can find vegetarian Worcestershire sauce in natural food stores.

1 tablespoon olive oil

1 medium-size yellow onion, halved and thinly sliced

1 medium-size red bell pepper, seeded and cut into thin strips

8 ounces seitan, thinly sliced

1 tablespoon vegetarian Worcestershire sauce

Salt and freshly ground black pepper

4 ounces mozzarella cheese or soy mozzarella, shredded

Two 6- to 7-inch sub rolls

1 Heat the oil in a large skillet over medium heat. Add the onion and bell pepper, cover, and cook, stirring a few times, until softened, about 5 minutes. Add the seitan and cook, turning once, until lightly browned on both sides, about 5 minutes. Add the Worcestershire and season to taste with salt and pepper. Sprinkle with the cheese and allow it to melt.

2 Split the rolls lengthwise and fill them with the seitan-and-cheese mixture. Serve hot.

Serves 2

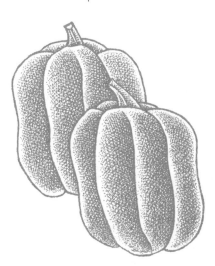

Grilled Portobello "Steak" Sandwiches

For a terrific meatless alternative to a steak sandwich, try a thick and juicy grilled portobello mushroom cap slathered with onions on a toasted hard roll. Serve with ketchup and Oven-Browned Steak Fries (page 213) for a hearty "meat and potatoes" meal.

1/3 cup olive oil

3 tablespoons balsamic vinegar

1 garlic clove, minced

1 teaspoon minced fresh thyme leaves or
  1/2 teaspoon dried

Salt and freshly ground black pepper

4 large portobello mushroom caps

1 medium-size red onion, halved
  lengthwise and thinly sliced

4 hard rolls

1 In a small bowl, combine the oil, vinegar, garlic, thyme, and salt and pepper to taste. Place the mushrooms and onion in a shallow bowl and pour the marinade over them. Marinate for 1 hour at room temperature, turning once.

2 Preheat the grill or broiler. Place the mushrooms and onion on the grill, or put them on a baking sheet and place it under the broiler; reserve the marinade. Grill or broil the mushrooms and onion, tuning once and basting with the reserved marinade, until just tender and browned, about 10 minutes.

3 Meanwhile, split the rolls open and toast them on the grill or under the broiler until golden brown.

4 Place 1 mushroom cap on each roll, top with the onions, and serve hot.

Serves 4

"Sausage" Subs with Peppers and Onions

Using green bell peppers instead of the recently popular red or yellow adds a taste of nostalgia: When I was young, my mother frequently made sandwiches using green bell peppers—sometimes combined with eggs, other times with sausage and onions.

2 tablespoons olive oil

1 medium-size yellow onion, thinly sliced

1 medium-size green bell pepper, seeded and cut into thin strips

8 ounces vegetarian sausage, coarsely chopped

Salt and freshly ground black pepper

Two 6- to 7-inch sub rolls

1 Heat the oil in a large skillet over medium heat. Add the onion and bell pepper, cover, and cook, stirring a few times, until softened, about 5 minutes. Add the vegetarian sausage and season with salt and pepper to taste. Cook, stirring a few times, until the sausage is browned and hot, about 5 minutes.

2 Split the sub rolls and divide the sausage mixture between them. Serve hot.

Serves 2

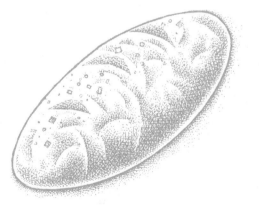

Sloppy Giuseppes

⁓⁓⁓

For years, my mom served a spicy concoction of Italian sausage and mushrooms simmered in tomato sauce on hard Italian rolls. It was only later in life that I realized this was sort of an Italian version of Sloppy Joes. I now make what I call "Sloppy Giuseppes" using frozen veggie burgers or vegetarian burger crumbles and bottled marinara sauce for a quick and hearty meal.

1 tablespoon olive oil

8 ounces white button mushrooms, chopped

3 frozen veggie burgers, thawed and chopped, or one 12-ounce package frozen vegetarian burger crumbles, thawed

3/4 teaspoon ground fennel

1/4 teaspoon cayenne

1/8 teaspoon red pepper flakes

Salt and freshly ground black pepper

2 cups bottled marinara sauce

4 hard rolls

1 Heat the oil in a large skillet over medium-high heat. Add the mushrooms and cook, stirring, until softened, about 5 minutes. Add the veggie burgers, fennel, cayenne, red pepper flakes, and salt and pepper to taste. Stir in the tomato sauce and simmer for 10 minutes to heat through and blend the flavors.

2 Split the rolls, and toast lightly if desired. Spoon the mixture over the rolls and serve hot.

Serves 4

The Convenience of Crumbles

One of the most convenient meat alternatives are the frozen vegetarian burger crumbles that can be substituted in equal measure for cooked ground beef. This precooked product, made with textured soy protein and available under a variety of brand names, is a great way to add texture and protein to vegetarian meals. Easy to use and great tasting, crumbles can be found in the freezer section of well-stocked supermarkets and natural food stores. With their chewy texture and meat-like appearance, they make a good stand-in for ground beef in such recipes as Sloppy Joes, chili, and spaghetti sauce. They make an ideal introduction to vegetarian meals for finicky children and "reluctant" vegetarians looking for familiar tastes and textures. If frozen "ground beef" crumbles are unavailable, substitute frozen veggie burgers, which can be cooked or thawed slightly and then chopped before adding to recipes.

Sizzling Soy Melts

T his recipe is a vegetarian incarnation of a famous fast food breakfast sandwich, although the English muffin is the only ingredient that remains the same. The rest of the ingredients are made with soy: a slice of tofu replaces the egg, which is then topped with vegetarian Canadian bacon and soy cheese.

1 tablespoon olive oil

2 slices vegetarian Canadian bacon

3 ounces extra-firm tofu, cut into 2 equal
   slices

$1/8$ teaspoon turmeric

Salt and freshly ground black pepper

2 slices mozzarella cheese or soy
   mozzarella

2 English muffins, split

1 Heat the oil in a medium skillet over medium heat. Add the vegetarian Canadian bacon and cook, turning once, until hot and lightly browned on both sides, about 2 minutes. Remove from the skillet and set aside.

2 Add the tofu to the skillet, sprinkle with the turmeric and salt and pepper to taste, and brown lightly on both sides, about 5 minutes. Place the bacon slices on top of the tofu slices and top each with a slice of cheese. Cover and cook for 1 minute to melt the cheese.

3 While the cheese is melting, toast the English muffins.

4 To serve, place a tofu-bacon-cheese patty on the bottom half of each muffin and top with the other half of the muffin. Serve hot.

Serves 2

The Shadrach

mm

Inspired by the classic Reuben sandwich made with corned beef, I came up with this vegetarian version made with tempeh, which I named "The Shadrach," after a Biblical captive in Babylonia who preferred to eat vegetables rather than the king's meat. The tempeh is simmered in water before using to mellow its flavor.

6 ounces tempeh, cut into $1/8$-inch-thick slices

2 tablespoons olive oil

4 slices rye bread

2 teaspoons Dijon mustard

$1/4$ cup sauerkraut

4 ounces Swiss cheese or soy cheese, thinly sliced

Quick Thousand Island Dressing (see below)

1 Place the tempeh slices in a saucepan of boiling water, reduce the heat to medium, and simmer for 10 minutes. Drain and pat dry.

2 Heat the oil in a large skillet over medium heat. Add the tempeh and cook, turning once, until lightly browned on both sides. Remove from the heat and remove the tempeh from the skillet.

3 Brush the oil from the skillet on one side of each slice of bread and spread the mustard on the other side of each slice.

4 Place 2 slices of the bread, oiled side down, in another large skillet. Layer with the tempeh, sauerkraut, and cheese. Top each with the remaining 2 slices of bread, oiled side up. Fry the sandwiches until golden on the bottom, about 2 minutes. Turn them over carefully and brown the other side.

5 Serve immediately, with the dressing on the side.

Serves 2

Quick Thousand Island Dressing

Combine 2 parts regular or soy mayonnaise with 1 part ketchup and 1 part sweet pickle relish.

Tempeh "BLT"

Everyone's favorite, the BLT, is made vegetarian with sizzling tempeh bacon—a delicious, smoky alternative that fries up crisp and brown. Tempeh bacon and other vegetarian bacon products are available at well-stocked supermarkets and natural food stores, where you'll also find soy mayonnaise. Most any bread will work for these sandwiches; use your favorite.

---

2 teaspoons corn oil

8 slices tempeh bacon

4 slices bread of choice

2 tablespoons regular or soy mayonnaise
 (page 309)

2 romaine lettuce leaves

4 slices ripe tomato

Salt and freshly ground black pepper

1 Heat the oil in a large skillet over medium heat. Add the tempeh bacon and cook, turning once, until crisp and browned on both sides, about 5 minutes. Transfer to paper towels to drain.

2 Toast the bread and spread with the mayonnaise. Place 2 slices of the toast on a work surface and top each with a lettuce leaf, 2 tomato slices, and 4 slices of the tempeh bacon. Season to taste with salt and pepper. Top each with the remaining slices of toast. Using a large serrated knife, cut each sandwich in half. Serve at once.

Serves 2

Chicken-Out Salad

Use this sandwich filling on a roll or croissant, in a pita pocket, or in a wrap sandwich. It's amazing how much this looks and tastes like chicken salad, but it's made with protein-rich tempeh. Poaching the tempeh before use mellows the flavor and makes it more digestible.

12 ounces tempeh, cubed

1 celery stalk, minced

2 tablespoons seeded and minced red
   bell pepper

1 large dill pickle, minced

2 or 3 scallions, to your taste, minced

1 tablespoon minced fresh parsley leaves

3/4 cup regular or soy mayonnaise
   (page 309)

1 tablespoon prepared mustard

1 teaspoon fresh lemon juice

1/2 teaspoon salt

1/8 teaspoon freshly ground black pepper

1 Place the tempeh in a saucepan of boiling water, reduce the heat to low, and simmer for 10 minutes. Drain and set aside to cool.

2 In a large bowl, combine the celery, bell pepper, pickle, scallion, and parsley.

3 Finely chop the cooled tempeh and add it to the bowl, along with the mayonnaise, mustard, lemon juice, salt, and pepper. Stir well to combine thoroughly. Cover and refrigerate for at least 30 minutes to allow the flavors to blend. This will keep in the refrigerator for 2 to 3 days.

Makes enough for 4 sandwiches

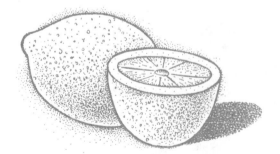

Tofu "Egg" Salad

This protein-rich sandwich filling tastes great and has an uncanny similarity to egg salad in texture and appearance. I especially like it on toasted whole-grain bread with lettuce and tomato slices, but it's also good on rolls or croissants or stuffed into pitas.

1 pound extra-firm tofu, drained

1 celery stalk, minced

2 scallions, minced

$^2/_3$ cup regular or soy mayonnaise
   (page 309)

2 tablespoons Dijon mustard

2 tablespoons sweet pickle relish

Pinch of turmeric

Salt and freshly ground black pepper

Crumble the tofu and place it in a medium bowl. Add the celery, scallions, mayonnaise, mustard, relish, turmeric, and salt and pepper to taste. Blend thoroughly, then cover and refrigerate for at least 30 minutes before using. This will keep refrigerated for 2 to 3 days.

Makes enough for 4 sandwiches

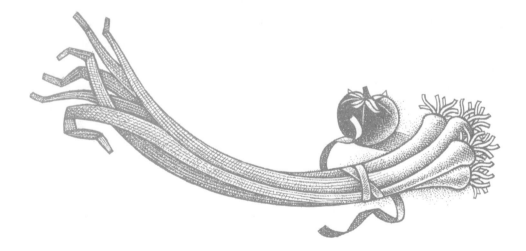

Nothin's Fishy "Tuna" Salad

I adapted this mock tuna salad from a recipe given to me by my friend Todd Ewen, a raw foods expert. Among my embellishments are cooked chickpeas and a small amount of flaxseed oil. The result is a nutritional powerhouse—complete with essential omega-3 fatty acids—that is amazingly similar to tuna salad in taste, texture, and appearance. Flaxseed oil can be found at natural food stores. If unavailable, use extra virgin olive oil. Kelp powder is also found in natural food stores.

$1/2$ cup unblanched whole almonds

$1/2$ cup shelled sunflower seeds

$1/4$ cup sesame seeds

1 cup cooked or canned chickpeas, drained and rinsed if canned

2 tablespoons fresh lemon juice

1 tablespoon water

1 tablespoon tamari or other soy sauce

2 teaspoons flaxseed oil

1 to 2 teaspoons kelp powder, to your taste

1 celery stalk, finely minced

$1/3$ cup finely minced red onion

2 tablespoons minced fresh parsley leaves

1 Soak the almonds, sunflower seeds, and sesame seeds overnight in water to cover, then drain well.

2 Combine the soaked and drained nuts and seeds, chickpeas, lemon juice, water, tamari, flaxseed oil, and kelp powder in a food processor and process until well blended but still retaining some texture. Transfer to a large bowl.

3 Add the celery, onion, and parsley and mix well. Cover and refrigerate for at least 30 minutes before serving. This is best eaten the day it is made.

Makes enough for 4 sandwiches

Sandwich Lore

The sandwich was supposedly invented in London in 1762 by John Montagu (the Earl of Sandwich), who is reported to have spent twenty-four hours at the gambling tables without leaving them to eat. By placing a piece of meat between two slices of bread, he was able to eat while continuing his gambling.

Sandwiches have come to be the epitome of simple food, often prepared—and eaten—on the run. They are thought of as portable meals, since they are typical brown bag and lunchbox fare. But they can be part of a well-balanced light supper when served with a bowl of soup or a salad. Sandwiches are taken along on picnics or road trips or enjoyed as quick late-night snacks, but this "everyman's" food also turns up (usually sans crust) on sterling silver trays at elegant parties and high tea. "Meaty" vegetarian sandwiches can be made using seitan, tempeh, tofu, or TVP. Grilled vegetables and bean spreads also make delicious meatless sandwich fillings.

Marinated Tofu Wraps

mm

O ne of the most appealing qualities of tofu is its ability to absorb surrounding flavors—it was made to be marinated! Lavash is a large Middle Eastern flat bread available at ethnic and specialty markets. If it is unavailable, large tortillas make a good substitute.

1/4 cup olive oil

1/4 cup balsamic vinegar

1 garlic clove, minced

1/2 teaspoon sugar

1/2 teaspoon salt

1/8 teaspoon cayenne

8 ounces extra-firm tofu, cut into
   1/4-inch-wide strips

1 small red bell pepper, seeded and
   chopped

1 medium-size carrot, finely shredded

1 large ripe tomato, chopped

1 lavash or 2 large wheat tortillas

1 cup shredded romaine lettuce

1 In a shallow bowl, combine the oil, vinegar, garlic, sugar, salt, and cayenne. Add the tofu and spoon the marinade over it. Set aside to marinate for 1 hour, turning once.

2 Heat a large skillet over medium-high heat. Remove the tofu from the marinade with a slotted spoon and transfer to the skillet. Stir-fry to sear the tofu, then remove and set aside to cool.

3 Add the bell pepper, carrot, and tomato to the reserved marinade and toss to coat. Remove the vegetables from the marinade with a slotted spoon, or drain in a strainer, and set aside; discard the marinade.

4 Place the lavash (or tortillas) on a work surface. Line the tofu strips across the lower third of the bread and top with the vegetable mixture and lettuce (if using tortillas, divide the filling evenly between them). Starting at the bottom edge, roll up the sandwich(es) into a cylinder. Cut in half and serve.

Serves 2

Southwestern Refried Bean Wraps with Avocado and Salsa

~~~

Sort of a burrito-taco hybrid, this sandwich has the great flavors of Mexico and the Southwest all "wrapped up."

One 15-ounce can refried beans

4 large flour tortillas, warmed

1/2 cup shredded Monterey Jack cheese or soy cheese

1 cup prepared tomato salsa of your choice

1 1/2 cups shredded romaine lettuce

2 ripe avocados, peeled, pitted, and sliced

1 Heat the refried beans in a medium-size saucepan over medium heat, stirring, until hot, about 5 minutes. Remove from the heat.

2 Place the tortillas on a work surface and spoon about 3 tablespoons of the refried beans across the lower third of each one. Top the beans with the cheese, salsa, shredded romaine, and avocado slices. Roll up the sandwiches, cut in half, and serve at once.

Serves 4

Seared Wheat-Meat Tortilla Wraps

Similar to a fajita, this sandwich is made with thin strips of seitan (wheat-meat) and vegetables encased in a soft tortilla. Serve with a bowl of salsa on the table.

2 tablespoons olive oil

12 ounces seitan, cut into 1-inch-wide
  strips

2 garlic cloves, minced

1/2 teaspoon ground cumin

1/2 teaspoon salt

Juice of 1 lime

1 large red bell pepper, seeded and thinly
  sliced

1 large red onion, halved lengthwise and
  thinly sliced

4 large flour tortillas, warmed

1 ripe avocado, peeled, pitted, and
  chopped

Chipotle Salsa (page 316)

1 Heat I tablespoon of the oil in a large skillet over medium-high heat. Add the seitan and sear on both sides. Add the garlic and season with the cumin, salt, and lime juice. Remove from the skillet and set aside.

2 Add the remaining I tablespoon oil to the skillet and heat over medium heat. Add the bell pepper and onion, cover, and cook, stirring a few times, until softened, about 5 minutes. Remove from the heat.

3 Lay the tortillas on a work surface. Place a few slices of seitan across the lower third of each tortilla and top with the onion-and-pepper mixture, avocado, and salsa. Roll up the tortillas to enclose the filling and serve at once.

Serves 4

Hungry-for-Hummus Pita

Rich and creamy, hummus is the quintessential Middle Eastern comfort food. High in protein and calcium and full of flavor, it's terrific as a vegetable dip and makes a great sandwich spread. I especially like it served with the classic pita bread.

1 small garlic clove, peeled

1½ cups cooked chickpeas or one 15-ounce can, drained and rinsed

¼ cup tahini (sesame paste)

3 tablespoons fresh lemon juice

1 tablespoon minced fresh parsley leaves

½ teaspoon salt

⅛ teaspoon cayenne

4 pita breads, warmed

1 Place the garlic and chickpeas in a food processor and process until finely ground. Add the tahini, lemon juice, parsley, salt, and cayenne and process until smooth and well blended. Transfer to a tightly covered container and refrigerate for at least an hour before serving to allow the flavors to blend.

2 Serve the hummus with the pitas.

Serves 4

Sunshine Burgers

These wholesome patties are called Sunshine Burgers because they are made with sunflower seeds and sunny yellow bell peppers and chickpeas. Serve on toasted burger rolls with all the trimmings.

1 cup cooked or canned chickpeas,
   drained and rinsed if canned

1/2 cup crumbled extra-firm tofu

1/2 cup shelled sunflower seeds

1/4 cup grated onion

1/4 cup seeded and finely minced yellow
   bell pepper

1/2 teaspoon salt

1/8 teaspoon cayenne

3/4 cup dry bread crumbs

2 tablespoons olive oil, or more if needed

6 burger rolls, toasted

1 Place the chickpeas, tofu, and sunflower seeds in a food processor, add the onion, bell pepper, salt, and cayenne, and process until well combined, leaving a little texture. Transfer to a plate.

2 Put the bread crumbs in a shallow bowl. Shape the tofu mixture into 6 patties and coat evenly on both sides with the bread crumbs.

3 Heat the oil in a large skillet over medium-high heat. Cook the patties, turning once, until golden brown on both sides, about 5 minutes. (If necessary, cook in batches, adding more oil as needed.) Place on the toasted burger rolls and serve hot.

Serves 6

Lentil Walnut Burgers

The rich flavors of lentils and walnuts combine in these hearty veggie burgers that are bound with creamy almond butter. These burgers are also great served as an entrée (without the rolls), topped with a mushroom sauce (see page 303). Instead of cooking the burgers on top of the stove, you can bake them in a preheated 350 degree F oven for 20 to 30 minutes. Look for almond butter in natural food stores.

3 tablespoons olive oil, or more if needed

1/2 cup minced onions

1 cup cooked brown lentils, drained well

1 cup finely chopped walnuts

1/2 cup cooked brown rice

2 tablespoons almond butter

2/3 cup dry bread crumbs

1 tablespoon minced fresh parsley leaves

1/2 teaspoon salt

1/8 teaspoon freshly ground black pepper

6 burger rolls, toasted

1 Heat I tablespoon of the oil in a large skillet over medium heat. Add the onion, cover, and cook, stirring a few times, until softened, about 5 minutes. Transfer to a food processor.

2 Add the lentils, walnuts, rice, almond butter, bread crumbs, parsley, salt, and pepper to the onion and process to blend well. Turn the mixture out into a bowl, and shape into 6 patties.

3 Heat the remaining 2 tablespoons oil in a large skillet over medium heat. Add the burgers and cook, turning once, until well browned on both sides, about 5 minutes per side. (If necessary, cook the burgers in batches, adding more oil as needed.) Place on the toasted burger rolls and serve hot.

Serves 6

Cajun Red Bean Burgers

Spiced with Tabasco and cayenne, these tasty burgers are especially good served with Ragin' Remoulade Sauce (page 311). Chilling the burgers before cooking helps to firm them up.

3 tablespoons olive oil, plus more as needed

¹/₂ cup minced onions

¹/₄ cup minced celery

1 large garlic clove, finely minced

1¹/₂ cups cooked dark red kidney beans or one 15-ounce can, drained and rinsed

³/₄ cup coarsely chopped pecans

1 teaspoon tomato paste

Dash of Tabasco sauce

¹/₂ teaspoon minced fresh thyme leaves or ¹/₄ teaspoon dried

¹/₂ teaspoon sweet paprika

¹/₂ teaspoon salt

¹/₈ teaspoon cayenne

³/₄ cup dry bread crumbs

6 burger rolls, toasted

1 Heat 1 tablespoon of the oil in a large skillet over medium heat. Add the onions and celery, cover, and cook, stirring a few times, until softened, about 5 minutes. Add the garlic and cook until fragrant, about 30 seconds.

2 Transfer to a food processor and add the kidney beans, pecans, tomato paste, Tabasco, thyme, paprika, salt, cayenne, and ¹/₂ cup of the bread crumbs. Process until well combined, leaving some texture. Turn out into a bowl, and shape into 6 burgers.

3 Coat the burgers lightly and evenly with the remaining ¹/₄ cup bread crumbs. Cover and chill for at least 30 minutes.

4 Heat the remaining 2 tablespoons oil in a large skillet over medium-high heat. In batches, add the burgers to the skillet and brown, turning once, on both sides, about 5 minutes per side, adding more oil to the pan as necessary. Place on the toasted burger rolls and serve.

Serves 6

Cardamom-Spiced Lentil-Potato Wraps

Inspired by the flavors of India, these sandwiches are best served on an Indian flatbread, such as roti, paratha, or naan. Paratha and roti are usually made with whole wheat flour and baked on a griddle. Naan is usually made with white flour and baked in a tandoor oven. If an Indian bread is unavailable, pita bread makes a good alternative. The Fresh Mango-Mint Chutney is the ideal condiment, but a store-bought chutney can be used if you prefer.

3 tablespoons olive oil

1/2 cup minced onion

1 cup cooked brown lentils, drained well

1 cup cooked potatoes

1/2 cup coarsely chopped cashews

2/3 cup dry bread crumbs

1 tablespoon minced fresh parsley leaves

1/2 teaspoon ground cardamom

1/2 teaspoon salt

1/8 teaspoon cayenne

4 loaves warm roti, paratha, or other
   Indian flatbread

Fresh Mango-Mint Chutney (page 318)

1 Heat 1 tablespoon of the oil in a large skillet over medium heat. Add the onion, cover, and cook, stirring a few times, until softened, about 5 minutes.

2 Transfer to a food processor and add the lentils, potatoes, cashews, bread crumbs, parsley, cardamom, salt, and cayenne. Process until well combined, leaving some texture. Turn out into a bowl, and shape the mixture into 8 small patties.

3 Heat the remaining 2 tablespoons oil in a large skillet over medium heat. Add the patties and cook, turning once, until browned on both sides, about 5 minutes per side. Place 2 patties end to end on the lower third of each flatbread, spread with the chutney, and roll up. Serve immediately.

Serves 4

Saucing It Up

When you think of "meat and potatoes" dishes, a sauce or condiment is often part of the picture. Consider hamburgers and ketchup, hot dogs and mustard, steak and steak sauce, and meat loaf and gravy. The same is true with vegetarian meat-and-potatoes dishes, for, in truth, it is often the sauce and other flavors that we crave in a dish, not necessarily the meat itself. For example, when I want the taste of barbecue, I let the spicy sweet flavor of the sauce enliven a vegetarian meat such as seitan or tofu, just as it does pork or beef.

Virtually all cuisines use condiments and sauces in their cooking. With the popularity of ethnic food on the rise, many international flavors are becoming commonplace in today's kitchens. Maintaining an arsenal of global condiments ensures variety in your meals. Often just a touch of a relish, chutney, or salsa can elevate foods to a higher level of sensory pleasure.

Although there is a wide variety of ready-made condiments available in supermarkets and specialty shops, you can easily—and more economically—make them at home. As you can see from the recipes in this chapter, many condiments are made simply by combining several readily available ingredients.

If you're looking for ways to wake up your taste buds and give a lift to your everyday meals, think condiments and sauces.

Red Wine Sauce

Good Gravy

Marvelous Mushroom Sauce

Lemon-Tahini Sauce

Spicy Peanut Sauce

Ginger-Soy Dipping Sauce

Spicy Ginger Sauce

Teriyaki Marinade

Soy Mayonnaise

Orange-Thyme Aïoli

Ragin' Rémoulade Sauce

Black Olive Tapenade

Basil Pesto

Asian Salsa Verde

Tomato Concassé

Chipotle Salsa

Strawberry-Mango Salsa

Tomato—Red Onion Salsa

Fresh Mango-Mint Chutney

Pineapple Chutney with Dark Rum and
   Crystallized Ginger

Cranberry Relish

Plum Crazy Ketchup

Red Onion—Green Apple Marmalade

Fresh Strawberry Coulis

Mad About Mango Sauce

Red Wine Sauce

This rich-tasting sauce lends an elegant touch to grilled vegetables. Simmer it with sautéed seitan and mushrooms for a quick entrée that tastes as if it took all day to prepare.

1 tablespoon olive oil

2 shallots, finely minced

1/4 cup finely chopped carrot

2 garlic cloves, minced

1/2 cup finely chopped mushrooms

3/4 cup dry red wine

1 1/2 cups vegetable stock (page 36)

1 tablespoon tamari or other soy sauce

1/4 teaspoon dried thyme, crumbled

Salt and freshly ground black pepper

1 tablespoon cornstarch, dissolved in
   1 tablespoon water

1 tablespoon minced fresh parsley leaves

1 Heat the oil in a medium-size saucepan over medium heat. Add the shallots, carrot, and garlic, cover, and cook, stirring a few times, until softened, about 3 minutes. Add the mushrooms and cook for 1 minute. Stir in the wine, then add the stock, tamari, thyme, and salt and pepper to taste. Simmer until the liquid is reduced by nearly half, about 15 minutes.

2 Strain the sauce through a fine-mesh strainer into a small saucepan, pressing on the solids with the back of a spoon to extract all the liquid. Place the saucepan on the stove and return to a simmer over medium-high heat. Taste to adjust the seasonings, then whisk in the cornstarch mixture and boil, whisking, for 1 minute, or until slightly thickened. Stir in the parsley, and serve hot.

Makes about 1 1/4 cups

Good Gravy

This flavorful all-purpose brown sauce is the perfect complement to Meat-Free Meat Loaf (page 172). It can also be used to enrich potpies, stews, and grain dishes or as a topping for veggie burgers or mashed potatoes.

2 cups vegetable stock (page 36) or
water

2¹/₂ tablespoons tamari or other soy
sauce

1 teaspoon minced fresh thyme leaves or
¹/₂ teaspoon dried

Salt and freshly ground black pepper

2 tablespoons cornstarch, dissolved in
3 tablespoons water

¹/₄ cup regular or soy milk

In a small saucepan, combine the stock, tamari, thyme, and salt and pepper to taste and bring to a boil over high heat. Reduce the heat to low, whisk in the cornstarch mixture, and boil, whisking, until the sauce thickens, about I minute. Slowly whisk in the milk; do not allow to boil. Taste to adjust the seasonings. Serve hot.

Makes 2¹/₂ cups

The Sauce Thickens

Most sauces require the use of a thickening agent, or liaison, in order to achieve the desired texture—it's what turns liquid ingredients into a sauce. Meat-based cuisines use heavy cream, cold butter, sour cream, and the classic flour-and-butter combination known as a roux, or *beurre manié*, a roux-like cousin made by kneading together equal parts of butter and flour. However, there are a number of vegetable-based thickeners available that are considerably more healthful. They come in a variety of guises, including starch thickeners, such as cornstarch, arrowroot, or kudzu, that get blended with water. Other vegetarian thickening agents include vegetable and fruit purees, soft tofu, even bread. Leaner still is the reduction method, whereby some of the liquid in the sauce is evaporated over heat and no thickening agent is used at all.

Marvelous Mushroom Sauce

Serve this sauce on seitan roasts, grilled portobello mushrooms, or Roasted Wheat-Meat with Oyster Mushroom and "Sausage" Stuffing (page 169). To achieve a darker brown color, add $^1/_2$ teaspoon or so of gravy seasoning liquid (such as Gravy Master, which contains no animal products) or molasses to the sauce near the end of cooking time.

---

1 tablespoon olive oil

1 small yellow onion, grated

1 garlic clove, minced

4 ounces mushrooms, sliced (about 1 cup)

2 tablespoons all-purpose flour

1$^1/_2$ cups vegetable stock (page 36) or water

2 tablespoons tamari or other soy sauce

1 teaspoon minced fresh thyme leaves or $^1/_2$ teaspoon dried

Salt and freshly ground black pepper

1 Heat the oil in a medium-size saucepan over medium heat. Add the onion and garlic, cover, and cook, stirring a few times, until softened, about 5 minutes. Add the mushrooms and cook, stirring, for 2 minutes longer. Stir in the flour and cook, stirring, for 1 minute.

2 Stir in the stock, tamari, thyme, and salt and pepper to taste. Cook, stirring, until thickened, 3 to 5 minutes. Serve hot.

Makes about 2 cups

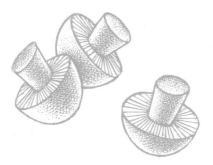

Lemon-Tahini Sauce

This rich and flavorful sauce is sublime on steamed vegetables or tossed with hot pasta. It can also be used as a dip or a spread, by reducing or eliminating the water.

1/3 cup tahini (sesame paste)

1/3 cup mashed silken tofu

1/4 cup minced fresh parsley leaves

1 garlic clove, minced

Grated zest and juice of 1 large lemon

2 teaspoons tamari or other soy sauce

1 teaspoon toasted sesame oil

1/8 teaspoon cayenne

About 1/2 cup water

Salt

1 Place the tahini, tofu, parsley, garlic, lemon zest and juice, tamari, oil, and cayenne in a food processor or blender and process until well combined. Slowly add up to $1/2$ cup water, until a smooth consistency is reached. Season to taste with salt.

2 To serve hot, transfer the mixture to a medium-size saucepan and heat through over low heat, stirring occasionally, just until hot; do not boil. Alternatively, the sauce can be used at room temperature.

Makes about 1 1/2 cups

Spicy Peanut Sauce

Served with the wheat-meat satays (page 14), this spicy dipping sauce is also the perfect complement to spring rolls or a variety of steamed vegetables—green beans are especially good. It can also be tossed with pasta or used to make a cold noodle salad; the recipe makes enough for 8 ounces of pasta. Adjust the amounts of chile paste and sugar according to personal preference.

1/4 cup creamy natural peanut butter

1/4 cup water, or more if needed

2 tablespoons tamari or other soy sauce

1 teaspoon fresh lime juice

1 teaspoon sugar, or to taste

1 teaspoon Asian chile paste, or to taste

In a small bowl or blender, combine the peanut butter, water, tamari, lime juice, sugar, and chile paste and stir or blend until well combined. Taste to adjust the seasonings. Add more water if the sauce is too thick. Use at once, or cover tightly and refrigerate until ready to use. Refrigerated, the sauce will keep for 4 to 5 days. It is best served at room temperature.

Makes about 2/3 cup

Ginger-Soy Dipping Sauce

The classic Asian flavor combination makes this an ideal dipping sauce for steamed or fried dumplings, egg rolls, and tempura, as well as tofu, tempeh, and seitan. It can also be used as a marinade. Mirin is a slightly sweet Japanese cooking wine that is available at Asian markets and well-stocked supermarkets.

2 teaspoons peeled and minced fresh
   ginger

1 large garlic clove, finely minced

1/2 cup tamari or other soy sauce

1/4 cup rice vinegar

2 tablespoons mirin (rice wine)

1 teaspoon toasted sesame oil

In a small bowl, combine the ginger, garlic, tamari, vinegar, mirin, and sesame oil, stirring to mix well. Cover tightly and refrigerate until ready to use. The sauce will keep well for up to a week, but the longer it stands, the stronger the flavors become.

Makes about 1 cup

Spicy Ginger Sauce

This sauce is ideal over Crispy Stuffed "Fillets" of Soy (page 143), but keep it in mind for other uses as well, such as adding rich flavor to a tofu or tempeh stir-fry. Hot bean paste is available at most Asian markets. If you can't find it, add a little extra Asian chile paste and tamari to compensate.

1 teaspoon peanut oil

1/4 cup seeded and chopped red bell
   pepper

2 scallions, chopped

2 tablespoons chopped mushrooms

2 tablespoons peeled and minced fresh
   ginger

3 garlic cloves, minced

1 tablespoon hot bean paste

1 teaspoon Asian chile paste, or more to
   taste

1 teaspoon sugar

1/2 teaspoon salt

1 1/2 cups water

1 tablespoon tamari or other soy sauce

1 1/2 teaspoons rice vinegar

1 tablespoon cornstarch, dissolved in
   2 tablespoons water

1. Heat the oil in a wok or medium-size skillet over medium heat. Add the bell pepper, scallions, mushrooms, ginger, and garlic and stir-fry until fragrant, about 30 seconds. Stir in the hot bean paste, chile paste, sugar, salt, water, tamari, and vinegar and simmer for 10 minutes over low heat.

2. Stir the cornstarch mixture into the sauce and boil, stirring, for 1 minute, or until thickened. Serve hot.

Makes about 2 cups

Teriyaki Marinade

When used with meat, marinades generally serve two functions: to tenderize and to add flavor. When used with vegetables and naturally tender vegetarian "meats," marinades can concentrate solely on the latter. This teriyaki marinade adds flavor to tofu, tempeh, and seitan, as well as vegetables destined for the grill. It is especially good with eggplant and portobello mushrooms. Marinate ingredients for about an hour, turning once. After removing the ingredients from the marinade, pour it into a saucepan and reduce by half. Use to baste the marinated ingredients as they cook, and drizzle any remaining marinade over the cooked ingredients as a sauce.

2 garlic cloves, mashed to a paste

2 teaspoons peeled and minced fresh
  ginger

1/2 cup tamari or other soy sauce

2 tablespoons toasted sesame oil

2 tablespoons dry sherry

2 tablespoons fresh orange juice

2 tablespoons firmly packed light brown
  sugar, honey, or brown rice syrup

In a small bowl, combine the garlic, ginger, tamari, oil, sherry, orange juice, and sugar, stirring to dissolve the sugar. If not using right away, cover tightly and refrigerate. The marinade will keep for up to a week in the refrigerator.

Makes 1 cup

Soy Mayonnaise

This mayonnaise relies on tofu instead of eggs for its creamy texture. Use it in any way you would use regular mayonnaise. A light flavorless vegetable oil such as sunflower works best in this recipe.

6 ounces firm silken tofu

1/4 cup sunflower oil or other light
   flavorless oil

1 tablespoon rice vinegar

1 tablespoon fresh lemon juice

1/4 teaspoon dry mustard

1/2 teaspoon salt

Freshly ground white pepper

In a food processor or blender, combine the tofu, oil, vinegar, lemon juice, mustard, salt, and pepper to taste and blend until smooth and creamy. Transfer to a tightly sealed container and refrigerate until chilled. Refrigerated, this will keep for up to a week.

Makes about 2 cups

wasabi mayonnaise: Add I teaspoon wasabi powder.

curried mayonnaise: Add I teaspoon curry powder.

lemon-dill mayonnaise: Replace the vinegar with I tablespoon additional lemon juice and add I tablespoon chopped fresh dill.

chipotle mayonnaise: Add I to 2 teaspoons pureed canned chipotle chiles in adobo sauce.

Orange-Thyme Aïoli

The sweetness of the orange balances the assertiveness of the thyme in this surprisingly versatile sauce. I like it on baked tofu, veggie burgers, and steamed broccoli, to name a few.

$^1/_3$ cup dry white wine

2 shallots, minced

1$^1/_2$ teaspoons minced fresh thyme leaves or $^3/_4$ teaspoon dried

$^2/_3$ cup regular or soy mayonnaise (page 309)

1 teaspoon grated orange zest

1 tablespoon fresh orange juice

Pinch of turmeric

Pinch of cayenne

Salt

1 Place the wine, shallots, and thyme in a small saucepan and simmer over medium-high heat until the liquid reduces by half.

2 Transfer the mixture to a food processor or blender and add the mayonnaise, orange zest, juice, turmeric, cayenne, and salt to taste and blend until smooth. Taste to adjust the seasonings. Cover and refrigerate until chilled. Stored tightly in the refrigerator, this will keep for 3 to 5 days.

Makes about 1 cup

Ragin' Remoulade Sauce

Remoulade sauce is traditionally served with cold seafood dishes, but I enjoy it with the Vegetable Carpaccio on page 22, or as a "special sauce" for veggie burgers.

3/4 cup regular or soy mayonnaise
   (page 309)
2 tablespoons tomato ketchup
2 teaspoons minced capers
2 teaspoons sweet pickle relish
2 teaspoons Dijon mustard
2 teaspoons minced fresh parsley leaves
1 teaspoon minced fresh tarragon leaves
   or 1/2 teaspoon dried
Splash of Tabasco sauce
Salt

In a small bowl, combine the mayonnaise, ketchup, capers, pickle relish, and mustard. Stir in the parsley, tarragon, Tabasco, and salt to taste. Blend thoroughly, then cover and refrigerate until chilled. Refrigerated, this sauce will keep for 3 to 5 days.

Makes about 1 1/4 cups

Black Olive Tapenade

A recipe is only as good as its ingredients, and tapenade is no exception. Use only good-quality, brine-cured olives, not the canned supermarket variety. Toss with pasta, spread on crostini or bruschetta, or use to top baked potatoes. If using a food processor instead of the traditional mortar and pestle, be careful not to overprocess—the tapenade should retain some texture. Both large, meaty Kalamata olives and the smaller, sweeter Gaeta variety are great in this recipe.

1¹/₂ cups Kalamata or Gaeta olives, pitted

3 tablespoons capers, drained

2 garlic cloves, finely minced

¹/₄ cup minced fresh parsley leaves

¹/₂ teaspoon salt

¹/₈ teaspoon freshly ground black pepper

¹/₄ cup extra virgin olive oil

In a food processor or mortar, combine the olives, capers, garlic, parsley, salt, and pepper. Slowly add the oil and pulse or work with the pestle into a coarse paste, retaining some bits of olive and caper for texture. Taste to adjust the seasonings. Stored tightly covered in the refrigerator, this will keep well for a week or two.

Makes about 2 cups

Basil Pesto

The basil leaves in pesto have a tendency to turn brown if in prolonged contact with the air. For that reason, if not serving the pesto fairly soon, spread a thin layer of olive oil on top of it before refrigerating in a tightly sealed container. Properly stored, pesto will keep for several weeks. Pesto sauce also freezes well for several months—but only if you do not add the cheese. For freezing, simply omit the cheese when making the pesto, then add it after the pesto is defrosted and ready for use. (If you prefer, the cheese can be omitted altogether with good results, but in that case, you may wish to add a little more salt.)

3 garlic cloves, peeled

1/3 cup pine nuts

3 cups firmly packed fresh basil leaves

1/2 to 3/4 teaspoon salt, to your taste

1/8 teaspoon freshly ground black pepper

1/2 cup extra virgin olive oil

1/4 cup freshly grated Parmesan cheese
   or soy Parmesan

1 Place the garlic and pine nuts in a food processor and process until minced. Add the basil, salt, and pepper and process until the mixture is ground into a paste. With the machine running, pour the oil into the feed tube in a slow, steady stream until well blended.

2 Transfer to a bowl and stir in the cheese. Cover and refrigerate until ready to serve.

Makes about 2 cups

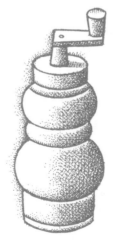

Asian Salsa Verde

This *salsa verde*, literally, "green sauce," is infused with the heady Asian flavors of cilantro, Thai basil, and sesame oil. A touch of sambal oelek, a fiery Indonesian chile paste, adds a bit of heat, but regular Asian chile paste can be used instead. If Thai basil, an especially aromatic variety, is unavailable, regular basil or mint can be substituted, for a somewhat different flavor. Serve this sauce with Tamari-Seared Tofu (page 140) or toss with pasta. It can also be used to perk up grilled vegetables or as a last-minute addition to a brothy Asian soup.

1/3 cup packed fresh cilantro leaves

1/3 cup packed fresh Thai basil leaves
   (see headnote)

1 large garlic clove, peeled

2 tablespoons rice vinegar

1/2 teaspoon salt

1/2 teaspoon sambal oelek or other Asian
   chile paste

1/4 cup toasted sesame oil

1/4 cup sunflower oil or other light
   flavorless oil

In a food processor, combine all the ingredients except the oils and process until ground into a paste. With the machine running, slowly add the oils, processing until well blended. This sauce is best used soon after it is made, to take full advantage of the flavor and color of the fresh herbs.

Makes about 1 cup

Tomato Concassé

A concassé is a sauce that retains some of the original texture of the primary ingredient (*concassé* means crushed), unlike a puree or coulis, which is smooth. A concassé can be either cooked or raw. To me, raw is best during the peak of tomato season, so the full flavor of the tomato can be enjoyed. Serve this with Eggplant Braciole (page 157) or use as a pasta sauce.

4 large ripe tomatoes, cored

Salt and freshly ground black pepper

1 tablespoon minced fresh parsley leaves

1 teaspoon extra virgin olive oil

1 Plunge the tomatoes into a pot of boiling water for about 15 seconds. Remove from the pot and place in a bowl of cold water. Drain.

2 Pull off the tomato skins with your fingers, then cut the tomatoes crosswise in half and remove the seeds. Coarsely chop the tomatoes and place in a medium-size bowl.

3 Season to taste with salt and pepper, sprinkle with the parsley, and drizzle on the oil, tossing gently to combine. For best results, cover the bowl and let stand at room temperature for 20 to 30 minutes to allow the flavors to blend before serving.

Makes about 2 cups

Chipotle Salsa

Chipotle chiles are dried jalapeños that add a smoky richness to recipes. They are commonly found canned in adobo sauce, a spicy red sauce made with ground chiles and vinegar. This salsa is best when made several hours in advance to allow the flavors to mingle. Serve it with Seared Wheat-Meat Tortilla Wraps (page 292) or Cilantro Polenta Wedges (page 254).

1 pound ripe tomatoes, peeled, seeded, and chopped

¹/₄ cup chopped onion

2 scallions, chopped

2 canned chipotle chiles in adobo sauce, chopped

1 teaspoon cider vinegar

1 teaspoon fresh lime juice

¹/₄ teaspoon salt

In a medium-size bowl, combine all the ingredients. Cover and refrigerate for at least 30 minutes before serving. Serve chilled or at room temperature. This salsa will keep for a week in the refrigerator.

Makes about 2 cups

Strawberry-Mango Salsa

In addition to serving it with Almond-Crusted Tempeh Cutlets (page 139), I like this fruity salsa as a colorful accompaniment to veggie burgers, as well as grain and bean dishes.

1 pint strawberries, rinsed and hulled

1 small ripe mango, peeled, pitted, and coarsely chopped

1 jalapeño chile, seeded and minced

1/4 cup minced red onion

1/4 cup seeded and minced red bell pepper

Juice of 1 lime

1 teaspoon balsamic vinegar (optional)

Salt and freshly ground black pepper

1/4 cup minced fresh mint leaves

1 Coarsely chop the strawberries and place in a medium-size bowl. Add the mango, jalapeño, onion, bell pepper, lime juice, vinegar, if using, and salt and pepper to taste. The salsa can be made a few hours ahead to this point. Set aside at room temperature, or cover and refrigerate to serve chilled.

2 Just before serving, add the mint and stir gently to combine. Taste to adjust the seasonings and serve.

Makes about 2 1/2 cups

Tomato–Red Onion Salsa

⁓⁓⁓

Make this when you have ripe tomatoes on hand and a craving for a zesty fresh-tasting salsa. If you prefer it on the hot side, add 1 or 2 minced hot chiles. Try it with everything from quesadillas or corn chips to Southwestern Refried Bean Wraps (page 291).

4 large ripe tomatoes, peeled, seeded,
  and chopped

1 small red onion, finely chopped

2 garlic cloves, finely minced

1/4 cup minced fresh cilantro leaves

1 teaspoon sugar

1/2 teaspoon salt

1/4 teaspoon freshly ground black pepper

Place the tomatoes, onion, and garlic in a large bowl. Add the cilantro, sugar, salt, and pepper and stir to combine. Cover and refrigerate at least 30 minutes, and up to several hours, before serving to blend the flavors. Serve chilled or at room temperature.

Makes about 2 1/2 cups

Fresh Mango-Mint Chutney

⁓⁓⁓

Because this is a no-cook chutney, the flavors remain as bright as the colors of the ingredients. It's a great way to use ripe mangoes when there's no time to make a cooked chutney. It can be used to perk up grain and bean dishes or as a condiment for Cardamom-Spiced Lentil Potato Wraps (page 297).

2 ripe mangoes, peeled, pitted, and cut
  into 1/2-inch dice

1 small shallot, finely chopped

1 small hot chile, seeded and finely
  chopped

2 tablespoons fresh lime juice

1 Place the mangoes in a medium-size bowl. Add the shallot, chile, lime juice, sugar, and salt and mix well. Cover and refrigerate for at least 30 minutes, and up to several hours, before serving.

1¹/₂ tablespoons sugar or a natural

   sweetener (page 330)

¹/₄ teaspoon salt

¹/₄ cup fresh mint leaves

2 Just before serving, finely chop the mint and stir into the chutney.

Makes about 2¹/₂ cups

A World of Condiments

Condiments can transform a meal from dull to dazzling right before your eyes. These zesty concoctions are designed to add a bold, complementary flavor to other foods, rather than being eaten on their own. Many condiments have a complexity that combines sweet, sour, hot, and spicy all in one.

Among the more familiar condiments are mustard, ketchup, and pickle relish. All-American ketchup actually has its origins in the tangy tomato-based Indonesian sauce called kecap manis, and pickle relish is a spin-off of the exotic relishes and chutneys of India. Mustard has long been used throughout the world in such diverse cuisines as French, German, and Chinese.

Another favorite condiment is salsa, which is said to have surpassed ketchup sales in the United States in recent years. Salsa—the word simply means "sauce"—is usually a spicy blend of tomatoes and seasonings. It is eaten as an accompaniment to Latin American foods and can also be used as a dip for chips, or as a flavoring for soups, stews, and chili.

A number of other exotic condiments are making their way into American pantries. For example, harissa is a fiery North African hot sauce that is traditionally used to flavor stews, while sambal oelek is a hot Indonesian chile paste. Hoisin sauce is an Asian condiment that is on the sweet side, a kind of Chinese "barbecue sauce" redolent of star anise and garlic.

Chunky vegetable condiments abound, such as chow chow, the lively corn relish popular in the United States, kim chee, the spicy Korean cabbage mixture, and caponata, the Italian eggplant relish.

Keep a variety of condiments, smooth or chunky, spicy or sweet, on hand to enhance your meals and add interest to everyday foods.

Pineapple Chutney with Dark Rum and Crystallized Ginger

───ᴡᴡᴡ───

The sweetness of the pineapple is accented by the bite of chile, rum, and ginger. Crystallized ginger is available at gourmet food stores or well-stocked supermarkets. Make this spicy-sweet chutney at least a day before you plan to serve it, as the flavor improves when the ingredients have a chance to steep together. This goes well with Indian Chickpea and Potato Stew (page 118) and other Indian-spiced dishes. Or try it as a condiment for veggie burgers or potato pancakes.

1 pineapple, trimmed, peeled, cored, and coarsely chopped

1/3 cup golden raisins

2 shallots, finely minced

1 small hot red chile, seeded and finely minced

2 tablespoons chopped crystallized ginger

1/2 cup firmly packed light brown sugar or a natural sweetener (page 330)

1/4 cup dark rum

2 tablespoons fresh lime juice

1/4 teaspoon ground cloves

1/8 teaspoon salt

1 Place the pineapple in a medium-size nonreactive saucepan over medium heat. Add the raisins, shallots, chile, ginger, brown sugar, rum, and lime juice and bring to a boil. Reduce the heat to low and simmer, stirring occasionally, until thick and syrupy, about 30 minutes.

2 Remove from the heat and stir in the cloves and salt. Allow to cool completely.

3 Transfer the chutney to a container with a tight-fitting lid, cover, and refrigerate, preferably overnight, before serving. Serve chilled or at room temperature. Refrigerated, the chutney will keep for several weeks.

Makes about 3 cups

Cranberry Relish

This zesty and colorful relish makes a nice change from ordinary cranberry sauce at Thanksgiving, but it's too delicious to reserve for only that time of year. Serve it in place of chutney with Indian food or as a condiment for veggie burgers or grain dishes.

One 12-ounce bag fresh cranberries

1 small red bell pepper, seeded and chopped

2 shallots, minced

3/4 cup firmly packed light brown sugar or a natural sweetener (page 330)

1/4 cup orange marmalade

Grated zest and juice of 2 lemons

3/4 teaspoon salt

1/8 teaspoon freshly ground black pepper

1 Pick through the cranberries to remove any stems, rinse them, and place in a large saucepan. Add the bell pepper, shallots, brown sugar, marmalade, lemon zest and juice, salt, and pepper. Simmer gently over medium heat, stirring occasionally, until the cranberries pop and the mixture thickens, about 30 minutes.

2 Transfer to a bowl, cover, and refrigerate to chill before serving. Stored covered in the refrigerator, this relish will keep for up to a week.

Makes about 2 cups

Plum Crazy Ketchup

In the kitchen of most "meat and potatoes" people, you're bound to find a bottle of ketchup. By making it from scratch, you can jazz up this all-American condiment. The plums add sweetness and a sophisticated nuance.

1 tablespoon olive oil

1 medium-size yellow onion, chopped

2 garlic cloves, chopped

6 cups diced ripe tomatoes (about
    4 pounds)

1¹/₂ cups pitted ripe or canned plums

¹/₄ cup sugar or a natural sweetener
    (page 330)

1¹/₂ teaspoons salt

1 teaspoon ground allspice

1 teaspoon sweet paprika

¹/₂ teaspoon ground cloves

¹/₂ teaspoon dry mustard

¹/₄ teaspoon cayenne

³/₄ to 1 cup cider vinegar, to your taste

1 Heat the oil in a large saucepan over medium heat. Add the onion and garlic and cook, stirring occasionally, until soft, about 5 minutes. Add the tomatoes and simmer until they cook down, about 15 minutes. About 5 minutes before the end of the cooking time, add the plums.

2 Put the mixture through a food mill or puree in a food processor, then strain through a fine-mesh strainer and return to the saucepan. Add the sugar, salt, allspice, paprika, cloves, mustard, and cayenne. Cook over medium heat, stirring occasionally, until thick, about 20 minutes.

3 Stir in the vinegar and cook until thickened again, about 10 minutes longer. Allow to cool, then refrigerate in a tightly sealed container. The ketchup will keep in the refrigerator for 2 weeks or in the freezer for several months.

Makes 4 cups

Red Onion–Green Apple Marmalade

An unlikely twosome combines to make a winning condiment that goes especially well with Sam's Truck-Stop Hash (page 222), veggie burgers, and grilled vegetables.

1 large red onion, chopped

1 large Granny Smith apple, peeled, cored, and chopped

1/2 cup firmly packed light brown sugar or a natural sweetener (page 330)

1/4 cup apple jelly

1/4 cup cider vinegar

Grated zest and juice of 2 lemons

1/2 teaspoon red pepper flakes

1/2 teaspoon salt

1/8 teaspoon freshly ground black pepper

1 Combine all the ingredients in a medium-size saucepan. Cover and cook over low heat until the onion softens and the mixture cooks down and thickens, 20 to 30 minutes. Stir occasionally to be sure the marmalade does not stick to the bottom of the pan; if it begins to stick, add a little water, and continue cooking until thick.

2 Taste to adjust the seasonings, then let cool to room temperature before serving or refrigerating. Refrigerated in a tightly sealed container, this will keep for up to 2 weeks. Serve at room temperature.

Makes about 2 cups

Fresh Strawberry Coulis

This ruby-red sauce, made with fresh strawberries and nothing else, couldn't be easier. If your strawberries are less than perfectly sweet, you can add a little sugar syrup (equal amounts of sugar and water heated to dissolve the sugar) and a dash of fresh lemon juice to brighten the flavor. Serve this with Peanut Butter Bread Pudding (page 339) or use it to adorn fresh-cut fruit or ice cream.

---

2 cups ripe strawberries, rinsed and
    hulled

Place the strawberries in a food processor and process until smooth. (Alternatively, the berries can be run through a food mill.) Strain through a fine-mesh strainer into a bowl. Cover and refrigerate until ready to use. I like to use this sauce on the same day it is made to fully enjoy the fresh strawberry taste.

Makes about 2 cups

Mad About Mango Sauce

~~~

This versatile and infinitely simple sauce can be used as a dessert topping for ice cream or cut-up fruit, or spooned alongside your favorite cake. It can also be transformed into a tropical smoothie by blending it with a frozen banana and a splash of orange juice. If you can find very ripe mangoes, no additional sweetener should be needed, although, of course, if you use orange juice the result will be a sweeter sauce than if you use lemon or lime juice. If you prefer it sweeter, add some sugar or a natural sweetener (see page 330), according to taste. The amount of juice added depends on how you will be using the sauce. For example, a thicker puree is better alongside a cake, a thinner sauce is better to top fruit.

---

1 large or 2 small very ripe mangoes,
   peeled and pitted
$1/4$ to $1/2$ cup fresh lemon, lime, or orange
   juice, according to taste and use

1 Place the mango flesh in a food processor or blender, add $1/4$ cup of the juice, and puree, adding more juice if needed to achieve the desired consistency.
2 Cover and refrigerate until chilled before serving. Stored in a tightly covered container in the refrigerator, this will keep for up to 5 days.

Makes 1$1/2$ cups

Sweet Endings

Chances are, the meat-and-potatoes people in your house also love rich desserts, many of which are loaded with sugar, butter, and eggs. If you're trying to eliminate dairy or cut down on sugar, you may be happy to learn that you can still enjoy many of the desserts your family loves by using dairy alternatives and natural sweeteners. Instead of saying "no" to desserts, say "yes" to healthier desserts made with soy and nut milks, tofu, egg replacers such as ground flaxseeds, and grain-based or natural fruit sweeteners.

In the interest of accommodating all tastes, most of these dessert recipes list alternate ingredient choices so you can decide for yourself which you want to include, whether it be sugar or a natural sweetener, milk or soy milk, eggs or equivalent egg replacer, and so on. Many alternatives can be substituted in equal measure. For convenience, substitution guidelines for sugar and for dairy and eggs can be found on pages 330 and 342.

Try the recipes in this chapter and see how delicious eating healthy can be. Although these desserts are not necessarily low in calories, they can be made cholesterol-free and low in saturated fat. In addition, many of the recipes contain significant amounts of protein and fiber. Best of all, they are loaded with great taste that everyone can enjoy without feeling guilty.

Soy Good Lemon Cheesecake

Pecan-Dusted Double Pumpkin "Cheese" Cake

Total Chocolate Eclipse Cake

Vanilla-Almond "Ice Cream" Cake with Chocolate Cookie Crust

Fresh Strawberry Pie

Sweet Potato Pie

Blueberry-Peach Galette

Granny Apple Crisp

Peanut Butter Bread Pudding with Fresh Strawberry Coulis

Creamy Rice Pudding with Slivered Almonds

Creamy Chocolate Pudding

Cranberry-Pistachio Scones

Pecan-Studded Chocolate Brownies

Egg-Free Almond—Chocolate Chip Biscotti

Five-Spice Oatmeal-Date Cookies

Mom's Butterballs

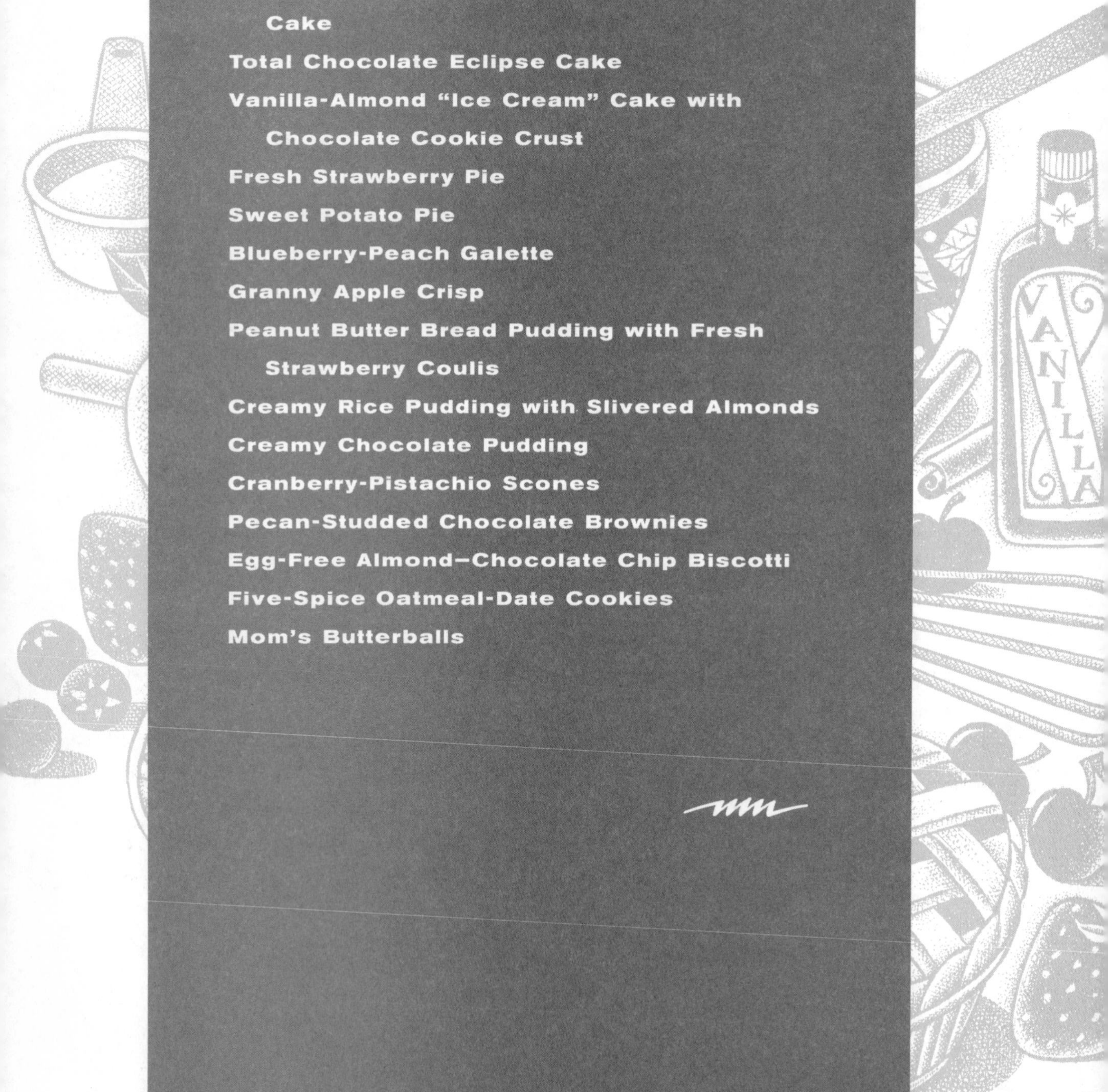

Soy Good Lemon Cheesecake

This creamy, fresh-tasting "cheese" cake is a lemon-lover's dream and a great way to enjoy heart-healthy tofu. The cake's refreshingly light flavor makes it a good dessert choice even after a heavy meal. For an elegant touch, garnish the cake with candied violets and lemon zest.

Crust:

1½ cups graham cracker crumbs

¼ cup corn oil

Filling:

1 pound firm silken tofu, crumbled, at
    room temperature

One 8-ounce package regular or tofu
    cream cheese, at room temperature

1 cup sugar or a natural sweetener
    (page 330)

Grated zest and juice of 2 lemons

1 teaspoon pure vanilla extract

1 Preheat the oven to 350 degrees F. Lightly oil a 9-inch springform pan.

2 *Make the crust:* Place the crumbs in the bottom of the prepared pan, add the corn oil, and toss with a fork until blended. Press the crumb mixture evenly against the bottom and partway up the sides of the pan. Bake for 5 minutes. Set aside to cool. Leave the oven on.

3 *Make the filling:* Put the tofu in a food processor and process until smooth. Add the cream cheese, sugar, half the lemon zest, the lemon juice, and vanilla and process until smooth (reserve the remaining zest for garnish). Pour the filling into the prepared crust.

4 Bake until the filling is firm, about 40 minutes. Turn the oven off and leave the cake in it for 45 minutes to 1 hour.

5 Remove the cheesecake from the oven and allow to cool to room temperature. Refrigerate for at least several hours, or overnight, before serving.

6 To serve, remove the sides of the springform pan and cut the cake into slices. Garnish with the reserved lemon zest.

Makes one 9-inch cake; serves 8

Sweet Alternatives

While some people need to avoid sugar for particular health problems, others wish to eliminate white sugar from their diet simply because it lacks nutritional value. Among the alternatives are grain sweeteners such as barley malt and brown rice syrup, and natural fruit sweeteners, available under a variety of brand names. Unlike sugar, grain sweeteners do not cause a sugar "rush," since they metabolize more slowly in the system. In addition to sweetness, natural sweeteners such as rice syrup, barley malt, maple syrup, pureed fruit such as raisins and dates, and concentrated fruit sweeteners provide nutritional benefits.

The sweetness level of sugar alternatives can vary greatly, so it is advisable to experiment to find ones you like best. In addition, certain sweeteners, such as molasses, barley malt, and maple syrup, have distinctive colors and stronger flavors and are suitable only for certain recipes. Artificial sweeteners should not be used at all, because they are "non-foods" that have been shown to be hazardous to one's health.

Substitution Guidelines for Sugar

- Sucanat (for "sugarcane natural") is an all-purpose sweetener with a mild flavor that can be substituted in equal measure for granulated sugar. Made from sugarcane juice, it retains the nutrients in the sugarcane, unlike white sugar.

- FruitSource is a widely available sweetener made from fruit juice concentrate and brown rice syrup. It is available in both liquid and granular forms, and it can be substituted in equal measure for sugar.

- Many liquid sweeteners, such as pure maple syrup, brown rice syrup, and barley malt, are about half to two-thirds as sweet as sugar. A good rule of thumb is to use $1^1/_2$ cups of liquid sweetener to replace 1 cup of sugar. When substituting a natural liquid sweetener for granulated sugar, it's a good idea to cut back on the other liquids used in the recipe by about $^1/_2$ cup so the finished product retains the intended texture.

- Soaked and pureed dates and raisins make good sugar alternatives and offer good nutritional benefits, but should only be used in recipes where their dark color and distinctive flavor will not interfere with the recipe. Again, these are only half to two-thirds as sweet as sugar and will need to be experimented with to suit your taste.

Pecan-Dusted Double Pumpkin "Cheese" Cake

Pumpkin two ways: in the cake and the sauce. Tofu stands in for cream cheese in this rich and elegant alternative to pumpkin pie. Serve on Thanksgiving, or any time the mood strikes.

Crust:

1½ cups graham cracker crumbs

¼ cup corn oil

Filling:

1 pound firm silken tofu, crumbled, at
   room temperature

One 15-ounce can pumpkin puree

¾ cup firmly packed light brown sugar or
   a natural sweetener (page 330)

1 teaspoon pure rum extract

1 teaspoon ground cinnamon

¾ teaspoon ground allspice

¾ teaspoon ground nutmeg

¾ cup finely ground pecans

Sauce:

¼ cup canned pumpkin puree

⅓ cup regular or soy milk

2 tablespoons firmly packed light brown
   sugar or a natural sweetener

½ teaspoon ground cinnamon

¼ teaspoon ground allspice

¼ teaspoon ground nutmeg

1 Preheat the oven to 350 degrees F. Lightly oil a 9-inch springform pan.

2 *Make the crust:* Place the crumbs in the springform pan, add the corn oil, and toss with a fork to combine. Press the crumb mixture evenly against the bottom and partway up the sides of the pan. Bake for 5 minutes. Remove from the oven and set aside to cool. Leave the oven on.

3 *Make the filling:* Place the tofu in a food processor and process until smooth. Add the pumpkin and process until well blended. Add the brown sugar, rum extract, cinnamon, allspice, and nutmeg and process until well blended. Pour the filling into the cooled crust.

4 Bake until the filling is firm, 40 to 45 minutes. Turn off the oven and allow the "cheese" cake to cool in the oven for 45 minutes to I hour.

5 Remove the cake from the oven and allow to cool completely. Refrigerate for at least several hours, or overnight, before serving.

6 *Make the sauce:* In a medium-size saucepan, combine the pumpkin puree, milk, brown sugar, cinnamon, allspice, and nutmeg. Heat over medium heat, stirring, until the sugar is dissolved. Set aside to cool.

continued

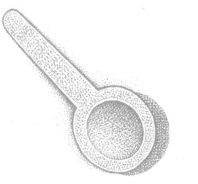

7 When ready to serve, remove the sides of the spring-form pan and spread the ground pecans evenly over the top of the "cheese" cake. Place a spoonful of sauce on each dessert plate, and top with a slice of cake.

Makes one 9-inch cake; serves 8

Total Chocolate Eclipse Cake

The rich flavor of chocolate eclipses the fact that no eggs, butter, or refined sugar are used to make this dense, fudgy confection. You'll need one 12-ounce package of silken tofu—half for the cake and half for the frosting. Flaxseeds are available at natural food stores.

Cake:

1¹/₂ cups all-purpose flour

³/₄ cup unsweetened cocoa powder

1 teaspoon baking powder

1 teaspoon baking soda

2 tablespoons flaxseeds

¹/₂ cup water

¹/₂ cup pitted dates, soaked in 1 cup
   hot water

6 ounces extra-firm silken tofu

1 Preheat the oven to 350 degrees F. Lightly oil two 9-inch round cake pans and coat with flour, tapping off the excess.

2 *Make the cake:* Sift together the flour, cocoa powder, baking powder, and baking soda into a large bowl. Set aside.

3 In a blender, grind the flaxseeds to a fine powder. Add the water and blend until thick and frothy, about 30 seconds. Add the dates and their soaking liquid, the tofu, maple syrup, oil, and vanilla and blend until smooth. Transfer to a large bowl.

1 cup pure maple syrup, unsulphured
molasses, or other natural liquid
sweetener (page 330)

1 tablespoon corn oil

1½ teaspoons pure vanilla extract

Frosting:

1 cup semisweet chocolate chips

½ cup raw cashews

⅓ cup water

6 ounces extra-firm silken tofu

¼ cup pure maple syrup or molasses

1 teaspoon pure vanilla extract

4 Whisk the dry ingredients into the wet ingredients, blending until smooth. Divide the batter between the prepared pans.

5 Bake until the cakes spring back when lightly touched, 20 to 25 minutes. Cool the cakes in their pans for 10 minutes, then invert onto wire racks to cool completely.

6 *Make the frosting:* Melt the chocolate chips in the top of a double boiler over gently simmering water, stirring frequently. Set aside.

7 In a blender or food processor, grind the cashews to a powder. Add the water and blend until smooth. Add the tofu, maple syrup, and vanilla and blend until smooth. Add the melted chocolate and process until smooth. Transfer to a bowl, cover, and refrigerate until well chilled.

8 To frost the cake, place one cake layer on a plate and spread about ¾ cup of the frosting over the top. Top with the second cake layer and spread the top and sides of the cake with the remaining frosting. Cut into wedges to serve.

**Makes one 2-layer 9-inch cake;
serves 8 to 12**

Vanilla-Almond "Ice Cream" Cake with Chocolate Cookie Crust

J ust a small wedge of this rich dessert is enough to satisfy any sweet tooth. Almond butter is available at natural food stores. Tofutti is a soy-based "ice cream" that can be purchased in natural food stores and well-stocked supermarkets.

Crust:

1¹/₂ cups fat-free chocolate cookie
    crumbs

¹/₄ cup corn oil

Cake:

1 quart vanilla Tofutti or other nondairy
    ice cream, softened

¹/₂ cup almond butter

¹/₃ cup pure maple syrup or other natural
    liquid sweetener (page 330)

Chocolate curls for garnish

1 Preheat the oven to 350 degrees F. Lightly oil an 8-inch springform pan.

2 *Make the crust:* Place the crumbs in the springform pan, add the corn oil, and toss with a fork to combine. Press the crumb mixture evenly against the bottom and partway up the sides of the pan. Bake for 5 minutes, then allow to cool completely.

3 *Make the filling:* In a large bowl, combine the softened Tofutti, almond butter, and maple syrup, mixing until well blended. Spoon evenly into the prepared crust. Freeze for at least several hours, or overnight.

4 To serve, let the cake sit at room temperature for 5 minutes, then carefully remove the sides of the pan. Sprinkle the chocolate curls around the edge of the top of the cake, and cut into wedges.

Makes one 8-inch cake; serves 8

Making Chocolate Curls

To make chocolate curls, run a vegetable peeler along one side of a room-temperature block of chocolate. Refrigerate the curls until ready to use.

Fresh Strawberry Pie

U se the sweetest, ripest strawberries you can find, and serve the pie within four hours of preparing it to experience the full flavor of the fresh berries.

Crust:

1½ cups raw almonds

1 cup pitted dates, soaked for 10 minutes
   in hot water and drained

Filling:

5 cups hulled and sliced strawberries

4 pitted dates, soaked for 10 minutes in
   hot water and drained

2 teaspoons fresh lemon juice

1 *Make the crust:* In a food processor, coarsely grind the almonds. Add the dates and process until thoroughly combined. Press the mixture into a lightly oiled 9-inch pie plate or springform pan.

2 *Make the filling:* Arrange 4 cups of the sliced strawberries on top of the crust in a circular pattern. Set aside.

3 In a food processor or blender, combine the remaining 1 cup strawberries with the dates and lemon juice and process until smooth. Pour the sauce over the strawberries and refrigerate for at least 1 hour, but no longer than 4 hours, before serving.

Makes one 9-inch pie; serves 8

Sweet Potato Pie

⌇⌇⌇

Try this version of a family favorite—you may start a new holiday tradition.

Crust:

1 cup all-purpose flour

1/8 teaspoon salt

1/2 cup corn oil, chilled

2 tablespoons ice water, or more if
    needed

Filling:

2 cups mashed cooked sweet potatoes

12 ounces extra-firm silken tofu, drained
    and patted dry

1 cup firmly packed light brown sugar or
    a natural sweetener (page 330)

2 large eggs or egg replacer for 2 eggs
    (page 342)

1 teaspoon pure vanilla extract

1 teaspoon ground cinnamon

1/2 teaspoon ground ginger

1/4 teaspoon ground nutmeg

1 Make the crust: Combine the flour and salt in a food processor. Blend in the corn oil with short pulses, until the mixture becomes crumbly. With the machine running, add the water through the feed tube and blend until the dough just starts to hold together; add a little more water if needed. Transfer the dough to a floured work surface and flatten into a disk. Wrap in plastic and refrigerate for at least 30 minutes, and up to 2 days.

2 Preheat the oven to 375 degrees F. Make the filling: In a food processor, process the sweet potatoes and tofu until well blended. Add the brown sugar, eggs, vanilla, cinnamon, ginger, and nutmeg and process until smooth and well combined.

3 If the dough has been refrigerated for longer than 30 minutes, let it stand at room temperature briefly to soften slightly before rolling it out. Roll out the dough on a lightly floured work surface to a 12-inch circle. Fit it into a 9-inch pie plate, trim off the excess dough, and flute the edges.

4 Pour the filling into the crust and bake until firm, about 50 minutes. Let cool completely.

5 Chill the pie in the refrigerator for at least 2 hours, and up to 8 hours, before serving.

Makes one 9-inch pie; serves 8

Blueberry-Peach Galette

A galette is a free-form tart, as delicious as a pie but much quicker to assemble and bake. It's a great way to prepare a special dessert in a hurry, using fresh seasonal fruit.

Crust:

1 cup all-purpose flour

1 teaspoon sugar or a natural sweetener
   (page 330)

$^1/_8$ teaspoon salt

$^1/_2$ cup corn oil, chilled

2 tablespoons ice water, or more if
   needed

Filling:

2 or 3 ripe peaches, peeled, pitted, and
   thinly sliced (about 2 cups)

1 cup blueberries, picked over for stems

1 teaspoon butter or soy margarine
   (optional), cut into tiny bits

1 tablespoon sugar or a natural
   sweetener

$^1/_2$ teaspoon ground cinnamon

1 Preheat the oven to 425 degrees F. Make the crust: Combine the flour, sugar, and salt in a food processor. Blend in the corn oil with short pulses until the mixture becomes crumbly. With the machine running, add the water through the feed tube and blend until the dough just starts to hold together; add a little more water if necessary. Transfer the dough to a lightly floured work surface.

2 Roll out the dough to a 12-inch circle. Place the dough on an ungreased baking sheet and arrange the peach slices in a spiral or concentric circles on the crust, leaving a 2-inch border. Scatter the blueberries over the peach slices. Fold the exposed edges of the dough up over the fruit, pinching the overlapping edges of the dough together. (The fruit in the center of the galette will remain exposed.) Dot the fruit with the butter, if using, and sprinkle with the sugar and cinnamon.

3 Bake until the fruit is bubbly and the crust is golden brown, about 25 minutes. Remove from the oven and let cool slightly. Serve warm.

Makes one 8-inch galette; serves 8

Granny Apple Crisp

The tart flavor of Granny Smith apples is accented by the cinnamon-sugar and the lemon mixture for a taste of apple pie without the bother of a piecrust. Serve warm with vanilla ice cream or a nondairy frozen dessert such as Tofutti.

5 Granny Smith apples, peeled, cored, and sliced

3/4 cup golden raisins

1 tablespoon all-purpose flour

1/2 cup firmly packed light brown sugar or a natural sweetener (page 330)

Grated zest and juice of 1 small lemon

3/4 teaspoon ground cinnamon

1 cup rolled (old-fashioned) oats

2 1/2 tablespoons corn oil

1 Preheat the oven to 375 degrees. Lightly oil a 10-inch baking dish.

2 In a large bowl, combine the apples, raisins, flour, 1/4 cup of the brown sugar, the lemon zest and juice, and 1/2 teaspoon of the cinnamon, mixing gently. Transfer to the prepared baking dish and set aside.

3 In small bowl, combine the oats, the remaining 1/4 cup brown sugar and 1/4 teaspoon cinnamon, and the oil. Mix with your hands to blend thoroughly.

4 Sprinkle the topping over the apple mixture. Bake until the fruit bubbles in the center and the topping is browned, 35 to 45 minutes. To serve, spoon into dishes while still warm.

Serves 8

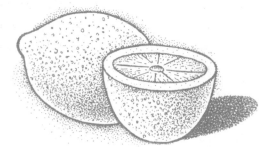

Peanut Butter Bread Pudding with Fresh Strawberry Coulis

Inspired by the all-American PB&J sandwich, this homey dessert is made even tastier with the addition of strawberry coulis and an optional garnish of chopped peanuts and fresh strawberries.

1/2 cup silken tofu

2 1/2 cups regular or soy milk

1 teaspoon pure vanilla extract

1/2 cup light brown sugar or a natural sweetener (page 330)

1/2 cup creamy natural peanut butter

1/3 cup strawberry jam

1/2 loaf sliced white bread, crusts removed

Fresh Strawberry Coulis (page 324)

1/2 cup chopped unsalted roasted peanuts (optional)

1/2 cup hulled and sliced strawberries (optional)

1 In a blender or food processor, process the tofu with 1/2 cup of the milk, the vanilla, and sugar until smooth. Set aside.

2 Spread the peanut butter and jam on the bread slices, then cut into cubes. Place the bread cubes in a large bowl and pour the remaining 2 cups milk over them, tossing to coat. Let the bread stand for 1 hour to soak up the liquid.

3 Preheat the oven to 350 degrees F. Lightly oil a shallow 10-inch baking dish.

4 Place the bread mixture in the baking dish. Pour over the pureed tofu mixture and bake until firm, about 45 minutes.

5 Allow the bread pudding to cool to room temperature before serving or refrigerating. Serve chilled or at room temperature, with the strawberry coulis spooned around the plates or drizzled over the bread pudding. Garnish with the peanuts and sliced strawberries, if desired.

Serves 6 to 8

Creamy Rice Pudding with Slivered Almonds

Using leftover cooked rice cuts the cooking time significantly, but this creamy rice pudding has all the flavor of a slow-cooked version.

2¹/₂ cups cooked basmati rice

2¹/₂ cups regular or soy milk

¹/₂ cup sugar or a natural sweetener (page 330)

¹/₂ teaspoon ground cinnamon

¹/₄ teaspoon ground nutmeg

¹/₄ teaspoon ground allspice

¹/₈ teaspoon salt

1 teaspoon pure vanilla extract

¹/₂ cup slivered almonds

1 In a large saucepan, combine the rice, milk, and sugar and simmer over low heat for 20 minutes, stirring occasionally until the sugar is dissolved. Stir in the cinnamon, nutmeg, allspice, salt, vanilla, and almonds and simmer until the desired consistency is reached, 5 to 10 minutes longer.

2 Allow to cool to room temperature and serve, or cover and refrigerate to serve chilled.

Serves 4

Creamy Chocolate Pudding

This pudding is a comfort food favorite at our house, and it's so easy to make. It can be also used as a quick and easy pie filling—just spread into a prepared pie crust and chill until ready to serve. A chocolate cookie crumb crust is especially good.

3/4 cup semisweet chocolate chips

1/2 cup sugar or a natural sweetener
   (page 330)

One 12-ounce package silken tofu,
   crumbled

1 teaspoon pure vanilla extract

Chopped nuts (optional)

1 Place the chocolate chips and sugar in the top of a double boiler and heat over gently simmering water until the chocolate is melted, stirring to blend. Set aside to cool.

2 Place the tofu in a blender or food processor and process until smooth. Add the cooled chocolate mixture and the vanilla and process until smooth, scraping down the sides if necessary.

3 Spoon the pudding into individual serving dishes. Cover tightly with plastic wrap and refrigerate for at least 1 hour before serving. This pudding tastes best on the day it is made.

4 When ready to serve, top each serving with chopped nuts, if desired.

Serves 4

Cranberry-Pistachio Scones

Cranberries and pistachios add a festive touch to these scones based on an old family recipe, which is made with raisins. Dried cranberries can be found in well-stocked supermarkets.

2 cups all-purpose flour

3/4 cup sugar or a natural sweetener
(page 330)

2 teaspoons cream of tartar

1 teaspoon baking soda

3/4 teaspoon salt

1/2 cup (1 stick) butter or soy margarine,
at room temperature

1/3 cup dried cranberries

1/4 cup shelled raw pistachios

1/4 cup regular or soy milk

2 large eggs or egg replacer for 2 eggs
(below)

1 Preheat the oven to 400 degrees F. Lightly oil a baking sheet and dust lightly with flour.

2 Sift the flour, sugar, cream of tartar, baking soda, and salt together into a medium-size bowl. Using a pastry blender, blend in the butter until the mixture resembles coarse crumbs. Add the cranberries, pistachios, milk, and eggs. Mix gently with a fork until just blended; do not overwork.

3 Divide the dough in half. One half at a time, transfer the dough to a floured work surface and, using a rolling pin, roll into a rectangle 1/2 inch thick. Cut the dough into 3-inch triangles and place on the prepared baking sheet.

4 Bake until golden brown, about 12 minutes. Serve warm.

Makes 16 scones

Egg and Dairy Alternatives

People avoid eggs for a variety of reasons, especially health and ethical concerns. While it may be easy enough to forgo the "over-easy" at breakfast time, it can be harder to avoid eggs when it comes to baked goods and other desserts. Fortunately, a number of egg alternatives are available. In many dessert recipes, eggs provide the moisture and fat content necessary to make the recipe work; however, silken tofu, applesauce, and other fruit purees can often stand in as nutritious and flavorful substitutes. Other egg replacers include the commercial product called

Ener-G Egg Replacer, made from vegetable starch, and a paste that you can make yourself from ground flaxseeds and water. Flaxseeds and Ener-G Egg Replacer are available at natural food stores. Non-vegans looking for ways to avoid the cholesterol in eggs may simply choose to use egg whites, which contain no cholesterol. If you do use eggs, I encourage you to buy only organic, free-range eggs.

If you're trying to eliminate or cut down on dairy products, baking is a great place to start. Many dairy alternatives can be substituted in equal measure for dairy. Soy, almond, or rice milk, as well as coconut milk when the flavor is appropriate, can be used instead of dairy milk. These products can be found in most supermarkets and natural food stores and can be used interchangeably with milk in most recipes. The taste difference is virtually indistinguishable in cooked recipes. Some brands of soy milk are found in the refrigerated section and should be refrigerated even if unopened, but most brands, as well as milks made with rice or almonds, are available in one-quart aseptic containers that can be stored unrefrigerated until opened. In addition to the regular flavor, many brands come in vanilla or chocolate, which can be used to heighten those flavors in particular desserts.

Butter can be replaced with chilled high-quality expeller pressed corn oil (it thickens under refrigeration). You could also try a nonhydrogenated spread, such as Spectrum Spread, which is made with soy protein isolate, or a high-quality soy margarine that contains no additives.

Substitution Guidelines for Replacing 1 Egg (in baking)

- Ener-G Egg Replacer: Blend $1^1/_2$ teaspoons of the powder with 2 tablespoons water.

- Ground flaxseeds: Combine 1 tablespoon ground flaxseeds with 3 tablespoons water in a blender and blend until the mixture becomes thick and frothy, about 1 minute.

- Soft tofu: Blend $1/_4$ cup soft tofu and $1/_4$ teaspoon baking powder in a blender with the other liquids in a recipe.

- Pureed fruit: Combine $1/_4$ cup pureed fruit, such as applesauce or mashed banana, with $1/_4$ teaspoon baking powder.

Pecan-Studded Chocolate Brownies

Chocolate lovers will enjoy the dense, chocolatey goodness of these fudgy treats. Carob powder and chips can be used instead of cocoa and chocolate if you prefer.

1/4 cup corn oil

3 tablespoons unsweetened cocoa powder

1/2 cup semisweet chocolate chips

2 large eggs or egg replacer for 2 eggs (page 342)

3/4 cup sugar or a natural sweetener (page 330)

1 teaspoon pure vanilla extract

3/4 cup all-purpose flour

1 teaspoon baking powder

1/2 cup chopped pecans

1 Preheat the oven to 350 degrees F. Lightly oil an 8-inch square baking pan.

2 Heat the oil in a medium-size saucepan over low heat. Stir in the cocoa until well blended. Stir in the chocolate chips until melted. Set aside.

3 Place the eggs in a large bowl. Add the sugar and vanilla and blend well. Stir in the chocolate mixture and blend well. Stir in the flour and baking powder, mixing well. Fold in the pecans, and spoon the batter into the prepared pan.

4 Bake until the top springs back when lightly touched, about 25 minutes. Allow to cool before cutting into squares.

Makes 16 brownies

Egg-Free Almond—Chocolate Chip Biscotti

My husband, Jon, loves biscotti, but most commercial varieties contain eggs—and are expensive. Fueled by the desire for eggless biscotti, Jon developed this recipe, which is both delicious and economical.

1/2 cup (1 stick) butter or soy margarine, at room temperature

2/3 cup sugar or a natural sweetener (page 330)

Egg replacer for 2 eggs (page 342)

1 teaspoon pure vanilla extract

13/4 cups all-purpose flour

1/2 cup unsweetened cocoa powder

1 teaspoon baking powder

1/2 cup slivered almonds

1/3 cup semisweet chocolate chips

1 Preheat the oven to 350 degrees F. Lightly oil a baking sheet.

2 In a large bowl, using an electric mixer, cream the butter with the sugar until light and fluffy. Blend in the egg replacer and vanilla. Beat in the flour, cocoa powder, and baking powder. Stir in the almonds and chocolate chips. Chill the dough for 10 minutes.

3 Divide the dough in half. Shape each half into a log about 2 inches thick and 10 inches long. Place the logs about 4 inches apart on the prepared baking sheet, and flatten slightly.

4 Bake until a toothpick comes out clean, 25 to 30 minutes. Remove the biscotti from the oven and reduce the oven temperature to 275 degrees F. Let the logs cool for 10 minutes.

5 Cut each log crosswise into 1/2-inch-thick slices. Place the sliced biscotti on their sides on an ungreased baking sheet and bake until they are dry, 8 to 10 minutes. Let cool completely before storing in an airtight container, where they will keep for several days.

Makes 3 dozen biscotti

Five-Spice Oatmeal-Date Cookies

These chewy cookies boast a quintet of aromatic spices, along with healthful oats and dates, making them good tasting and good for you.

1 cup all-purpose flour

¹/₂ teaspoon ground cinnamon

¹/₄ teaspoon ground nutmeg

¹/₄ teaspoon ground allspice

¹/₄ teaspoon ground ginger

¹/₄ teaspoon ground cloves

¹/₂ teaspoon baking powder

Pinch of salt

¹/₂ cup corn oil

¹/₂ cup firmly packed light brown sugar or
    a natural sweetener (page 330)

2 large eggs or egg replacer for 2 eggs
    (page 342)

2 tablespoons cold water

1 teaspoon pure vanilla extract

1¹/₄ cups rolled (old-fashioned) oats

³/₄ cup chopped pitted dates

1 Preheat the oven to 350 degrees F. Lightly oil two baking sheets.

2 In a medium-size bowl, whisk together the flour, cinnamon, nutmeg, allspice, ginger, cloves, baking soda, and salt. Set aside.

3 Place the oil and brown sugar in a large bowl and, using an electric mixer, beat until well blended. Beat in the eggs, water, and vanilla until blended. Add the dry ingredients and beat just until blended. Stir in the oats and dates.

4 Drop the batter by rounded tablespoonfuls about 2 inches apart onto the prepared baking sheets. Bake until golden, about 15 minutes. Allow the cookies to cool completely before storing in an airtight container.

Makes 2 dozen cookies

Mom's Butterballs

My mother made these sublime cookies for holidays and other special occasions. They are especially fun at Christmastime, since they look like miniature snowballs, and they taste so delicious that it's hard to stop eating them. One Christmas, a cousin planted himself in a corner of the room with a huge platter of butterballs and ate them all!

Although butter is a central ingredient here, vegans and those watching their cholesterol can use soy margarine. A natural sweetener can be used instead of sugar in the cookie dough itself, but the final dusting of confectioners' sugar is hard to duplicate—so if sugar's a problem, simply eliminate that final flourish.

1 cup (2 sticks) butter or soy margarine, at room temperature

3/4 cup confectioners' sugar or a natural sweetener (page 330)

1 teaspoon pure vanilla extract

1 3/4 cups all-purpose flour

1 3/4 cup finely ground walnuts

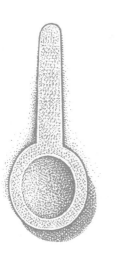

1 In a large bowl, using an electric mixer, cream together the butter, 1/2 cup of the confectioners' sugar, and the vanilla. Add the flour and walnuts, stirring until well combined.

2 Divide the dough into thirds. Using your hands, roll each piece of dough into a 12-inch-long rope. Wrap in plastic and refrigerate for 1 hour to chill.

3 Preheat the oven to 350 degrees F. Remove the dough from the refrigerator. Cut each rope into 1-inch pieces, roll into balls, and arrange about 1 inch apart on ungreased baking sheets.

4 Bake until golden brown, 16 to 18 minutes. Remove from the oven and allow to cool to room temperature.

5 Place the remaining 1/4 cup confectioners' sugar in a sifter and sift over the cookies until they are dusted with sugar. Store in an airtight container.

Makes 3 dozen cookies

Index

Oils, in recipes, xii
Olive, Black, Tapenade, 312
Olive oil, cooking with, xii
Onion(s), 105
 Five-, Soup, Baked, 49
 Red, −Green Apple Marmalade, 323
Orange-and-Sesame-Tossed Penne Salad
  with Red Beans and Watercress,
  84
Orange-Thyme Aïoli, 310
Oyster sauce, about, 15

P

Pad Thai, 252
Pakoras, Potato-Scallion, 11
Pancake(s). *See also* Latkes
 Chinese Noodle, 251
 Plan-Ahead Potato Cakes, 232
 Potato, with Apples and Cinnamon,
  231
Parsley
 Couscous Tabbouleh, 78
 Tried and True Tabbouleh, 77
Parsnips, 105
 Underground Vegetable Sauté, 274
 Winter Vegetable Stew with Potato
  Gnocchi, 108
Pasta. *See also* Noodle(s)
 Baked Macaroni with a Twist, 248
 Baked Ziti and Eggplant, 244
 and Broccoli Bake, Creamy Tahini,
  249
 Call It Macaroni Salad, 85
 Fettuccine with Potatoes and Pesto,
  224
 Kasha Varnishkas, 261
 Layered Vegetable Lasagna, 246-47
 Orange-and-Sesame-Tossed Penne
  Salad with Red Beans and
  Watercress, 84
 Pepper-Stuffed Peppers, 191-92
 Salad, Tuscan Summer, 82
 Spaghetti and "Meatballs," 241-42
 Ziti with Mushroom and Green
  Peppercorn Sauce, 243
Pâté, Country-Style Lentil, 32
Pâté, Red Pepper−Walnut, 29
Pâté, Three-Stripe Vegetable, 30-31
Peach-Blueberry Galette, 337
Peanut Butter
 African Groundnut Stew, 113
 Bread Pudding with Fresh
  Strawberry Coulis, 339

Bronzed Tempeh with Broccoli and
  Spicy Peanut Sauce, 136
 Creamy Peanut Soup, 61
 Spicy Peanut Sauce, 305
Peanut oil, cooking with, xii, 15
Peanut(s)
 African Groundnut Stew, 113
 Chili-Spiced, 23
 Hoisin Eggplant Balls, 8
 Sauce, Spicy, Bronzed Tempeh with
  Broccoli and, 136
 Soup, Creamy, 61
Pea(s)
 Caribbean Couscous Salad, 80
 Roasted New Potato Salad with Pine
  Nuts, Mint, and, 67
 Soup, Thick as, 54
 and Sweet Potato Salad, 76
Pecan(s)
 -Cranberry-Stuffed Wheat-Meat
  Ballotine, 170-71
 Curried, 23
 -Dusted Double Pumpkin "Cheese"
  Cake, 331-32
 Rum-Kissed Sweet Potato Sauté with
  Cranberries and, 219
 -Studded Chocolate Brownies, 344
Pepperoni Pizza, Pile-It-On, 195
Pepper(s). *See also* Chipotle
 Bean and Chile Burritos, 267
 Gutsy Gazpacho, 47
 Pepper-Stuffed, 191-92
 Red, −Walnut Pâté, 29
 Roasted Ratatouille, 272
 Roasted Red, and Potato Napoleons,
  17
 Roasted Yellow, and Black Beans,
  Cilantro Polenta Wedges with,
  254-55
 Stuffed, on Sliced Potatoes, 193
Pesto
 Basil, 313
 Basil, Mushroom-Stuffed Seitan Rolls
  with, 132
 Fettuccine with Potatoes and, 224
 -Potato Pizza, 199
 Potato Salad, 72
Piccata, Tofu and Mushroom, 141
Pie
 Flaky Vegetable Potpie, 177
 Fresh Strawberry, 335
 Indian-Spiced Sweet Potato Potpie,
  175-76

Quiche and Tell, 178
 Shepherd's Vegetable, 174
 Sweet Potato, 336
Pierogi, Potato-Onion, 229-30
Pilaf, Fruity Bulgur, 263
Pineapple and Potatoes, Thai Tofu
  Curry with, 106-7
Pineapple Chutney with Dark Rum and
  Crystallized Ginger, 320
Pinto beans
 Bean and Chile Burritos, 267
 Chili con Frijoles, 121
 Mexican Tortilla Bake, 184
 Spicy Southwestern Rice Salad, 88
 Three Sisters Corn Chowder, 48
Pistachio-Cranberry Scones, 342
Pistachios and Dried Cranberries,
  Couscous with, 253
Pizza
 Artichoke, Fennel, and Mushroom,
  197
 Calzone Crazy, 200
 Dough, Basic, 194
 Grilled Vegetable, 196
 Pesto-Potato, 199
 Pile-It-On Pepperoni, 195
 Spicy Eggplant Calzones, 201
 White on White, with Baby Spinach,
  198
Plantain Bites, Spice Island, 10
Plum Crazy Ketchup, 322
Polenta
 Baked, with Porcini Mushrooms,
  256-57
 Triangles with Chipotle Salsa, 16
 Wedges, Cilantro, with Black Beans
  and Roasted Yellow Peppers,
  254-55
Portobello(s)
 cooking with, 5
 -Eggplant Chili, "Meaty," 122
 Fajitas, Chipotle-Glazed, 154
 Great Stuffed Mushrooms, 155
 Grilled, with Garlic and Herb-
  Infused Olive Oil, 152
 Mushroom-Stuffed Seitan Rolls with
  Basil Pesto, 132
 Steaks, Ginger-Sesame-Glazed, over
  Sesame-Wasabi Mashers, 153
 "Steak" Sandwiches, Grilled, 280
Potato(es), 203-37. *See also* Potato
  Salad; Sweet Potato(es)
 Baked, Chili-Topped, 211

continued